BREAKING
CLAYS

BREAKING
CLAYS

Chris Batha

SWAN·HILL
PRESS

First published in the UK in 2005
by Swan Hill Press, an imprint of Quiller Publishing Ltd
Reprinted 2006

British Library Cataloguing-in-Publication Data
   A catalogue record for this book
   is available from the British Library

ISBN 1 904057 43 8
ISBN 978 1 904057 43 7

Printed in China

Swan Hill Press

An imprint of Quiller Publishing Ltd
Wykey House, Wykey, Shrewsbury, SY4 1JA
Tel: 01939 261616 Fax: 01939 261606
E-mail: info@quillerbooks.com
Website: www.countrybooksdirect.com

Contents

Acknowledgements

My grateful thanks go to the many editors, writers and authors (living and deceased) whose works have helped build the knowledge to write this book and to the fellow coaches and clients who have helped create the experience to know what works:

Cyril Adams, Dolph Adams, Bob Allen, Gil and Vicki Ash, Lionel Atwill, Lanny Bassam, Fred Baughan, Paul Bentley, John Bidwell, Bryan Bilinski, Stephen A. Blumenthal, Bruce Bowlen, Robert Braden, John Brindle, Bob Brister, Bruce Buck, Nash Buckingham, Louise Burke, Major Sir Gerald Burrard, Dan Carlisle, G.L. Carlisle, Robert Churchill, Charles Conger, George Conrad, Chris Craddock, Dr Debbie Crews, Milhaly Csikszentmihalyi, Fred Neal David, Ken Davies, Bob Decot, Steve Denny, Chuck DeVinne, George Digweed, Andy Duffy, George Evans, Julian Murray-Evans, Richard Faulds, Alister Ferguson, Marty Fischer, John Gosselin, Rob Gray, Les Greevy, John Gregson, B. C. Hartman, Robert R. Hartman, Macdonald Hastings, John Hawley, Arthur Hearn, Gene Hill, Roger Hill, Charles Hillman, Tony Hoare, Dave Holmes, Mick Howells, Susan Jackson, Christopher Janelle, Alan Jarrett, David Judah, Nick Karas, Michael Kayes, Bill Kempffer, John King, Mike King, Richard Alden Knight, Frank Kodl, Charles Lancaster, David Leathart, Ernie Lind, John R. Linn, Frank Little, David Lloyd, Tom Mack, Robin Marshall-Ball, Dr Wayne F. Martin, E.S. McCawley, Jr, Michael McIntosh, Jerry Meyer, E. Migdalski, Tom Migdalski, Chris Miles, Brian Miller, Fred Missildene, Jack Mitchell, Peter Munday, Andrew A. Montague, Bob Nichols, Tony Norman, Steve Nutbeam, Jack O'Connor, George G. Orberfell, Michael Pearce, Tom Penman, Neal Phillips, Richard Rawlingson, Mike Reynolds, Michael Rose, Micky Rouse, Bob Rottella, Major J.E.M. Ruffer, Ed Scherer, Dan Schindler, Bruce Scott, Robin Scott, Roger Silcox, A.J. Smith, Ronald W. Stadt, Percy Stanbury, Jackie Stewart, Ralph Stuart, Dale Tate, Douglas Tate, John Taylor, Mark H. Taylor, Charles E. Thompson, John Topliss, David Trevallion, Vic Venters, Doug Vine, Billy Walker, Sam Wilkinson, Mike Williams, John Wooley, Mike Yardley, and Don Zutz.

I am grateful for the help given to me by a number of people and companies in the writing of this book:

Michael Brunton for his permission to use the original artwork illustrations from *Clay Shooting* magazine.

Black's Wing and Clay for their permission to use original artwork illustrations and tables from their publication.

Mike Barnes for his permission to use original artwork from *Pull* magazine.

Rob Gray of *The Shooting Times* and *Country Magazine* for his permission to use original artwork from the magazine.

Beretta, Brownell's, Browning, Electronic Shooters Protection, Magna-port International, Promatic Traps, Ranger Shooting Glasses, White Flyer Targets, Winchester (Olin Corp) Inc for photographs and reference materials.

The CPSA and NSCA for the publication of their rules and regulations.

Sara Gump of Redfield & Associates for original photography and help and support – without her the book would never have been written.

John Beaton for his editorial efforts in transforming my illegible scribbling into legible print.

Trudy Abadie-Fail for her excellent work in transforming ordinary photographs into handsome photo-illustrations.

Glyn Griffin, designer, and Rob Dixon, Production Manager, for their patience and dedication to creating an interesting and accessible layout and design.

Jeff Love, for his outstanding cover design.

Louis LaSorsa and his team at Phoenix Colour Corporation for his extraordinary generosity and assistance in printing this book.

And finally, my thanks go to Andrew Johnston of Quiller Publishing for his foresight and confidence in making the decision to publish *Breaking Clays*.

Author's Foreword

I am a lucky man… I enjoy my work. When I am not coaching, I am shooting and shooting has been my life-long passion. I still feel the same sense of anticipation and excitement entering a competition today as I did twenty-plus years ago.

My passion for shooting has taken me all over the world, offering more fantastic experiences and long-lasting friendships than I could ever have dreamed of. I often reflect on how this all came about – it was not planned – I never woke up one morning and decided to become a shooting instructor. I had never even considered it, it just happened. On reflection, instructing evolved from my own shooting. Being limited by my budget, I wanted to shoot more and thought working at a shooting ground would give me the opportunity. Silly me! As it ended up, I shot less!

I began by refereeing and helping with corporate entertainment and quickly recognised that there was a great deal of difference between being able to shoot a target and teaching someone else how to. Then I saw an announcement in the *Pull* magazine for a CPSA One Day Coaches Course and thought that this would help me to help the corporate clients break a few more targets.

I had opened 'Pandora's Box'! I am a competent shot, not a great shot. I can, more often than not, straight skeet and trap and average in the mid-eighties at sporting clays. This one day course taught me that I knew next to nothing about how I did it. I was intrigued, curious and wanted to learn more. I began to read everything I could on teaching shooting: books, magazines, videos – I bought and studied them all! At the same time, I continued to take CPSA coaching courses, one after another. These courses were held in the spring, followed by an examination in the autumn. The skills taught required practice to learn, so throughout the summers, I worked at any and every shooting ground or corporate entertainment company that I could.

You can learn any skill, but nothing teaches like experience. During the five years of courses that led to my receiving the CPSA Senior Coaches Award, I learned from every instructor I worked with, every client I coached, every article and book I read and every video I watched.

The contents of *Breaking Clays* are not only my thoughts and ideas but are a distillation of all that I have learned from these many sources. I would like nothing better than to list and credit each and every one, but it would take another book in its own right to do so! Just let me offer a very big 'Thank you' to you all and recognise that, if it were not for your willingness to share your knowledge, in person or on paper, I could not have written this book. I hope you may recognise a little of your input in my interpretation of how to break clays.

Introduction

When asked to write this book, I had to make a decision as to its direction and content. During my life I have worked alongside many good instructors and shot in many competitions. Through these experiences I have had the opportunity to study the best shots in the world in action. I have always given special attention to anyone who had won two or more championships and observed the similarities among them in their approach to the game.

My intention is to share with you some of the secrets of successful clay shooting that I've learned from years of studying the best. I have focused most of my attention on the fundamentals for this is where you will see the greatest similarities among the best shooters…this is where you see what the top shots consistently do that the also-rans do not. Secondly, I decided it would be impossible to do justice to all the disciplines in one book so I have chosen to concentrate on the three main or domestic games – sporting clays, skeet and trap.

The difference between the disciplines is in the titles and rules, not in the actual shooting. In every game a target is thrown and needs to be broken to score. The technique used does not need to change because the name of the discipline being shot does. I accept that there are techniques, methods, guns and equipment which make the shooting of each more consistent, but the actual mechanics remain constant. It is the speed, angle and distance that determine the technique and the method best suited to breaking the target, not the title of the game.

When you miss, it has little to do with the ballistics of the shotgun – choke and cartridges give you inches where you miss in feet. A miss is more often caused by a breakdown in the fundamentals. All the top competitors demonstrate consistent fundamentals that they have grooved and practised for so long that they have assigned them to their subconscious. As a result, he or she can be forgiven for not emphasising the importance of these fundamentals in their teaching, instead of focusing on the technique that made them a winner. However, co-ordination, reaction time, and visual acuity are individual skills and what works for one will not necessarily work for another. Techniques and methods will vary with the individual as well as the target being shot. Mastering the fundamentals and learning which technique works best for you is the key to successful shooting.

The real purpose of this book is to help you recognise where and why you miss and to give you the knowledge to make the changes necessary to correct your mistakes. 'Fault, Cause, Correction' is the primary focus.

Chapter by chapter, the contents will insure a sound start for the beginner, improved performance for the intermediate, and perhaps even provide a few insights to help the advanced shooter…beginning with the mechanical and progressing through to the visual and mental skills required to shoot straight in competition.

Breaking Clays is intended to be used as a workbook that can be returned to time and time again to help with the 'falling off' of form and the correction of mistakes…to help you to become your own coach. To perform to the best of our ability in any activity requires knowledge, it is my hope that this book will go some way to increasing yours.

CHAPTER 1
History of the Clay Target Games

C lay target games have their origins in live bird shooting, when wing shooters of the nineteenth century began to engage in games of chance shooting at live pigeons. That is why a clay pigeon is called a 'bird' and the electric trap that throws the clay is called a 'trap'.

The format was, at first, simple. A group of gentleman would gather, often at one of the their London clubs, of which the Hurlingham in Fulham was the most famous. They began by placing live pigeons under their hats on the ground in front of them. They then would stoop, pick up the hat, place it on their heads and, only then, shoot at the departing bird. As the shooters' skill increased, the birds were placed in 'traps', further from the guns. The 'trap' was a collapsible metal box with a release string attached, into which the live pigeon was placed, through a hole in the top. Five of these metal 'traps' would be placed in an arc facing the shooter. On the shooter's call of 'pull!', the 'trapper' would select a string at random and pull it firmly. This would 'spring' the box and it would collapse. The pigeon would explode out of the 'trap'. The shooter had to shoot and kill the bird so it dropped within a fenced area.

This became the fashionable sport of the era. It was so popular that the gunmakers of the time designed guns specifically for 'trap' shooting. Though still shot in many parts of the world today, live pigeon shooting was banned in Britain in 1921. In many countries, and in particular the United States, access to sufficient live pigeons for an event was often a problem, so enthusiasts began to experiment with a variety of inanimate targets. Glass balls filled with feathers and other imaginative 'birds' were tried.

It wasn't until 1880 that an American, George Ligowski, invented the now universally-accepted replacement for live birds – the clay target. Legend has it that Ligowski was skipping clamshells with his grandchildren at a lake and that he modelled his clay targets after the clamshells.

Over the next few years, Ligowski's clay 'pigeon' improved and evolved. When the use of pitch replaced the more fragile clay, this 'bird' quickly became the standard, replacing the feather-filled balls, at that time, the only alternative to live birds. The clay target became so popular and was so practical, it slowly began to replace live pigeon shooting altogether.

Disciplines

Shooting clay targets led to the development of numerous games in their own right, with three distinct disciplines emerging: trap, skeet and sporting clays. The worldwide popularity of these target sports has resulted in further multiplication and diversification of the games. Attempting to classify and define the proper approaches to all these various disciplines in one book would do justice to none. I have, instead, chosen to stick to the original three, as these are still the most popular and widely-shot.

Trap

Trap is the first clay pigeon game. Imitating live pigeon shooting, it had and still retains much of the original format in its setup and rules. It is called Trap after the devices, or traps, that were originally used to hold and release live birds.

The first US National Championship was held in 1885; and 'The Inanimate Bird Shooting Association' was formed in 1892 in Great Britain. The type of Trapshooting described herein is known as Down-the-Line. It is the oldest and most basic of all the trap disciplines. Down the Line is shot over one trap machine that has a fixed elevation but constantly changing angles. The clay target is thrown away from the shooter and must travel 55 yards. The height of the target is adjusted so that at a distance of 10 yards from the trap, its height will be 10 feet. The angles at which the targets are thrown, (to the left and right of the shooter), are constantly changing and the targets should appear random and unpredictable. The maximum target angle is normally 22 degrees either side of the centre of the trap house.

A round of trap consists of twenty-five shots, with groups of five shots being taken from five shooting positions. The maximum of five people shooting per round is called a squad. Each shooter on the squad shoots five shots from each of the five shooting positions. The shooters take turns shooting: the first shooter will shoot one shot, the second shooter takes his shot, and so on, until all five shooters have shot five shots from a given shooting position. The shooters then rotate to the next shooting position and repeat the process. Most competitions consist of 100 targets or four rounds.

Skeet

In 1920, a group of American upland bird hunters got together to shoot clay targets as practice for their wing shooting. During their practice, competitions began among the wing shooters. Charles E. Davies of Andover, Massachusetts, generally acknowledged as the creator of the original game, set out rules establishing the order and number of shots that could be taken, so the competitions would be fair to all the participants…and Skeet was born.

A competition was held to give the game a recognised title. Gertrude Hurlbutt of Dayton, Montana won the contest with her entry, 'Skeet', which comes from the Scandinavian word for 'shoot'. (The winner was chosen from thousands of suggestions; among the losing entries were 'Bye-Bye Blackbird' and 'Bang'!)

At first the game was shot from twelve stations set in a circle, using only one trap. This was referred to as Clock Shooting. These twelve stations gave the guns every conceivable angle of target flight. However, this setup took up a great deal of space and the decision was made to add an additional trap and, in effect, 'fold' the course in two, creating the same number and variety of targets but halving the space needed for shot fall out.

Like Trap, Skeet is a game of twenty-five shots. There are two houses, one low and one high, set 44 yards apart. They each throw a standard single target 67 yards. The thrown targets must pass through a 3-foot hoop, 19 feet high, placed at the centre of the range, 22 yards from the seven stations.

A squad of five shooters starts at Station 1, directly under the High House. Each person shoots one bird from the High House, then one bird from the Low House. Then a pair of birds is launched simultaneously, one bird from each house. Four targets are presented at Stations 1, 2, 4, 6 and 7. Singles, one each, high and low, are shot at Stations 3 and 5.

In the USA, there is no double on Station 4, so singles are shot at Stations 4 and 8. That adds up to only twenty-four shots, so the first missed shot is an option and can be retaken. If the competitor completes the round without missing, they can choose their last target to complete the round of twenty-five shots. Most competitions consist of one hundred targets or four rounds.

Sporting Clays

In America, birds were primarily shot for the table, whereas in England, birds were shot for sport. In the 1800s, being recognised as a good shot had great social impact on one's place in society, opening many doors and creating an equal number of invitations.

The gunmakers of the time were quick to recognise that, not only did they need to make guns for their clients, they also needed to teach their clients how to shoot. A number of shooting schools sprang up, quickly recognising the potential of Ligowski's clay pigeons. Initially designed to re-create the flight of the different game birds, this type of 'game' target shooting soon became a game unto itself, like Trap and Skeet.

At first, the Sporting Clays Competitions were rather simple affairs, locally organised and regionally

Clay Pigeon and Glass Ball Traps

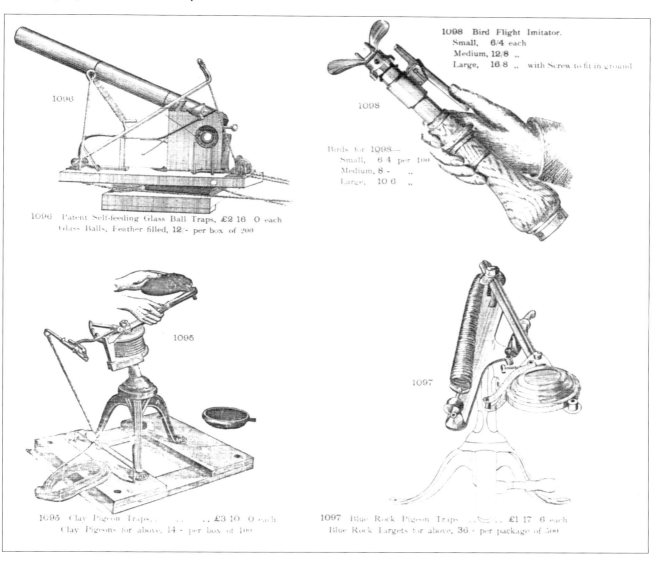

1096 Patent Self-feeding Glass Ball Traps, £2 16 0 each
Glass Balls, Feather filled, 12/- per box of 200

1098 Bird Flight Imitator.
Small,   6/4 each
Medium, 12/8 ,,
Large,   16/8 ,, with Screw to fit in ground

Birds for 1098—
Small,   6 4 per 100
Medium, 8 -   ,,
Large, 10 6   ,,

1095 Clay Pigeon Traps.. .. .. £3 10 0 each
Clay Pigeons for above, 14 - per box of 100

1097 Blue Rock Pigeon Traps .. .. £1 17 6 each
Blue Rock Targets for above, 36 - per package of 500

shot. The first International Sporting Clays Tournament was held in Carlisle in 1925, between England and Scotland with the Scots emerging victorious. Over time, Sporting Clays has evolved into the present-day shooting game in which clay targets are presented to mirror the flight patterns of game birds, or, occasionally, rabbits, in their natural habitats.

The Sporting Clays course is laid out in Stations or stands, usually ten or more. At each Station, clay targets in varying sizes are thrown in pairs – five or so pairs to the station. The traps at each stand are set to represent the flight of one type of bird, a combination of two birds, or a rabbit and a bird. It is this great variety of trap positions, trap speeds, shooting positions, and flight paths of the different types of targets that makes this game so challenging. In the typical Sporting Clays Course, 100 birds will be presented, divided by the number of Stations and shots over the course.

Five Stand or Compact Sporting

All the major competitions feature side events, often referred to as Pool Shoots. Here a competitor can warm up for the main event and place a wager on his score to be the highest of the day or event. These so-called Five Stand events, because of land restrictions, are often overlaid on a Trap or Skeet field. Six to eight automatic traps throw a variety of targets, in varying degrees of difficulty, to be shot from the different stands. There is very little walking in a Five Stand event as shots are taken from a series of adjacent stands, similar to the FITASC parcours layouts.

These events have become very popular and as many shooting grounds added a Five Stand to their course, it was inevitable that specific competitions would evolve. Today, Five Stand has become a miniature Sporting Clays course, offering a wide range of targets in a compact area. There are three levels of difficulty in Five Stand target presentations:

1. Five single targets are thrown with full use of the gun for scoring.
2. Three single and a simultaneous pair are thrown.
3. One single and two simultaneous pairs are thrown.

Participants take turns shooting each of the Five Stands (hence the name). Various combinations of targets can be thrown from the traps; a 'menu card' at each stand describes the sequence of targets. Five Stand Sporting can be, and often is, referred to as Compact Sporting.

FITASC

Federation Internationale de Tir aux Armes Sportives de Chasse or FITASC, was developed in France as practice for field shooting. Evolving from the same origins as Sporting Clays, FITASC is shot in squads of up to six, with a fixed order of stands (*parcours* in French) that are shot in strict rotation. A competition normally consists of 200 targets, shot over two days, in eight rounds of twenty-five. In each round of twenty-five, shots are taken from a minimum of three different stations.

A gun mount is compulsory. The shooter is required to hold the butt of the gun below armpit level (the shooting vest is marked with a line) until the target is seen. The entire squad shoots single targets first, then, after the entire squad has completed the singles, combinations of singles are presented as doubles.

The variety of types and sizes of targets are thrown at longer ranges than in Sporting Clays and this plus the continuously changing speeds, angles and distances, make FITASC the most challenging of the Sporting Clay disciplines.

CHAPTER 2
Safety

Clay pigeon shooting has one of the most enviable safety records of any sport, and it is important to maintain this high standard. When a newcomer is introduced to the sport, the first lesson should cover safety and gun handling. Because we use a shotgun in a recreational sport in the same manner as a golf club or tennis racquet, we must never forget its lethal qualities.

Carrying the Shotgun

There are only two ways in which a gun can be carried safely.

1. Unloaded, in a closed gun slip, where it is impossible to access the trigger.
2. Open and seen to be empty.

The open gun should be carried over the crook of the arm and not, as is too often seen, over the shoulder. Though it is comfortable and easy to carry a gun over the shoulder, there is every chance of striking a fellow competitor with the stock of the gun as you turn around. Never

A gun is safest unloaded in a closed gun slip

The correct technique for taking a gun in and out of a gun slip

The correct technique for taking a gun in and out of a gun slip

An open gun is best carried over the crook of an arm

An open gun carried over the shoulder is comfortable, but beware of striking a fellow competitor with the stock

carry the gun with the barrels sticking back over your shoulders!

Semi-automatic shotguns that cannot be broken open should have a flag or a piece of cloth placed in the open breach to draw attention to the fact that the chamber is empty and a cartridge cannot be placed in it. The best way to carry a semi-automatic is with the stock placed in the pocket of your shooting vest, muzzles pointing up, with the open breech facing out. It is best to carry your shotgun from station to station in a gun slip. It is comfortable, easier to manage and the slip protects the gun in transit.

__Never__ carry the gun with the barrels pointing backwards over your shoulder

The semi-automatic is safest carried with the stock in your shooting vest pocket, barrel pointing up, the open and flagged breech facing out

General Shooting Ground Rules

The governing body rules for all disciplines are explicit in requiring that all shotguns be open and empty except when the competitor is on the shooting stand and the referee has given permission for shooting to commence. Ear and eye protection is compulsory when on the shooting ground. Never touch another person's gun without their knowledge and permission.

Ear and eye protection is compulsory

The Ten Commandments of Safety

1. Every gun should be considered loaded and treated with the utmost respect at all times. There are only two safe guns: one that is broken and seen to be empty; one that is in a zipped and closed gun slip where access to the trigger is impossible. Treat every closed gun as if it were loaded and respect its lethal qualities.

2. When carrying a gun out of its slip, it should be open and visibly empty at all times. Semi-automatic shotguns should be carried with the bolt back and the muzzles pointing up. A flag or other indicator should be placed in the chamber to help others recognise its safe condition.

3. Horse play is not tolerated and alcohol should never be consumed while shooting, only after the event or practice is over and your gun is safely locked away.

4. Use only cartridges of the correct gauge and chamber-length to match the gun you are shooting.

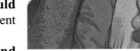

A gun out of its slip should always be open and empty

Make sure you have the appropriate shot size for the target being shot. Never use shot sizes larger than No. 6 and never mix different gauge cartridges in your bag or pockets.

A twenty-gauge cartridge can pass through the chamber of a twelve-gauge shotgun and lodge in the barrel, or even worse, allow a twelve-gauge cartridge to be loaded on top of it! The results can be disastrous!

Cartridges of different gauges should be stored separately, both at

Use only cartridges of the correct gauge and chamber length for your gun

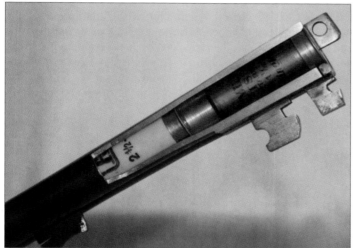

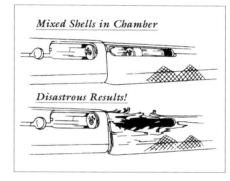

Mixing cartridges can have disastrous results

home and on the shooting ground. With the exception of some foreign imports, all twenty-gauge cartridges are yellow with other gauges being assorted colours.

5. Check your gun to make sure that it is in safe and sound condition, with no dents or pitting in the barrels; that it is in proof and has been nitro-proofed, and the correct cartridge is to be used.

All guns sold in the UK, by law, have to be submitted to proof-testing either by the London or Birmingham proof houses or their European counterparts. At the proof house, the guns are subjected to a pressure test and, if passed, stamped with the appropriate marks. Also the manufacturer will have engraved or stamped the chamber size and gauge on the gun.

If in any doubt regarding the above information, contact a reputable gun dealer who can give you a report on the condition and safety of your gun.

6. Never point or fire a gun at anything other than a clay pigeon. Any violation of this rule will automatically lead to your expulsion from the shooting ground. There are no exceptions to this rule.

All guns should be proofed, and in safe and sound condition

7. Always check that the gun is empty, pointing the muzzles up-range before loading, when taking the gun from or replacing it in its slip or gun rack. Also, always check the barrels for obstructions. Any blockage, no matter how small, can cause pressure to be generated in the barrels, with potentially dangerous results.

8. Muzzles must be kept pointing up the range at all times and only when you have opened your gun and ensured that it is empty, may you turn and leave the firing point.

9. There are three gun malfunctions you should be aware of while shooting.

(1) Anytime you pull the trigger and the gun fails to discharge, do not instantly open the gun. Keep it closed and pointing down range for thirty seconds before opening the gun and safely disposing of the cartridge. This is referred to as a 'hang fire'. In the governing body rules if a gun fails to discharge, the referee is required to take the gun from you to be sure it is a malfunction and not operator error. If you open the gun yourself, you will lose a target and this could affect both your safety and your score.

(2) You fire the gun and get a strange discharge, i.e., a soft 'ploof' sound instead of the normal loud crack. Stop and open the gun and check the barrels for blockage. The cartridge may have not had sufficient energy to push the wad clear of the muzzle. Both of these phenomena are, fortunately, rare occurrences with modern ammunition however you should be alert to them if they occur.

(3) If a gun is in poor condition, badly maintained or has developed a fault, closing the gun may cause the hammer to fall, accidentally discharging the gun. If this should happen, it is important to have control of the gun. The best way to do this is to hold the gun stock on your hip, the right forearm hand gripping the stock, but your finger off the trigger. The barrels are then brought to the action.

This closing technique, with the gun down and pointed down-range, ensures that if the gun *should* discharge, it will do so harmlessly, into the ground some two yards in front of you. This hip and hand grip allows you to keep control of the gun at all times – especially important if two cartridges are loaded.

In FITASC, where you may shoot from a hoop placed on the floor and not in a cage, this closing technique is required. If any accidental discharge occurs, the shot is safely controlled.

When shooting in a stand, keep your muzzles pointed down range at all times until you have opened and emptied the gun. Then, and only then, you may turn around and leave the stand.

10. You are responsible for the safe handling of yourself and your gun at all times. You are also responsible for the behaviour of any family, guests and animals when they are in your company.

Good shooting is no accident! Let us all try to do our bit to keep it that way!

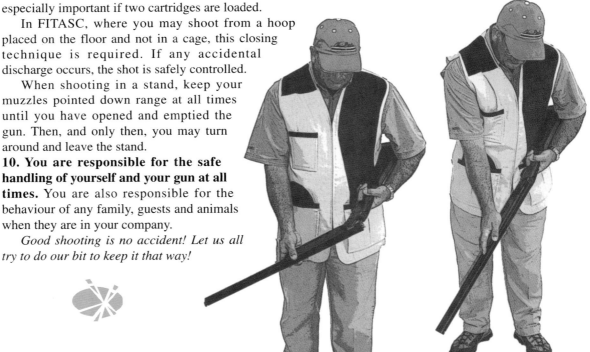

The correct way to open and close a shotgun

Chapter 3
The Shotgun

The Shotgun Defined

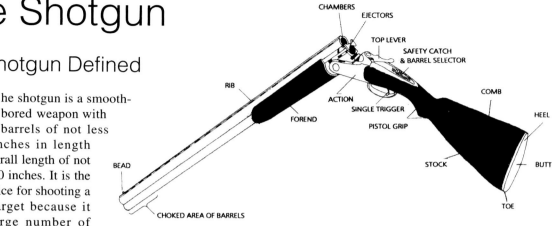

The shotgun is a smooth-bored weapon with barrels of not less than 24 inches in length and an overall length of not less than 40 inches. It is the gun of choice for shooting a moving target because it fires a large number of projectiles (shot) instead of a single projectile (bullet). The shot pattern, created by the shot stream, gives a greater margin of error. The shot strings out and spreads as it leaves the barrel. The amount of spread is controlled by the degree of 'choke' at the muzzles. Choke is a variable constriction at the end of the barrel. The more choke, the longer the effective range of the shotgun.

Shotguns come in many shapes and sizes

Types of Shotguns
Break Action
Side by Side – Over and Under

Fixed Action
Semi-Automatic – Pump

All types have their proponents, but for the clay shooter, there are advantages and disadvantages to the different types.

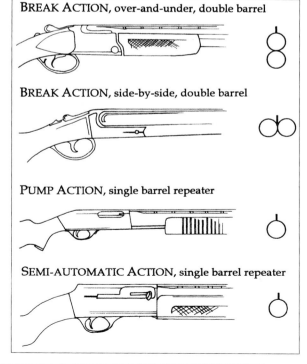

BREAK ACTION, over-and-under, double barrel

BREAK ACTION, side-by-side, double barrel

PUMP ACTION, single barrel repeater

SEMI-AUTOMATIC ACTION, single barrel repeater

Disadvantages

The Side by Side The broad barrel configuration of the side by side obstructs vision and the angled recoil and muzzle flip reduce control.

The Pump The time taken in working the pump, and the movement of the action, takes the barrels off the target line.

The Semi-Automatic The fixed action cannot readily be seen as unloaded and safe. Many find the mechanism movement in reloading distracting.

Advantages

The Semi-Automatic Preferred for their light recoil and fast handling characteristics, the relatively low-cost of the semi-auto makes it an attractive choice for beginners, ladies and the young shooter.

The Over and Under The single sight plane of the Over and Under complements our natural pointing ability, placing both hands in line, in synchronised movement to the target. The rigid barrels offer direct recoil and reduced muzzle flip. The break action is easily seen as safe from any distance.

Competitions are won by small margins – there is often only one target separating the winner from the pack. The inappropriate type of gun could cost you that one target. The only real choice for a competition gun is between the over and under and the semi-automatic.

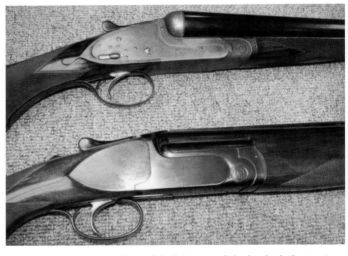

Shotgun actions

There are three types of actions in a break-action sporting gun.

The Sidelock

The firing mechanism in the sidelock is on plates let into the head of the stock and action bar. This design offers superior trigger pulls and has the advantage of intercepting sears that prevent accidental and double discharges.

The sidelock (top) and the boxlock (bottom)

The Boxlock

The over and under boxlock differs from the side by side in that the firing mechanism is between the top and bottom straps behind the action, concealed by the head of the stock.

The Trigger Plate

In this design, the firing mechanism is fixed to the trigger plate and, by working a catch, can be released through the bottom of the action for cleaning or maintenance.

The removable trigger plate action allows easy cleaning and maintenance

Buying a Shotgun

Your biggest decision and investment in clay target shooting is the purchase of a shotgun. For the beginner, the choices are many and a little bewildering. You should take your time, and do some research. Read the gun reviews in the different magazines and on-line. Talk to more experienced shots and ask them their opinions and suggestions.

Visit gun shops, examine and handle the guns that match your criteria to find the gun that feels right and seems to fit you well. The gun shop owner is usually an enthusiast and probably also shoots and can offer advice in the process. If the opportunity arises to shoot the chosen gun, then, by all means, do so. This advice also applies to the intermediate or advanced shot interested in upgrading his gun. Armed with the results of your research and enquiries, you should be able to begin to compile a short list of guns, by type and features, to match the discipline you intend to shoot. The list should also suit your budget parameters and physical requirements.

New or Second-Hand?

To buy new or second-hand is another decision. If you are buying a new gun, it will come with both a warranty and be in new condition. You can get a gun specifically designed for your discipline and some manufacturers offer a custom stock or some custom fitting options.

If, however, you are purchasing a second-hand gun, you should be aware that a gun is mechanical, like your car. Just as your car requires regular cleaning and maintenance, so does a gun. If this has been neglected, the gun could be in poor condition and, in extreme cases, not safe to shoot. A used trap gun is often a good choice. They are usually better priced and the money you save can be used to fit an adjustable comb, allowing some degree of custom-fitting.

A registered dealer has both legal responsibilities and a reputation to maintain. So, buying a second-hand gun through a dealer allows you to purchase with confidence. If you consider purchasing a used gun from a private party, you must carefully examine the gun to check proof, safety and condition. If you are unsure of how to do this, ask a more experienced friend or a dealer.

Some Words of Advice

You will be spoiled for choice in gun selection. There are as many choices in guns as there are cars on the road! This is really a two-edged sword. Yes, there is a wide selection, but it is so wide, that it's as easy to make the wrong choice as the right one.

Make haste slowly is the best advice! Take your time, don't be led by fashion. Make an informed decision. Make every attempt to 'try before you buy'. Ask friends if you can try their guns…use the club guns and, if possible, attend manufacturers' 'Have-A-Go' days.

Avoid excesses. Too heavy a gun will cause fatigue, too light a gun will create excessive recoil. Try to achieve balance, not only in the gun's handling, but in its overall design, length, weight, fit and feel.

Analyse your personal requirements, both physically and mechanically. Too often we are drawn to the gun being shot by the current champion or the one tricked out with all of the 'bells and whistles', which sometimes little suits our own needs. The 'hot' gun of today can often cause a slump which, due to a stubborn belief in the gun's championship-winning pedigree, can be a long-lasting and frustrating slump as well.

What makes a straight-shooting gun is a combination of elements - a harmonious balance. Once you have found the gun that best suits you, take the time to learn how it shoots, and when you have, stay with it.

Selecting the best gun for you

There are three requirements that a gun needs to fulfil. If you achieve all three, you will have a gun that works *with* you rather than *against* you. To find the right tool for the job for you, you need to first answer these questions:

1.   Does the gun **fit your budget?**
2.   Does it **fit the discipline** you intend to shoot?
3.   Will the gun allow you to **shoot to your full potential?**

Fitting your Budget

You get what you pay for in life. Nowhere do these words ring more true than in selecting your first gun or trading up. Always try to buy the best gun your budget will allow. I urge you to consider that the difference between the entry grade and the top gun in any particular make is nothing more than better wood and elaborate engraving. Neither of these 'up-grades' will help you shoot one target more. It is better to buy a plain, quality gun at your entry level price, than an elaborately engraved shotgun of poorer quality. If you buy a gun that is made of quality components, it will give you years of good service, stand up to a lot of shooting, be better balanced, with improved trigger pulls and reliable ejectors. The multi-choked gun costs a little more and is an individual choice, though it most certainly gives greater flexibility, especially in the sporting disciplines.

You do not have to break the bank to be a successful shooter! More competitions are won with good quality, entry level guns than with the expensive custom-made variety. (I will take it for granted that any gun you purchase complies with the Rules of Competition.)

Fitting the Discipline

It is amazing how many people I see shooting with an inappropriate gun for the discipline being shot. Many of them are doing an adequate job of it, but I can only wonder how much better they might be with the right tool for the job. Different disciplines require different characteristics and performance in a gun. These can be broken down into three types:

Trap

In Trap, the target is always at distance, rising and going away, so the classic Trap gun is high-stocked and often high-ribbed. The rising target needs a gun that prints its pattern a little high, building in lead, and allowing the target to be shot without being blocked out by the barrels. A 70 per cent over, 30 per cent under pattern placement is normal in Down the Line. In International Trap, because of the lower target presentations, competitors prefer their guns to shoot a little flatter at 60 per cent over, 40 per cent under.

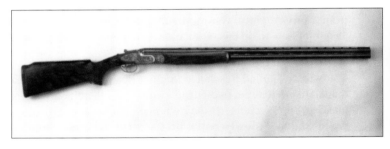

The trap gun

The average DTL gun weighs about 7½ to 8 lb and has the longer, 30, 32, or 34 inch barrels. Most of these guns are choked modified and improved modified or fitted with multi-chokes. This ensures the steady handling characteristics perfect for the target presentations of DTL. The International disciplines will require a gun with more life and tighter chokes; improved, modified and full.

The majority of Trap guns are over and unders. In the USA, where single 16-yard and Handicap shooting replaces DTL, the single-barrelled gun, both adapted over and under and purpose-made, are used, as are the pump and semi-automatic. USA shooters also show a preference for heavier guns and 9 to 10 lb competition guns are not uncommon.

Skeet

With its close targets, great variety of angles and number of stations, Skeet requires a gun that is far more dynamic than a Trap gun. In Trap, a gun is designed for inherent steadiness, the Skeet gun needs to have a

The skeet gun

combination of swift swinging characteristics and sufficient weight to control recoil. A good starting weight for a Skeet gun is around 7½ lb, though I know of some top competitors who favour a 9 lb-plus gun.

Skeet targets present a much flatter trajectory and the guns are set up to shoot a little flatter, with a 60 per cent over, 40 per cent under pattern. This allows the target to be kept in view, but the gun will still shoot to point of aim.

Barrel lengths of 28, 30 and 32 inch are now, by far, the most common. Multi-chokes have given the shotgun such flexibility that the same gun can even be used for both Skeet and Sporting Clays by just opening the chokes for the close Skeet targets. In the Olympic disciplines, fixed chokes are still preferred, these are very open and highly specialised. Once again, over and unders are the main gun of choice. But semi-autos and, in the US, pumps are also widely used.

Sporting Clays

This sport places the most demands on a competition shotgun because of the wide range of target presentations that are encountered. The type of targets thrown at sporting have evolved over the last two decades and have been very much influenced by the increased shooting skill of the competitors. Just look back at the scores that won the British Open in the seventies compared with the winning scores of today!

The sporting gun

Shooting ground owners, club members and competitors now demand far more challenging target presentations. This situation has created an almost infinite variety of targets, many at the very limits of a shotgun's range. The average course today is, without a doubt, more demanding than it was thirty years ago. As target distances have increased, it is not uncommon to see competitors carrying two guns; a short-barrelled, fast-handling Skeet gun, open-choked for the close shots, and a long-barrelled Trap gun, tight-choked for the longer targets.

It was not long before a distinct hybrid emerged, about the same time the technique for fitting interchangeable chokes was refined. The multi-choked gun gives the shooter the flexibility to use one gun throughout a sporting course, without being at a disadvantage. The Sporter or Sporting Shotgun, as it is most commonly referred to, should have choke tubes of the extended type, with knurled ends to ease changes and a manual barrel selector.

The Sporter started out with 28 to 30 inch barrels, weighing around 7½ lb. To keep within that optimum weight for the gun and to achieve that perfect combination of steadiness and dynamics, limited the length of the barrels. But with the introduction of cold-forged barrels, new steels and modern rib-less and vented construction, barrel weight was reduced to a point where it is now possible to find 34 inch Sporters, no heavier than older guns with the shorter barrels.

Advice on barrel lengths for Sporting Clays has made for interesting discussions over the years. You will receive as many opinions as there are barrel lengths. Only you can make the decision on the correct barrel length for you. But here is a list of opinions for and against the use of long barrels:

For the Longer Barrels
1. It is easier to point with a long gun than a short one.
2. Once under way, the gun will hold its course and line, giving a good follow-through.
3. The length and balance help control recoil and muzzle flip.
4. It is well-suited to the FITASC discipline and the longer sporting targets.

Against the Longer Barrels
1. Overcoming the dead gun or inertia is required (slow to start).
2. A deliberate timing of swing and trigger pull are required.
3. The gun requires a more deliberate style and the lead pictures must be re-learned.
4. At closer, incoming targets, as well as low driven presentations, the gun can be at a disadvantage and practice is required to overcome it.

Timing and swing-speed are, indeed, subtleties in shooting Sporting Clays. Rhythm and coordination are essential. They must be applied with an understanding of and a familiarity with the gun's weight and dynamics. You must be able to shoot a gun without upsetting your timing, regardless of the gun's barrel-length. I believe that those who struggle with a longer-barrelled gun do so because of a lack of this understanding.

Shooting to your Full Potential
It must seem obvious that if you are a petite lady or slight of build, the choice of a heavy, long-barrelled gun would be inappropriate. Likewise, if you are a six foot-plus weightlifter, a light, fast short-barrelled gun will be an equal handicap.

Try to find a gun that complements, rather than handicaps, your shooting. Choose a gun of a suitable length and weight to match your physical capabilities. 'A bad workman blames his tools' but if he does not have the correct tool for the job he cannot expect to do his best work.

If you shoot Trap, purchase a Trap gun, Skeet, a Skeet gun and Sporting Clays, a Sporting Clays gun. This may seem simplistically obvious, but the reality is: you will never shoot to your true potential in a given discipline, using a gun designed for another discipline. The improvements in the modern competition shotgun referred to earlier, have been mainly in the refinement of the gun for its particular discipline. The only proviso to this statement is the use of a suitable Trap gun for Sporting Clays; i.e., one that has been custom set-up for the Sporting discipline.

Barrel Length
Barrel length is determined by your physical size and strength, not the target presentation. While long barrels might help on the long distance crosser, they are not going to help on the close, fast incomer. Improved control is worth more than length, any day.

Strength
The modern shotgun has improved immeasurably! They are 20 per cent better balanced, 30 per cent stronger and 40 per cent more reliable than the guns being made thirty years ago. Modern metallurgy and manufacturing techniques have created guns of maximum strength and superior shooting qualities. This has been achieved, not so much by reducing weight, but by better distribution of the weight throughout the whole shotgun.

The better barrels and actions, barrel-boring and the advances in chokes, together with improved cartridges have created guns that shoot impressive patterns, balanced with low recoil.

Mechanics and Ballistics
The mechanics comprise the components of the gun, the lock, the stock and the barrel, but it is the interaction between the barrel and the cartridge – the ballistics – that allows the consistent shooting of a moving target.

Because a shotgun fires a large number of projectiles – the shot – instead of a single projectile – a bullet – the pattern created allows a larger margin for error.

The shot strings out and spreads as it leaves the barrel. The amount of spread is controlled by the degree of 'choke' at the muzzles. This is a variable constriction at the end of the barrel – the tighter the choke, the longer the effective range of the shotgun. The optimum degree of choke present in the gun depends on the type of target presentation being shot. You should purchase a gun with the correct choking for the targets you intend to shoot.

Velocity and Patterns

It is the long forcing cones, back-boring and choke-taper technology, combined with the choice of cartridge that creates the pattern, not the length of the barrels. All velocity is generated within a few inches of the chamber, and any increase as the charge progresses through the barrel, is minimal – at most, a foot-per-inch of the barrel length.

The pattern is regulated at the muzzle, independent of barrel length. It makes no difference if the gun has 26 or 34 inch barrels, the velocity is minimally affected and the pattern quality is regulated by the amount of choke present in the muzzles.

Ribs, Beads and Optical Illusions

Ribs and beads have a big impact on apparent barrel length; a narrow rib and small bead will make a short-barrelled gun look long when mounted, whereas a wide rib and large bead will make the long-barrelled gun look short. In fact, ribs and beads can create an optical illusion! They are a very personal addition, and you should experiment to find the combination that gives you good muzzle awareness while being minimally distracting when shooting.

The rib's other purpose is to dissipate heat and avoid the 'mirage effect'. Ribs are cross-filed to reduce distracting reflection. One-eyed shooters who tend to be 'aimers', favour a narrower rib, while two-eyed shooters being pointers, prefer a wider rib. The tapered 8mm to 11mm rib seems to suit all.

There are as many combinations of ribs and beads as there are types of shotgun

Weight, Balance and Ease of Handling

Once the gun is mounted, it can be made to feel longer by moving the moment of inertia, or balance point, in front of the hinge pin. This makes the barrels feel a little heavier and swing more freely, controls muzzle flip and can help

Shotgun rib styles

on second targets especially in true pairs and longer crossers. A smooth swing is more easily obtained when the point of balance is between the hands. A properly-balanced gun feels alive and much lighter than it actually is.

Triggers

Often taken for granted, triggers are a very important part of the gun. Their importance and effect on timing is immense. Too light and there is every chance of accidental discharge, especially on cold days when gloves may be worn. Too heavy and the effort of pulling the trigger can cause loss of timing, the swing can check and the result is a miss behind.

The single selective trigger is a necessity in a Sporting Clays gun. Instant selection makes best use of the gun chokes for the different sequence in target presentations. Single triggers are complex in design. After the first shot, the trigger must be released to

The single selective trigger shown on a Beretta sporting clays gun

allow the engagement of the second lifter. This is referred to as the 'dead pull'. Without this 'dead pull', the recoil from the first shot would cause an involuntary firing of the second barrel.

This trigger release can cause some shooters to develop a twitch which can become a problem, causing a miss-fire of the second barrel. Correct regulation, with crisp pulls and the correct poundage will allow unconscious firing of the gun with minimum lock-time.

Weights of trigger pulls are a personal choice, but I would never recommend a pull of less than 3½ lb for the front trigger, with an additional ½ lb on the second trigger. That is my personal preference: 3½ lb on the front and 4 lb on the back. The ideal trigger pull is like a stem of fine-spun glass snapping with no drag or sponginess.

Adjustable triggers are a good addition to a gun. They can be adjusted to achieve proper grip and finger placement.

Stocks

Manufacturers differ greatly in their standard stock dimensions. You may be lucky and find one that fits, but the odds are against it. Many shooters struggle for years with a gun that does not properly fit. As far as the way a gun fits, all measurements are important but the drop at face (measured half-way between the drop at

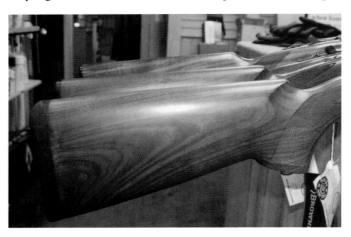

Stock dimensions vary greatly from one manufacturer to another

comb and heel) is critical to straight shooting. Too low a drop will cause cross dominance, too high a drop will cause misses over the target.

The correct eye-rib alignment is essential. The comb, at face, should be as parallel as possible, negating the effect of involuntary head movement as the target elevations change. The Monte Carlo stock (it gets its name from the famous European city of Monaco, once the Mecca of live pigeon shooting) has a parallel comb. This is particularly advantageous to people with long necks. The adjustable comb serves the same purpose and allows an element of custom-fitting for cast and drop.

Grips

The shape of the grip on the stock and the fore-end needs careful consideration. They must be of a shape and size that gives a natural, relaxed hand position allowing full articulation throughout the shooting action. If the radius of the pistol grip is too sharp, it places the hand in an unnatural position – the hand is under tension and its movement is constricted.

The straight-hand grip, also known as the 'English' grip

The semi-pistol grip, also known as a half-pistol grip

A full pistol grip

The splinter fore-end is a small wedge-shaped piece of wood

The beavertail fore-end curves upward along the barrel's contou

A deep beavertail fore-end on a repeater

Basic shotgun stock grips and fore-end styles

The thickness of both grip and fore-end should be comfortable, put the hand in a good shooting position and enhance gun control. A palm swell is only required for people with very large hands. The distance between the comb nose and the breech is what matters in hand placement. If this distance is too small, it forces the hand into an unnatural position and, combined with a too-full grip, can be very bad indeed.

Recoil

Newton's Third Law of Motion states: 'For every action, there is an equal and opposite reaction'. So, in the shotgun, the rearward thrust of the gun equals the velocity of what goes out of the front.

Recoil Type and Effect

I personally believe that recoil has a greater impact on our shooting than we are aware of, perhaps even as much as impact as gunfit does. The right gun goes a long way to controlling recoil.

There are two types of recoil:

1.   Conscious: where you feel it on every shot.
2.   Subconscious: where you are *unaware* of its impact.

Subconscious recoil, even though you may not physically feel it, can affect your shooting by throwing off your timing, swing and rhythm.

Recoil Cures

If we are suffering from conscious, or felt, recoil, we need to learn what alterations or additions can be made to the gun to minimize and control it. The first criteria is that the shotgun should fit not only your build and height, but also strength and reaction capabilities. The word that best sums up the cure for hidden or felt recoil is *balance*.

Too light or too heavy a gun can result in similar actions. Barrel length should be considered in this equation, as well. It is possible that a light gun with long barrels can have worse recoil characteristics than a heavier, short-barrelled gun.

A longer-barrelled gun of the correct weight will always have the advantage of recoil control. Here you find the inertia of the longer, heavier barrels helps to minimize recoil as well as muzzle flip. A well-fitted gun is one of the best cures for excessive recoil. However, the good gun fit must be accompanied by a good gun mount. A poorly-mounted gun can negate even the best gun fit and increases felt recoil. There are many alterations and additions that can be done to a shotgun to reduce recoil. Be aware that while some of these changes can suppress recoil very well, they can also increase weight and affect balance.

Factors that help control recoil:
1. Individual physical build.
2. Stance and posture.
3. Grip or how we hold the gun.
4. Cartridge load.
5. Gun type.
6. Noise.
7. Gun fit.
8. Balance of the gun.
9. Barrel length.
10. Forcing cones.
11. Back-boring.
12. Porting.

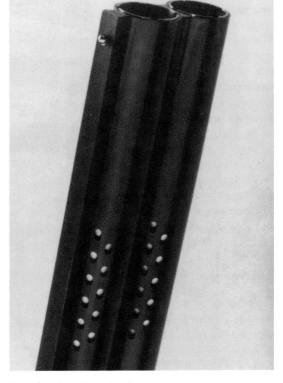

BELOW: *Mercury recoil reducer*

Ported and multi-choked barrels

Additions and Alterations for Recoil Control
Spring recoil reducers and mercury recoil suppressors work by slowing the recoil force down but they can add 8 to 10 ounces-plus of weight which can affect or disturb balance and handling.

Custom recoil reducers Either spring, air or hydraulic, are fitted to the stock and then the recoil pad through a piston or plunger connection. They are adjustable and offer the most *effective* recoil suppression and reduction. But most custom recoil reducers weigh, on average, 12 ounces. This extra weight affects balance and handling. It can actually be so effective in suppressing recoil that it causes the inertia single trigger to fail to pick up the second barrel.

Barrel porting A series of holes are drilled, laser-cut or spark-eroded at angles and in shapes into the top half of the barrel or barrels, so that a percentage of gas is released, countering both recoil and muzzle flip. Ported barrels offer more benefit in controlling muzzle flip than recoil. With porting, noise is increased considerably. This has led to a ban on ported guns for use in competition by some clay shooting governing bodies.

Back boring The barrel is over-bored from the normal 729. to between 735. and 739. This improves the patterns and helps reduce recoil. The increased nominal boring requires a cartridge with a plastic wad to create an effective seal in the barrel to avoid shot balling and deformity. Felt or fibre wads do not work well in a back-bored gun.

Forcing cone This is a cone that forces the shot from the chamber into the barrel. Lengthening and polishing the forcing cone improves patterns and reduces recoil by easing the shot's transition from the shell into the slightly smaller barrel. The improved performance has the same effect as back boring – it reduces pressure and recoil. Every gun should be factory-fitted with lengthened forcing cones.

Trigger Properly-regulated trigger pulls are very effective in reducing recoil. This is not a job for a machine in a factory, but should be done by hand by an expert.

Chokes Long chokes that have a smooth parallel progression into the barrel restriction will improve patterns and reduce recoil.

Balance Placing the moment of inertia between the hands creates balance. The combination of the gun's weight and the shape of the stock and fore-end allows correct placement of the hands. Good balance gives the hands a good grip and lets the arms act like a car's suspension, absorbing recoil. A well-balanced gun ensures a smooth and steady swing.

Recoil Pads The traditional pads for reducing recoil come in many shapes, patterns and materials. The amount of recoil absorption the pad provides is in direct proportion to the material in the pad. Some rubber pads can be as hard as the wood itself and have little dampening effect on recoil. Other pads are too soft and can even be sticky, hanging up on clothing and making the gun mount difficult. A smooth, mid-way pad is the best choice.

The Last Word on Recoil Reduction

Recoil control is vital to straight shooting. The addition of any recoil reducer which adds weight to the gun will affect its balance and handling. It may be better to consider a combination of several recoil reducing methods which would work better and have less impact on balance and handling than one heavy, mechanical solution.

The Ideal Combination

My preference for the ideal Sporter would be a 7½ lb gun with 30 to 34 inch barrels, back-bored to .735, with 3 inch, lengthened forcing cones, well-polished and extended chokes that exactly match the bore of the gun.

Trigger interior parts should be polished and set to a crisp 3½ to 4 lb with no creep or drag. The point of balance should be on, or fractionally in front of, the hinge pin. A ⅝th inch Kick Eez sporting pad rounds off the package. The butt of the stock should be fitted so that as much of the surface as possible is in contact with the shoulder, to spread and diminish the impact of recoil. Now you have a gun that is easy to mount, comfortable to shoot and not excessively heavy.

Keeping it Working

Your shotgun represents a considerable investment and we take for granted that this investment, along with balanced handling, gives the reliability to deliver perfect function shot after shot, year after year. We are totally depending upon this reliability during a competition. Well, in the same manner that a car requires regular servicing to give reliable performance and decrease depreciation, so does your shotgun.

A regular cleaning and maintenance regime takes little time and effort but will ensure the reliability, safe functioning and long life of your shotgun. There are two corrosive and damaging actions:

1. Fouling:

(a) Every shot made creates an actual fire in the chamber, the resultant residue, no matter how clean burning the powder, fouls actions, chambers and bores, if allowed to accumulate will clog moving parts, cause corrosion affecting performance and safety.

(b) Plastic wads leave residue in the barrels.

(c) Lead shot can leave residue, particularly at the muzzle and, if allowed to accumulate, will affect choke and hence patterns.

2. Moisture:

(a) Accumulated fouling left in the action, chambers and bores wicks moisture from the air.

(b) Moving your gun from cold to warm air creates condensation.

It is the combination of the two, fouling and moisture, that causes the most corrosion, with rust beginning to form within 24 hours of contact with metal.

Shotgun Terms

action - the moving parts that allow you to load, fire and unload your shotgun. (See Breech, Chamber, Trigger)

barrel selector - detemines which barrel of a double barrel gun will fire first.

blacking/blueing - the blue coloration applied to protect gun barrels

bore - in simple terms the interior diameter of a gun barrel, which will vary according to the gun's design and intended use. The size of the bore is indicated by the term gauge.

box-lock - a type of gun action, often recognizeable by its squared appearance.

breech - the end of the barrel nearest the stock.

broken gun - in a hinge type gun, where the barrels are dropped open and clear of the action, exposing the chambers to view.

butt - the rear of the shoulder end of the gun's stock

comb - the side of the stock that fits against your cheek.

chamber - the part of the action, at the breech end of the barrel, into which the shot shell is placed.

choke - the degree of narrowing or constriction of the bore at the muzzle end of the barrel, intended to increase the effective range of the gun. (See examples of chokes: Full, Modified, and Improved Cylinder)

ejector - the mechanism on shotguns by which spent shot cases are automatically ejected from the gun when it is opened after firing.

forearm - the part of the stock that lies under the barrel.

full choke - the tightest constriction or narrowing of the bore, producing the greatest effective range.

grip - the narrow portion of the stock held with the trigger hand.

gauge - the term used to describe the interior diameter of the bore. The smaller the gauge number, the larger the bore size. Modern shotguns are available in 10, 12, 16, 20 and 28 gauge. An exception is the .410 bore shotgun, which is actually a 67 gauge.

hinge - a type of action in which a hinge mechanism separates the barrel from the standing breech block, providing access to the chamber.

improved cylinder - less constructed than a modified or full choke - a good all around choke for sporting clays.

modified choke - moderate constriction or narrowing of the bore.

muzzle - the end of the barrel from which the shot exits.

over-and-under - a two-barrelled shotgun with one barrel placed over the other. (The American version of the standard British game shooting gun.)

pump - a type of action that loads and ejects shells by pumping the forearm of the stock back and forth.

recoil - the force with which the gun moves backwards into the shoulder when fired.

safety - a safety device that, in the "on" position, prevents the gun from firing. In many field guns the safety is automatically engaged when the gun is opened; in other guns, particularly competition grades, the safety must be manually engaged.

semi automatic - a type of action in which gas from the burning gunpowder in the shell automatically ejects the spent shell and loads another. Semi-automatics are noted for minimal recoil.

shot - round projectiles, usually of lead or steel. Depending on shot size and load, a shell can contain from 45 to 1,170 shot.

shot pattern - the concentration of shot measured in a circle at a given range, usually 30 to 40 yards.

side-by-side - a shotgun with two barrels sitting side by side. In Great Britain, the standard game shooting gun.

stock - the "handle" of the shotgun, the part held to the shoulder, comprising the butt, comb, grip.

shotshell or shell - the ammunition fired by shotguns, consisting of five components: the case, primer, powder charge, wad, and shot.

trigger - finger-pulled lever in single, double or trigger that drives the firing point forward and fires the gun.

You should clean your gun each and every time that you use it, if it is in storage it should be removed on a regular schedule and inspected and given a further application of oil. If a gun has been stored for a protracted period of time it should be thoroughly examined and cleaned before use.

If the gun is used in the rain, it should be wiped off and allowed to stand for several hours to allow any water to sweat out, before the normal cleaning regime is performed.

Never leave guns for prolonged periods in fleece-lined gunslips and especially when wet.

Gun safes should have electric dehumidifiers fitted or a sack of silica crystals placed inside to remove any moisture created from condensation.

Gun Cleaning Kit:

1. Cleaning rod, bronze brush, jag, wool mop, patches of the correct bore size for the gun.
2. Bore cleaning solvent.
3. Gun oil, which has two roles – lubricant for moving parts and protective coating.
4. Clean lint-free cloths.
5. Small brush (toothbrush).
6. Cotton buds or a feather.
7. Kitchen roll.

Cleaning Sequence

Check that the gun is unloaded; dismantle it into its component parts of stock and action, barrels (remove multi-chokes if fitted) and fore-end. Either spray bore cleaner into the barrels or dip the brush in the solvent. Using the rod, run the brush through the barrels from the breech end to the muzzles several times. Next, using balled kitchen roll or patches with the jag, dry the bores, using clean material in each pass until they emerge clean. Multi-chokes are cleaned in the same manner; if badly fouled, they can be soaked in solvent to soften up residue. Taking a small brush or feather, clean all debris from between the ribs and in the action. Check all screws and fastenings to ensure tightness (they can become loose in use). Coat all metal surfaces including interior bores (rod and mop) with fine gun oil, multi-chokes require a smear of gun grease before reinstallation and a little grease should be used an all bearing parts of the action and fore-end.

Woodwork should be wiped off and polished using one of the stock care products.

The gun can now be reassembled and safely stored.

Note: Before using, always run a rod and mop through the bore to remove oil residue.

It is recommended that you should give your shotgun to a competent gunsmith once a year for a strip and clean, where the interior parts are inspected for both reliability and safety.

In Conclusion

Everyone will change guns several times during their learning curve. As shooting skills and knowledge of the differences in guns improve, you will change guns to better match your current level. However, once you have found the gun that fits and functions well for you, keep it.

Targets come in many shapes and sizes. The colour is chosen to make the target stand out against different backgrounds.

Chapter 4
Targets, Chokes and Cartridges

T he target's type and presentation determines the amount of choke and the size of the shot you need to break it. The correct combination of choke and cartridge is what produces hard-hitting patterns which translate into better-broken targets.

An understanding of the various types of targets used in the different disciplines will help you choose the best choke and cartridge combination to break them. We also will take a look at the best place to break those targets, as well as how they are thrown.

Targets

Target Types
There are six different target sizes and configurations:

1. **Standard** 4½ inches in diameter and 1⅛ inches thick; dome shaped. Used in Skeet, Trap and the majority of Sporting Clays presentations.
2. **Midi** 3½ inches in diameter, ⅞ inch thick. Used in Sporting Clays. Its smaller size makes it appear farther away than it actually is; it retains its initial velocity longer than larger targets.
3. **Mini** 2⅜ inches in diameter, ⅝ inch thick. Used in Sporting Clays. Very deceptive because its small size makes it appear to be moving faster than it actually is; slows equally quickly because it is so light.
4. **Rabbit** 4½ inches in diameter; ⅝ inch thick. Used in Sporting Clays. Rolls and bounces on the ground; thick rim density prevents it from shattering on the ground; often presented as a Chondel.
5. **Battue** 4½ inches in diameter; ⅜ inch thick. Used in Sporting Clays. Called the 'flying razor blade'; difficult to pick up edge-on; because of the lack of a dome is unstable in flight and rolls to show the full face to the gun.
6. **Rocket** 4½ inches in diameter; ⅝ inch thick. Used in Sporting Clays. Deceptive in flight, it appears to float, but retains far more velocity than the standard clay.

Colours
Standard targets come in a variety of colours: orange, yellow, green, white and black. They are chosen based on their visibility against different backgrounds. The other target types are predominantly black.

Vulnerability
The target can be shown to the gun in three presentations, each offering a different degree of vulnerability. These are described in descending order of breaking difficulty:

1. **Shoulder** This is the thickest part of the clay and the hardest part to break. Added to this is the fact that it offers a very small target area. The target is spinning at many revolutions per second and the shoulder deflects the energy and direction of the shot from the strike point. The target shoulder requires a solid hit from multiple pellets to break it.

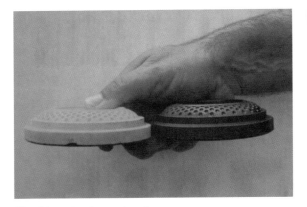

Shoulder – hardest to break

Dome – less hard to break

2. **Dome** This is the next thickest area, and offers a much larger target to the gun. At the dome, the spinning effect is reduced and the target will break from a strike by a moderate number of pellets.
3. **Belly** The underside offers the thinnest and largest target area. Its revolutions have little effect to the gun and only a few pellets are required to break it.

Deceptive Targets

The course setter often sets the trap so that the target is changing flight at the place you are naturally inclined to shoot it. This transition can result in a target that deceptively shows a mixture of areas. For example, in a quartering-away shot, only half the

Belly – easiest to break

dome will show. These targets are always best shot with the choke and cartridge best suited for the hardest part of the target.

Traps

The target is, to all intents and purposes, a flying saucer. It sustains level flight through its speed, revolutions and shape, in the same manner that a frisbee does. It is thrown by a machine known as a trap and these can be manually or automatically operated.

The trap itself is simply a large spring and an arm; the target is placed on or against the arm. The spring is compressed and released, driving the arm at great speed and throwing the clay, like a discus thrower. The speed at which the clay leaves the trap is determined by the tension 'wound on' the spring.

Trap settings are fully adjustable for distance, elevation, and angle and many can also be tilted. Course setters can offer as many different targets, in as many

Automatic trap

varied and challenging presentation as their imagination (and the shooters) will allow.

Chokes
Origin

The invention of the choke in 1866 is generally credited to an English gentleman, Mr W. R. Pape. There is additional evidence that Sylvester Roper, an American gunsmith, patented the invention of choked barrels in April of 1866, several weeks before Mr Pape received his patent. All this was contested by Fred Kimble, an American, who claimed to have invented choking in 1867. Then in 1874, W. W. Greener, another Englishman, researched and developed the concept even further. Whoever gets the ultimate credit, the choke has done more to increase the effective range of the shotgun than any other invention since!

Automatic rabbit or Chondel trap

The early chokes increased the shotgun's range from 30 to 50 yards and subsequent refinements have extended the effective range even farther. Cartridge innovations, such as the addition of antimony to the lead shot, added buffers and coatings, plus the invention of the plastic wad and the star crimp, have all been factors in the shotgun's increased range. But without the presence of choke, cartridge improvements alone would have little impact.

How Choke Works

'Choke' means to constrict – to create a tightening effect – and that is exactly what choke does in the barrel of a shotgun. The walls of the shotgun barrel are parallel from the chamber to the muzzles. The addition of choke gradually increases the wall thickness of the barrel, so gradually *decreases or constricts* the inside diameter at the muzzles.

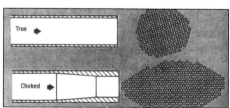

DIAGRAM 1:
An exaggerated diagram showing how choke works.

The amount of this constriction is measured in thousandths of an inch as added to the nominal boring of the barrel. Before the invention of choke, all barrels where simply straight tubes, hence the expression 'true cylinder'.

DIAGRAM 2:
The difference in patterns achieved by different chokes at 25 yards.

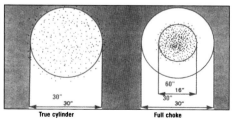

(This is the most open barrel with '0', or no choke.) The amount of choke restriction is measured in increments of ten thousandths of an inch, with the tightest or 'Full' choke, measuring forty thousandths of an inch.

Terminology and Sizes

Different countries have different terminology for the different amounts of choke: (measurement in thousandths of an inch)

UK		Europe and America	Symbol
True Cylinder	0	True Cylinder	Cyl
Quarter	10	Improved Cylinder	****
Half	20	Modified	***
Three Quarter	30	Improved Modified	**
Full	40	Full	*

Note: There are choke constrictions designed specifically for Skeet. While manufacturers differ on this amount, it is typically five to eight thousandths of an inch. This is usually marked SK1 and SK2. These marks are most often found on the barrel at the breech.

Range and Distance

The more choke present in the barrels, the greater the shotgun's effective range. This is achieved by holding the shot column together longer, so as it leaves the barrel it is narrower and more air resistant, reducing the amount of spread. The accepted Optimum Range of different chokes is:

30-inch pattern at:
40 yards	Full
35 yards	Improved Modified or ¾
30 yards	Modified or ½
25 yards	Improved Cylinder
20 yards	True Cylinder or Skeet

You can see that a cylinder choke would be of little use at 40 yards and, conversely, a full-choke, little use at 20 yards.

Further Choke Developments

Since the discovery of chokes' major impact on the range of a shotgun, there have been many variations and permutations. Several different designs were patented by E. Field White, inventor of the Poly Choke, others by Col Cutts of the Cutts Compensator, and W.R. Weaver of the Weaver choke. Other manufacturers tried other choke designs: swaged, conical, recessed, cylindro-conical, bell, trumpet, retro, and Tula, among others.

But the innovation destined to match the impact of the choke itself, was the Winchester Company's introduction of the first internal multi-choke, the Winchoke. This concept had been tried earlier by Sylvester Roper, but the Winchester multi-choke system would change the game of Sporting Clays shooting forever.

During the 1960s and 70s, many Sporting Clays competitors carried two guns; a Trap gun with tight chokes for long shots and a Skeet gun with more open chokes for the close shots. This way, they could choose the gun best-choked for the target presentation.

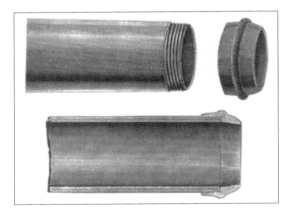

Roper's original mult-choke

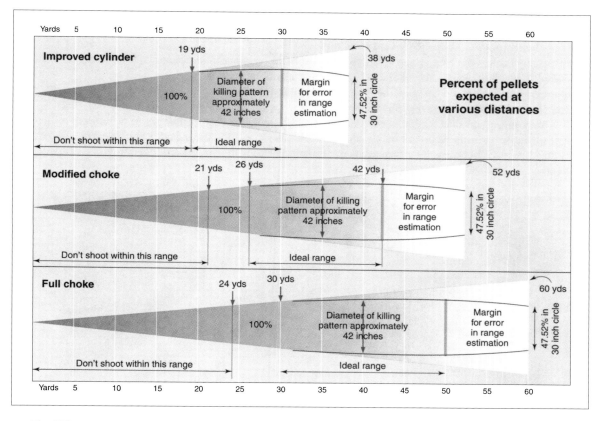

The Winchester system was followed by the work of another American, Jess Briley of Houston, Texas. Briley refined the development of the screw-in choke. He created a system wherein any shotgun could have the barrels machined and threaded, and, by screwing in matched tubes, the *choke could be adjusted to suit the target!* This ultimately revolutionised the clay target gun.

This Briley System is now an industry standard and is factory-fitted in many shotguns. Other specialist companies also offer retro-fitting to a fixed-choked gun or they can adapt and install their own system to replace the manufacturer's. In the USA, Briley, Rhino, and Seminole are suppliers of these specialist choking services. In the UK, Nigel Teague has built a sterling reputation for his products.

These after-market installations have given greater flexibility to choke selection and many competitors today choose to install personalized degrees of choke to their guns such as Light Modified, which is fifteen thousandths of an inch and half-way between IC and Mod. This is a good selection for the semi-automatic single-barrel, as it is an extremely flexible choking.

Choke works because of the difference in the diameter of the choke to the nominal boring of the barrel. This difference creates a problem: as the shot column is propelled down the barrel, it suddenly runs into a restriction to its passage. At this point, many of the pellets become crushed and deformed. This deformation means the pellets are slowed down and deflected off-path by the effects of air resistance (flyers). Every pellet crushed in this way fails to reach the target.

It was quickly learned that the more gradual the lead-in to the choke constriction, the fewer pellets were deformed. Today's specialist choke suppliers have refined their product to minimize the deformation of the shot charge. Modern chokes, whether parallel or gradually-tapered, are much longer than the early Victorian versions.

Multi-Choke Options

Multi-chokes with interchangeable tubes are screwed into the muzzles of the shotgun, increasing the flexibility of choke options. These come in several types:

Flush-fitting chokes have castellations in them to facilitate installation and removal with a key or wrench.

Extended tube chokes are knurled and are put in and taken out by hand.

Wad–stripping chokes are designed to strip off the wad.

Ported chokes reduce muzzle flip and recoil.

It is very important that the multi-chokes match the nominal boring of the gun to accurately reflect the amount of choke present. The amount of choke in the tube is marked on its side. Because this is obscured when they are installed, they are either grooved around their top edge or colour-coded to tell you the degree of choke.

Multi-Choke Markings
Number of grooves
None:	True Cylinder
One:	Full
Two:	Improved Modified
Three:	Modified
Four:	Improved Cylinder

Written Markings:
SK 1 & SK 2 Skeet

Some of the extended multi-chokes have a colour-coding or the degree of constriction is written out on the choke.

Choke versus air resistance
As the shot leaves the barrel, it encounters air resistance. In fact the loud 'bang!' heard when a shot is fired, does not all come from the exploding powder, it is the sound of the shot stream breaking the sound barrier as it leaves the end of the gun!

This air resistance acts upon the shot charge, slowing it down and forcing the component pellets apart. The deformed pellets or 'flyers' peel away first. Then, in progressive erosion, the outer layer of pellets stretches out, forming the shot string. It is this string that gives a shotgun the margin for error that allows us to shoot a moving target. But this shot string needs to be balanced, if it is too thin, there are gaps big enough for the target to pass through untouched.

It is important to choose the appropriate choke for the distance at which the target will be broken. A slightly tighter choke than the distance might dictate will deliver a dense, accurate shot string, with breaking capabilities along its entire length. This is preferable to depending on a wider, longer shot string, full of gaps, to try to make the hit.

Cartridges
Choke and its effectiveness can be very much affected by your choice of cartridge, and you can easily be overwhelmed by the number and variety of cartridges available on the market today. Each brand and formula promises better performance, more speed, improved patterns and harder shots. For the beginner and intermediate shooter, this can lead to constant experimentation, changing brands and loads, trying to find the cartridge solution to improve their performance. The reality is all cartridges contain the same components; the differences are in the type, amount and quality of those components, and how they are constructed, to achieve what level of performance. The component parts are the case, primer, powder, wad, shot and crimp.

The cartridge, when fired, acts like the plunger or piston in a bicycle pump. The primer is struck and ignites the powder, which creates combustion, similar to the fuel and air mixture in a petrol engine when ignited by the spark plug. This, combined with the crimp, or the way the cartridge is closed, creates the pressure that propels the shot charge along the barrel. At this point, the wad performs a very valuable task, both protecting the shot charge from the heat of the powder combustion and acting as the piston and seal to ensure that the best use is made of the pressure generated.

As the shot travels down the barrel at great speed and under high pressure, it is inevitable that there will be some shot deformity. The more deformity, the more 'flyers', and the poorer the pattern or 'string'. Passage through both the forcing cones and choke tubes creates many more deformed pellets or flyers. In fact, when choke was first used in shotguns, it actually resulted in worse patterns! The shot itself must be of sufficient hardness to resist deforming while being pushed through the barrel at several hundred miles per hour.

It was only with the discovery and introduction of antimony into the mixture of lead shot that it became hard enough to resist these damages. Like all things in life, the best costs more. Antinomy is ten times the price of lead. When you see a cartridge that has an antimony content of 5 per cent or more, that's the reason that cartridge is a little more expensive.

The high antinomy cartridges are the premier marques within every brand and, if the manufacturer elects to use high antinomy shot in a cartridge, they often use better quality components in the rest the cartridge. However, until you master the basics of shooting straight, there is little to be gained between buying the budget and the best.

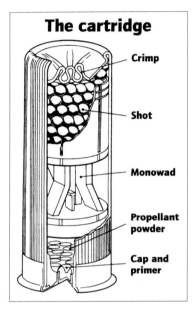

Cartridge Components Impact Choice

When choosing a cartridge, you should consider:

1. Wad.
2. Shot Size.
3. Recoil.

Taking them in order:

Wad

The wad is made from either felt or plastic. Some shooting grounds insist on bio-degradable felt wads for environmental reasons. However, from the shooter's stand point, the plastic wad will always be superior to the fibre. The plastic wad has a cup with a built-in seal and shock-absorbing piston to protect the shot on its journey down the barrel. There have, however, been many advances in the felt wad cartridge, including a small orbitrator or seal, so its performance is now only a small percentage short of the plastic wad cartridge.

Shot Size

The main shot sizes used for clays include No. 9s, 8s and 7½s. *The larger the number, the smaller the diameter of the individual pellet and the less energy is generated per pellet.* If you cut open a cartridge of each size and micrometer the shot, you will find very little difference in the sizes of the pellets. As the No. 8 pellets are smaller in diameter, there are a greater number in a 28 gram load. But what you gain on the swings you inevitably loose on the roundabouts. If you shoot No.7½s, yes, you have bigger shot and more striking power, but fewer pellets in the cartridge than if you shot No. 8s.

Shot size 9.

Shot size 8.

Shot size 7½.

A simple rule of thumb is out to 35 yards, use No. 8s. Past 35 yards, use No. 7½s. Some competitors favour No.9s for wider, denser patterns at really close targets. But the main shot sizes used for clays, now that the compulsory use of No. 9s for Skeet has been removed, will be No. 8s and No. 7½s.

Recoil

Recoil is a big factor in your personal choice of shell. Recoil is both fatigue-inducing and the cause of many second barrel misses. Comparing two shells with equal feet per second ratings, one can be smooth, with little recoil when fired, while the other can give you a punch of which a boxer would be proud.

This is due to the burning properties of the powder; one ignites in a steady, powerful progression, one simply explodes. The differences can be compared to the acceleration of a Rolls-Royce and a Hot Rod. Both get up to 60 miles per hour, the ride is just more comfortable in the Rolls. The powders that are capable of both speed and reasonable pressure are as in the automobile analogy: the smoother the recoil, the more expensive the cartridge.

Cartridge Speed's Affect on Lead

Compare the average cartridge and the fastest cartridge on the market: the difference between the two in lead required to hit a target at 40 yards is but a few inches. When you consider a target travelling at forty miles per hour, at this distance, it would require nine feet of forward allowance! Surely the faster cartridge in and of itself would not give you any great advantage. It is better to find a cartridge that is comfortable to shoot and stick with it, rather than continuously experimenting with the 'rocket science' of velocity's small affect on lead.

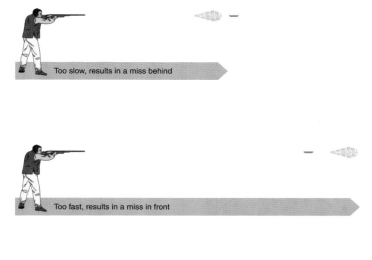

Too slow, results in a miss behind

Too fast, results in a miss in front

Flight Testing the Cartridge-Choke Combination

The only way to determine precisely how your cartridge-choke combination performs in your shotgun is at a patterning board. Here you can determine if you have the correct mix of choke and cartridge to match the target flight and distance of your chosen discipline.

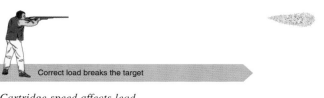

Correct load breaks the target

Cartridge speed affects lead

Pattern Plate

The 'pattern' is the distribution of the pellets shot onto a vertical surface. The pattern plate, usually a vertical steel plate that is painted or greased, is shot at from a set distance of 40 yards away. The resulting shot pattern reveals the interaction between your chosen choke and cartridge.

The pattern plate is used to check the following:

1. Point of impact
2. Choke and cartridge performance
3. Choke regulation
4. Barrel regulation
5. Gun mount
6. Gun fit

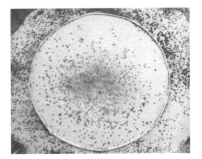

If your technique and gun fit are correct, poor ballistics can make or break the outcome of a competition. Consistency can only be achieved with a gun that throws good patterns, and which choke does so at set distances.

Traditional Patterning

A typical pattern plate is usually a four foot square sheet of ⅛-inch-thick steel, with the centre eight feet above the ground. The surface is painted or greased, and is fired upon to determine the number of pellets hitting the target at specific yardages. Traditionally, the distance was 40 yards, but it is more useful to shoot at the yardage that suits the targets presented in your discipline.

A 30-inch circle is drawn around the centre of the pattern and divided into four quarters. The number of pellet strikes in one quarter is counted and multiplied times four to determine the total number of pellets that hit the plate. The process is then repeated five times, painting the plate between shots. If you own a digital camera, take a picture of the five patterns, download them into a file on your computer and you can do the pellet count at home at your leisure.

Next, several of the cartridges being tested need to be cut open, a tedious but necessary task, and the number of pellets counted in each cartridge. This will give you the average number of pellets per cartridge for that brand and load. That number of pellets in the cartridge is then compared to the number of pellets in the pattern. The number that hit the plate is expressed as a percentage of the number of pellets in the cartridge. That number determines the density of the pattern. Seventy to eighty per cent is considered a very good density.

To complete the evaluation, the pattern should be checked for evenness of pellet distribution. The pellet pattern should not be in one small bunch, but spread evenly across the 30-inch circle, with no holes or gaps.

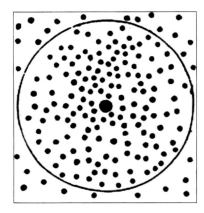

Analysing the Results

Armed with the information gleaned from the pattern board, you can determine the following:

1. How good or bad any given cartridge patterns in your gun or guns; how the cartridge interacts with the choking present; or, if a multi-choke, which choke gives the best pattern. Ideally, you would see up to seventy per cent or more of the pellets from the cartridge evenly distributed over the 30-inch circle.

2. How the different degrees of choke correspond with the laid-down averages, which traditionally are as follows: cylinder forty per cent, half choke sixty per cent, full choke seventy per cent. This way you can determine the actual choking in a gun. If it is throwing sixty per cent, it is half choke, regardless of the degree of choke present at the muzzle.

PATTERN DENSITY

You can calculate the number of pellets in a 30 inch circle at a given range for any combination of shot, size and choke constriction by using the table below (total pellets in the charge) and the following table:

PERCENTAGE OF TOTAL PELLETS IN 30 INCH CIRCLE

American	CHOKE English	Constriction	Range in Yards 20	25	30	35	40	45	50	55	60
True Cylinder	True Cylinder	.000"	80	69	60	49	40	33	27	72	18
Skeet-1	Improved Cylinder	.005"	92	82	72	60	50	41	33	27	22
Improved Cylinder	1/4	.010"	100	87	77	65	55	46	38	30	25
Modified	1/2	.020"	100	94	83	71	60	50	41	33	27
Improved Modified	3/4	.030"	100	100	91	77	65	55	46	37	30
Full	Full	.040"	100	100	100	84	70	59	49	40	32

Example: Say you'd like to find the pattern of a 1 oz. Charge of No. 6 shot at 40 yards for a modified barrel. First determine the number of pellets in the charge by using the table below. Answer: 225. Using the table above you can determine that the percentage of total pellets for a modified barrel at 40 yards is 60. Multiply the total number of pellets, 225, by 60 and divide by 100. Answer: 135 pellets in the 30" pattern at 40 yards.

PATTERN SPREAD

Diameter in inches covered by the bulk of the charge at various distances for different chokes.

DIAMETER IN INCHES

American	Choke English	Constriction	Range in Yards 10	15	20	25	30	35	40
True Cylinder	True Cylinder	.000"	20	26	32	38	44	51	58
Skeet-1	Improved Cylinder	.005"	15	20	26	32	38	44	51
Improved Cylinder	1/4	.010"	13	18	23	29	35	41	48
Modified	1/2	.020"	12	16	21	26	32	38	45
Improved Modified	3/4	.030"	10	14	18	23	29	35	42
Full	Full	.040"	9	12	16	21	27	35	40

Example: The diameter of spread covered by the bulk of the charge for an improved cylinder or 1/4-choke at 30 yards is 35 inches.

APPROXIMATE NO. OF SHOT IN VARIOUS LOADS

Shot Size	Shot Diameter	2 oz.	1⁷/₈ oz.	1⁵/₈ oz.	1¹/₂ oz.	1³/₈ oz.	1¹/₄ oz.	1¹/₈ oz.	1 oz.	⁷/₈ oz.	³/₄ oz.	¹/₂ oz.
#9	● .08	1170	1097	951	877	804	731	658	585	512	439	292
#8	● .09	820	769	667	615	564	513	462	410	359	308	205
#7¹/₂	● .095	700	656	568	525	481	437	393	350	306	262	175
#6	● .11	450	422	396	337	309	281	253	225	197	169	112
#5	● .12	340	319	277	255	234	213	192	170	149	128	85
#4	● .13	270	253	221	202	185	169	152	135	118	101	67
#2	● .15	180	169	158	135	124	113	102	90	79	68	45

3. Regulation, which is accomplished by altering the degree of choke or cartridge used until you achieve the exact distribution desired for the target to be shot with a particular gun. For example, for Trap, sixty per cent in a 30-inch circle at 40 yards, regardless of the choke actually in the gun, would give the best results.

Misleading Information

There are many things that can negatively impact your pattern testing and can result in misleading pellet counts and percentages. Be aware of the following:

1. Poor gun fit or inability to shoot straight.
2. Inaccurate pellet counts. Accurate pellet counts can only be obtained from cutting open several cartridges and physically counting the pellets.
3. Variation in cartridge performance. You should shoot more than once. A minimum of five patterns per choke and cartridge combination should be obtained.
4. Inaccurate pattern distances. Patterning is traditionally done at 40 yards, but patterns should be double checked at the ranges at which you actually shoot your targets.
5. Inaccurate chokes. Choke can only be measured by comparing the nominal boring to the restriction present. The advances in choke tapering technology, together with back boring and the lengthening of forcing cones can have Skeet choke throwing a modified pattern.
6. Cartridge variations. Cartridges of the same specifications but from different manufacturers can vary greatly. Find a brand that patterns well in your gun and stick with it.

Chokes and Cartridges in Trap and Skeet Guns

I believe that you cannot discuss one separately from the other. In Trap and Skeet, the distances and angles that the targets are thrown are fixed. The guns for these disciplines should be choked and regulated to maximize the pattern at those set distances. For example, the close Skeet target is best shot with open chokes and smaller shot like No. 9s, where the distant Trap target requires tight chokes and a larger shot size like No.7½s or No. 8s. Although many are, there is no requirement for Trap and Skeet guns to be multi-choked.

Chokes and Cartridges in Sporting Clays Guns

Sporting Clays does not have set angles or distances and presents an almost infinite variety of targets. Most often the targets are a combination of two presentations, one near and one far, and the degree of choke and shot size needs to be decided for each target. Because of this, the Sporting Clays gun needs to be flexible and should always be fitted with multi-chokes.

Ask yourself the following questions:

1. Are your target breaks chips and edges?
2. Are they balls of dust?
3. If safe to do so, when you collect whole missed targets, are any holes in them?
4. Do you shoot different disciplines with the same gun?
5. Do you miss more than you hit?
6. Do you shoot a fixed-choke gun?

If you answer 'yes' to one or more of these questions, then a better understanding of choke and cartridge choice could definitely improve your scores.

Chapter 5
Equipment and Accessories

L ike any sport, you need the correct equipment to compete to the best of your ability. You will need to invest in a variety of items, and it is important that it is the right equipment as it can have considerable impact on your performance. It is well worth giving careful consideration to selecting the various items you will need. Equipment can be broken down into two categories: Essential and Recommended.

Essential Equipment
Shooting Glasses

The first and most essential piece of equipment is shooting glasses which perform three distinct functions.

1. Provide protection from the impact of a shotgun pellet and debris from broken targets. Clay target pieces can often fly in erratic paths; they are extremely sharp and you only need to take a look at the facing wall of the high house on a skeet field to see the scrapes and gouges caused from the pieces of broken targets. This positively demonstrates the requirement for eye protection. Even when the direction of shooting is strictly controlled, there is an inevitable, but minor, risk of being struck by a stray pellet or ricochet.

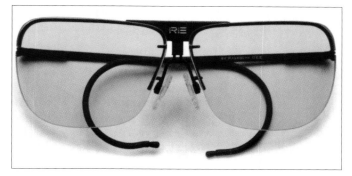

Essential protection with the added benefit of improved target contrast

2. Targets come in many colours and are thrown against a variety of backgrounds in ever-changing light conditions. Shooting glasses with interchangeable lenses offer the distinct advantage of being able to put in the correct tint of lens to enhance target definition in any situation.

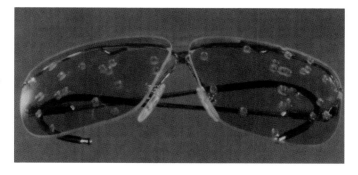

3. Clay shooting is an outdoor sport and protection for the eyes from the harmful UV rays in sunlight is a necessity.

It should also be noted that shooting glasses have a large frameless lens that allows the eye to see the target without obstruction. If prescription lenses are required, they should be ordered in single vision, for distance, only. Bifocal, trifocal, or Varilux lenses can cause problems in seeing the target.

Hearing Protection

The second essential piece of equipment is hearing protection, and with the modern digital systems, this also can offer more than simple blockage of damaging noise.

Basic Ear Protection

1. The report of a shotgun, though just a milli-second in duration, is louder than a jet plane as it takes off. Repeated exposure to this level of noise will cause permanent hearing loss. You could compare this to a large rock under the constant drip of water – it may take years, but eventually the rock will be eroded away. Hearing damage is permanent and once sustained, can never be replaced. Simple foam plugs or ear-muffs, well-fitted and of good quality, should always be worn when shooting or even observing shooting.
2. Anticipated recoil is greatly contributed to by the noise generated at the discharge of the gun, and good hearing protection helps eliminate this and the tendency to flinch.

Custom electronic

Advanced Ear Protection

3. The modern digital hearing protection allows full stereo input at all frequencies, but at any harmful noise above 0-82 decibels, has an automatic shut-off. This type of ear protection eliminates the blocked-up sensation created with ordinary plugs and ear muffs, often the reason ear protection is prematurely removed. Digital ear protection gives the further advantage of being able to hear the traps being released and the benefit of enhanced communication with the referee and other competitors, which can be of particular importance in FITASC.

Head Protection

A brimmed hat, be it a baseball cap or other design, is a simple piece of clothing that offers many benefits.

1. The extended brim covers the gap between your forehead and glasses offering essential protection from broken shards of clay which can potentially enter the eye area.
2. The brim helps by shading the eyes from strong sunlight, aiding your vision. It is always easier to look out from shade into light. The brim also helps keep the rain off your glasses.
3. In hot weather, a hat protects you from strong sunlight and a ventilated hat helps to dissipate heat. In the cold, a great deal of heat is lost through the top of the head, and a hat reduces this loss which can result in fatigue.

Recommended Equipment

Shooting Vest

The first recommendation is a shooting vest, and many would consider it an essential. The skeet or shooting vest is unique to the clay shooting games, and it fulfills several necessary functions.

1. A proper shooting vest should facilitate the smooth and consistent mounting of the gun. It is required to be cut to allow the unrestricted articulation of the shoulders, but it should not be so loose as to fold and cause the gun to snag or hang up. The waist should be adjustable so that any slack can be taken up and help when the pockets contain cartridges. Pockets should not move during the swing and mount. A leather or synthetic pad, fully extending from the shoulder to the pocket and stitched vertically every one inch, is the best design to promote a smooth gun mount.

Hot weather ventilated vest   *Standard international skeet vest*   *Down shooting vest*

2. Vests come with a variety of pockets, hooks, and compartments. The front two pockets are the only essential ones, and they should be of a bellows design, stitched and riveted and large enough to accommodate a box of shells. Some competitors like to carry everything they may need on their person, and the other pockets are merely for storage.

3. If the majority of your shooting is in hot weather, look for a vest with a ventilated back panel. Vests offer little weather protection and should your shooting be predominantly in the cold or wet, choose a shooting jacket of the same specifications instead. Be sure that it too has a bellows back and raglan-sleeve design to allow the arms ample freedom to swing.

Some who want only recoil protection, prefer a half-vest that comes to the waist with the option of carrying their ammunition in a pouch or 'shooting apron' fastened at the waist.

Shoes for Shooting

There is a considerable amount of walking and standing around during any competition, and this is more so in Sporting Clays. Here, instead of the concrete stations of the Skeet and Trap fields, you will be walking a wooded course that is often wet and slippery. I do not know of any shoes made specifically for shooting, but the following are my suggestions for choosing a pair of shooting shoes.

1. They must be light and fit well, not too tight, but not so loose that they allow the feet to move around inside them. Cushioned insoles and padding at the ankles will help during a long day. They should have a little height at the heels so they encourage a good shooting posture with the weight forward on the balls of the feet.
2. Good gripping soles are essential, both for smooth concrete on a wet day, but even more so on a well-worn Sporting Clay station on the side of the hill. However, the sole of the shoe should not have such aggressive cleats that they could impede the movement of the feet when required, such as in FITASC.
3. From the list of requirements, you can see that the 'sports trainer' or light hiking boot is an excellent choice. I particularly like the all-terrain type that have a more rigid design offering greater stability and support of both foot and ankle.

Cross trainers with ankle support make excellent shooting shoes

Shooting Gloves

Shooting gloves offer improved gripping control as well as protection from hot barrels. They should be of thin and supple leather and should fit closely. For hotter weather, the cut-a-way back and fingerless type, similar to a racing cyclist's, are a good choice.

Shooting Clothing

Clothing comes in two categories: good weather and bad weather.

1. Good Weather Clothing: Wear cotton and it should be loose-fitting and comfortable. The shirt, like the shooting vest, should allow good arm and shoulder articulation but not have so much slack as to impede the gun-mount. In very hot weather, wear shorts and ventilated shirts, and remember to carry a towel to wipe off perspiration.
2. Bad Weather Clothing: Many will choose to wear a waterproof overcoat and remove it before shooting at every station. I much prefer to wear layers, starting with thermal underwear. Over that wear regular loose and comfortable clothing, substituting a thin polo-neck sweater for the shirt, finishing with a rain- and waterproof 'golf suit'. These are cut to allow the freedom to swing a golf club and offer the same advantage of protection and movement to the shooter. I then wear my skeet vest over the top. A large golf umbrella to stand under while waiting to shoot and a towel to dry hands and equipment are sound additions. A second pair of shooting gloves to change into half-way around the course in poor weather is also advisable.

Cotton or natural fabrics for fine weather shooting

Weatherproof Ventile or Gore-tex® shooting jacket and extra layers for cold weather

The Gear Bag

A gear bag allows you to have all of the equipment that you need or might need to be at hand during a competition. It also means that you can put the bag down and take only the essentials into the station that you are shooting. This eliminates any unnecessary weight that can interfere with your shooting action. A gear bag can be anything from a gym bag to a custom-designed tote bag with a reinforced bottom for carrying ammunition, with pockets for accessories. The bag must have a wide, padded shoulder strap and be comfortable to carry.

The following is a list of what you would find in the average competitors' bag, depending on the weather and the country where the competition is being held.

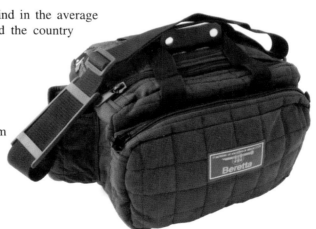

Hearing protection
Shooting glasses and spare lenses
Hat
Ammunition
Multi-chokes and choke key for changing them
Water or other drinks or snacks
The Leatherman or other multi-tool
Sun block
Insect repellent
Pen and pencil
Towels
Gloves

To carry everything including the kitchen sink!

The list of equipment could go on, but beyond the essential and the recommended, there are a couple of additions that are popular, convenient, and useful.

SHOE PROTECTORS

Leather shoe protectors prevent wear on shooting shoes where the muzzles of the guns rest on the tops of the shoes. This is mainly a Trap and Skeet shooting accessory where an open over and under is often placed muzzle-down on the toe...a comfortable way to wait your turn to shoot.

Equipment Carts

These carts, often called a gear caddies, are simply converted golf carts that allow all a shooter's equipment to be carried on two wheels, avoiding fatigue.

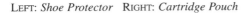

LEFT: *Shoe Protector*   RIGHT: *Cartridge Pouch*

Chapter 6
Eye Dominance

Beginner

The essential test before beginning to learn to shoot is to establish which is your Master or Dominant Eye. This will determine the shoulder you will shoot off, the stance you will adopt, your clothing and equipment choices, and how you will have your gun fit.

Intermediate

It is incredible how many intermediate and even advanced shots have come for lessons and gun fittings with eye dominance conflicts. Often they are either totally unaware of any problems, or adamant that they are dominant in one eye or the other, often the wrong one.

Advanced

The failure of the advanced shooter or his instructor to diagnose Eye Dominance at the beginning of his shooting career, has often resulted in frustration and dramatically impacted his progress. Helping a clay shooter to understand and correct the interaction between his eyes and the gun will improve where his shotgun points and throws its pattern, and will enable him to shoot better scores.

What is Eye Dominance?

Understanding the impact of Eye Dominance and how to correctly diagnose the Dominant or Master Eye is the first essential to straight shooting.

The human being is designed with two eyes which can be compared to two television cameras, yet we have only one receiver or television screen. The brain knits these two independent camera pictures seamlessly together, allowing us to see one clear and sharp picture. The brain actually considers the two eyes to behave like a single 'Cyclopean' eye, but the images arrive into the brain separately, one fractionally in front of the other. The first registered image is the 'Dominant' or 'Master Eye'.

It is this binocular vision, with both eyes open, (stereoscopic – three dimensional) that is perceived in the visual cortex of the brain where the focusing mechanisms of the two eyes are linked together. This gives us the ability to place objects in space by size and distance and is called Stereopis, or as it is more commonly known, Depth Perception.

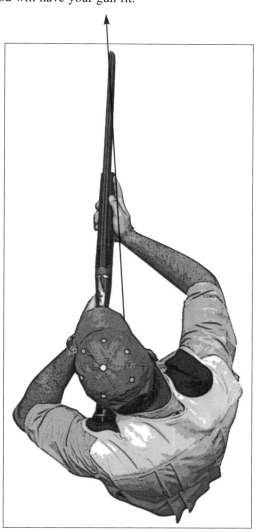

Left-handed shooter, right-eye dominant will miss to the right of the target

If you shoot off the shoulder opposite to the Dominant Eye, you disrupt the process of binocular vision, this causes confusion in the eye's focusing mechanisms. This usually results in a shot missed some six inches to four feet off-centre.

It is the master eye that decides which shoulder you should shoot off, not, as you would think, whether you are right or left-handed.

Diagnosing the Master Eye

There are many ways in which to determine your eye dominance. The simplest method is, with both eyes open, pick out an object in the distance. Raise your arm and point at it with your forefinger. Close first one eye, then the other. You will find that your finger will remain firmly pointing at the object with one eye (the Master Eye)

Left eye dominant

Right eye dominant

Central vision

A tube allows for more accurate diagnosis

Another method of diagnosis

and move off line with the other (Non-Master Eye). Occasionally, your finger will appear an equal distant on either side of the object. This is referred to as 'Central Vision', where there is no dominant eye.

Another test is to use a piece of card with a hole pierced in it. Look through the hole to the distant object. Bring the card back towards the face. It will come to the Master Eye.

There are several variations on this theme, and all are useful. I personally prefer to use a used kitchen or toilet roll – this allows a more accurate diagnosis of the degree of dominance. Others choose to consult their optometrist to determine their Master Eye.

Eye dominance, however, is not cast in stone and is not affected by visual acuity. The Master Eye can often be the weakest eye when measured optically. Fluctuations in dominance can occur with fatigue and especially at the onset of middle age.

If you find that you can shoot straight on most targets but certain angles or directions cause you trouble, or if you inexplicably lose sight of the target or stop the gun on certain presentations, these may be the symptoms of dynamic or shifting dominance.

Gun Interference

These tests do not allow for the visual interference created by the gun. Gun barrels, their configurations and rib design can greatly impact eye dominance and the initial Master Eye test results need to be rechecked with the gun correctly mounted on the shoulder. Please give consideration to the fact that at the most critical moment of taking the shot you are placing a three foot-long object directly between your eye and the point of focus (target). This can create a number of master eye conundrums, which, in the split second of taking the shot, often result in a miss.

Though you should never be looking directly at the gun, your subconscious has to be aware of it in your peripheral vision to recognise where it is pointing. The various configurations of barrels and ribs can influence this by drawing the Non-Dominant Eye's attention away from the point of focus. This often is the explanation as to why you can shoot well with one gun but fail to do so with another gun of a different design.

LEFT: *Visual interference created by the gun impacts on eye dominance*

ABOVE: *The barrels should be a subconscious awareness in your peripheral vision*

Pattern Plate

The pattern plate is a four-foot square steel plate which is greased or painted so when shot, shows the exact degree and impact of the eye-barrel alignment. It is only at the pattern plate that you can see the impact of your pattern and its relation to the target. Corrections needed to the interaction between eyes and gun can be determined at the pattern plate and the right adjustments can dramatically improve your scores.

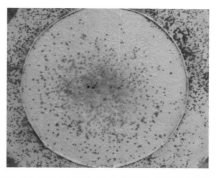

Definitions, Faults and Fixes

True Dominance

You are able to shoot with both eyes with all the benefits of full binocular vision.

True Cross Dominance

The first and best option is to start off learning to shoot from the correct shoulder under the Master Eye. With a beginner who has no muscle memory established, this is easily achieved. But to switch to shoot from the opposite shoulder later in life requires great determination and diligent practise – retraining and grooving the mount, readjusting the swing and timing of each shot to reach previous levels of performance. It will take some time before the benefits of the shift to the dominant eye shoulder can be appreciated.

The Fix: Switch shoulders wherever possible or implement one of the solutions.

Central Vision

Where there is no dominant eye, one could be forgiven for thinking that this would be the perfect scenario. Unfortunately, though most people with central vision can shoot tolerably well, they are constantly making adjustments to do so. Their lead pictures are, in effect, doubled. Take Station Four in Skeet: the lead required on both the Low and High House is approximately four feet on both targets, but the person with central vision compensates by shooting two feet in front of one target and six feet in front of the other.

The Fix: Do not switch shoulders, but implement one of the solutions.

Partial Dominance

With the onset of middle age, someone who has been True Dominant in one eye all of their life can experience an increased interference from the Non-Dominant Eye.

The Fix: Do not switch shoulders, but implement one of the solutions.

Fluctuating or Shifting Dominance

These symptoms of eye dominance are difficult to detect. They can occur when you generally shoot well but have days where, for no explanation, you under-perform, especially on certain target presentations. It is caused by stress, fatigue or the inability or failure to maintain hard focus on the target.

The Fix: Do not switch shoulders, but implement one of the solutions.

Solutions

The primary solution to eye dominance problems is to close, block or obscure the vision of the Master Eye to allow straight shooting off the opposite shoulder. This has drawbacks in that the binocular vision (stereoscopic – three dimensional), so valuable to shotgun shooting, is seriously disrupted.

The closing or blocking of one eye completely is not the best option. The most simple and effective cure is the application of a small piece of opaque scotch tape (do not block the whole lens), cut in a triangular shape. This is placed on the lens of the shooting glass of the Dominant Eye, so that when

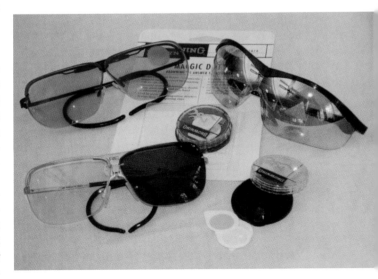

Verious methods of correcting cross dominance

the gun is correctly mounted, the head on the stock, ready to shoot, one of the corners of the tape is directly on the center of the pupil.

This solution means that until the shot is ready to be taken, the brain is receiving binocular signals, both central and peripheral, and can best coordinate the target acquisition. There are many alternatives to the tape: a patch, blinkers, a smear of ChapStick or Vaseline or proprietary products like the 'Magic-Dot' work equally well.

When someone has had a stroke, their vision is often impaired. A series of lens coatings has been developed to help correct this problem. I have been experimenting with this system to see if it can be used to correct Dominant Eye problems. So far the tests have been very positive and the great strength of using the coated lens is that it allows the person to shoot with both eyes open.

Blinking

If the dominance is central, partial or fluctuating, a technique can be learned whereby both eyes can be kept open during target acquisition (binocular) and initial movement to the target. Then the non-shooting eye is blinked on the completion of the gun mount and when the shot is being taken. This requires that the correct timing be learned as to the right time to blink the eye. This timing can be different on the various target presentations. Also, be aware that closing an eye can result in aiming.

Cross Over Stocks

It is possible to have the stock of a gun shaped in such a way as to be able to shoot off the shoulder opposite the Dominant Eye. This requires a considerable degree of cast or bend in the stock so that the rib of the gun is placed in line with the Dominant Eye. The degree of this cast or bend depends entirely on the degree of dominance. In cases of Partial Dominance, a little extra cast can work wonders. Central Vision would require a semi-cross over stock and True Cross Dominance would need a full cross over stock. You should be aware that excessive cast creates more felt-recoil.

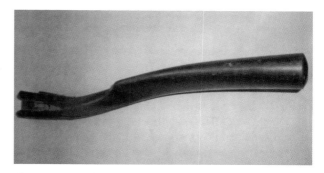

Cross over stock

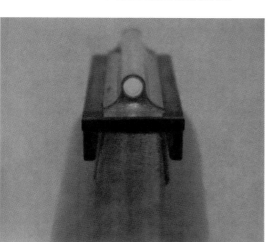

Fibre optic sight

Fibre Optic Sight

There are fibre optic rods now available that channel light down a narrow tube along the sight plane of the shotgun. When the gun is correctly mounted, a bright fluorescent red dot appears that can only be seen by the eye in line with the rib because of the tunnel effect created by the tubing. This 'sight' can allow Cross Dominant shooting.

Shooting Glasses

Like the ability to focus, there is much individual variation in perceived contrast and the amount of low light vision that enters the eye. A number of trap shooters have been experimenting with the control of eye dominance by fitting lenses of different colours and intensities to their shooting glasses. The most common combination is a dark lens (bronze or purple) over the Dominant Eye, and a light colour (vermillion, orange or yellow) over the eye in line with the gun.

Gun Fit

The drop at comb (the height between the eye and rib alignment) is the most important aspect of a gun fit. If this is too low, it will cause the wrong eye to take over (Cross Dominance).

Centreing

Dr Wayne M. Martin, author of *An Insight to Sports*, writes that Cross Dominance is caused by faulty movement in centreing and that we can learn, with either eye, to complement the hand and side chosen for shooting. His basic philosophy is that if golfers, tennis and baseball

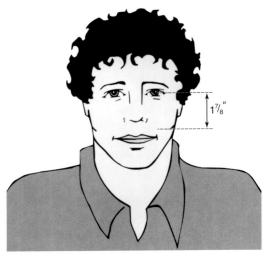

Too much drop at comb will cause cross dominance

players have little, if any, problems with Cross Dominance, why should shotgun shooters?

To understand his theory, you have to understand the basic actions of hand and eye coordination. These are three basic skills that compose good shooting vision:

1. Accommodation: Adjusting the eye's focus to see targets clearly at varying distances.
2. Convergence: Having two eyes fixed on the target at the same time to maintain a single image.
3. Centering: Intense focus on one part of an object without being distracted by peripheral images.

His advice is to centre our vision on the targets' primary zone to the exclusion of anything in the peripheral zone – in effect, suppressing the secondary or ghost image in the periphery of our vision. This takes great discipline and practice.

There are as many ideas for controlling Cross Dominancy as there are varying degrees of that dominancy. They range from the muscular, i.e. changing the shoulder shot off to simply blinking or closing the offending eye, to the mechanical, where stocks are bent and cast to extremes to compensate.

Proprietary and homemade obstructions which can correctly assist the centering of the eyes are another option. There is no one cure-all and you will need to experiment to find the single solution or combination of solutions that work for you. Then you must have the patience and the strength to practice until your solution fits your chosen discipline and personal shooting style.

Chapter 7
The Fundamentals of Shooting Straight

he components and quality of your starting position are the nuts and bolts of consistent and successful competition shooting. A proper set-up allows a smooth swing in the direction that the target is travelling and is the key to better scores.

Setting Up

Establishing a proper address to the target is the first thing that determines how easily you are able to build and repeat a sound swing. The body angles you create at your set-up determine the quality of your pivot. You should place your body in a position to rotate correctly around the constant axis created by your feet.

Correct Foot Position

You should address the target so you can start and complete the shot in balance. This begins with the feet.

Stand with your feet an armpit's-width apart and your belt buckle facing the break point of the target. Then simply turn forty-five degrees to your right (for the right handed, to your left for the left-handed).

If you visualise yourself standing in the centre of a clock, your leading or left foot would be pointing at the break point at just past twelve o'clock and your right foot would be pointing just short of the three o'clock mark, with six to eight inches between your heels. An imaginary line drawn from your right heel and passing though the big toe of the left foot would point directly at the break point of the target.

This position places the gun at a forty-five degree angle to the body and opens the shoulder pocket up nicely for an unimpeded gun mount. Too narrow a stance is far better than too wide. A wide-spread stance causes the shoulder nearest the direction of rotation to drop, resulting in the windscreen-wiper effect of rolling off the target line.

In FITASC and certain Sporting Clays presentations, some combinations of pairs will involve footwork; you will have to step from one target break-point to another. This should be practised in your gun mounting drills.

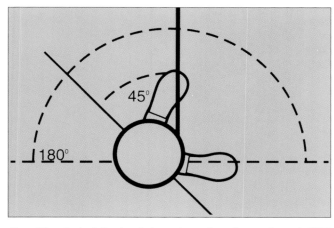

Gun 45° to body following balanced rotation of torso through 180°

Correct Foot Position Benefits

1. **Balanced Movement**. You can rotate, in balance, around the pivot of your leading leg through 180 degrees–90 degrees either side of the breakpoint of the target. This achieves the first basic requirement of a smooth swing: *balanced movement*, keeping the shoulders level with the target line, maintaining good head position and rotation.

2. **Good Body Shape**. Proper foot position creates a good body shape and allows an unimpeded gun mount.

Correct Posture

To ensure the maximum mobility and control, the weight should be well-balanced and distributed seventy per cent on the ball of the front (left) foot and thirty per cent on the back foot. There should be a slight forward inclination of the body from the waist up, towards the target, like a boxer ready to throw a punch. The head should be slightly forward and to the right with the chin angled down. (For the right handed.)

This set-up ensures that the head is in the correct position to receive the comb and stock into the face without any head movement. It also has the advantage of keeping the head forward and down while taking the shot. This forward weight can be increased on those shots where head lifting is most prevalent, even slightly bending the knee of the front leg to keep the weight forward. This works well for shooting rabbits, targets beneath the feet and low, quartering targets.

There will be subtle differences in each individual's set-up to allow for the differences in physique and the specific demands of the discipline being shot.

Correct Posture Benefit

1.**Good posture leads to a good gun mount**. The correct posture allows the gun to be mounted correctly to the cheek without any unnecessary and unwanted head or body movement.

Richard Faulds, Olympic Gold Medallist, is an excellent example of stance and posture complementing each other to produce a consistently good gun mount and solid head position. Learn from the top shots by watching how they set up for a shot and begin to incorporate their methods into your own shooting practices.

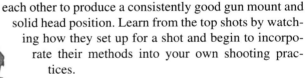
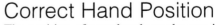

Correct Hand Position

The position of your hands on the gun is an important consideration. To set up correctly, place your hands in position to take the target that requires the most gun movement: the high driven bird. Take up your stance and then mount the gun into your shoulder replicating the taking of the high overhead shot. Then adjust your left hand on the fore-end so that the angle between the wrist and fore-end is approximately forty-five to fifty degrees.

The stock and fore-end of the gun should allow the rear hand to sit well back, giving the first pad of the trigger finger correct placement on the trigger. The thumb should be rolled over the grip as if shaking hands with the gun to assure proper control. The fore-end should be laid diagonally across the palm of the left hand from the outside edge to the forefinger. The three fingers and thumb support and control the gun, while the extended forefinger is laid along the side of the fore-end accentuating our natural ability to point.

Place the gun in the shoulder one-handed...

... take your grip on the fore-end creating an angle of 45° between the wrist and gun

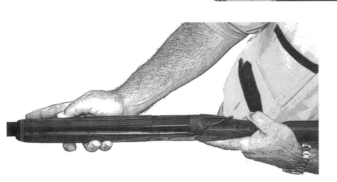

Correct Hand Position Benefit

Works for every target. With your hands in the correct position, you will always have enough movement to both control the gun and maintain a constant swing on any target presentation.

The Grip

A sound grip makes a secure coupling between you and the gun, but your grip should be subtle and not too stiff. The wrists must be free to hinge without restriction to ensure a smooth-swinging motion. The hands must learn to work as a unit, joined together so they can swing with power and control.

Grip pressure is important; the arms need to be relaxed to be able to move freely – this is affected by the pressure you apply in your grip. A too-tight grip will cause tension and create a muscle gridlock in your wrists, arms and shoulders.

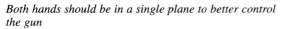

Both hands should be in a single plane to better control the gun

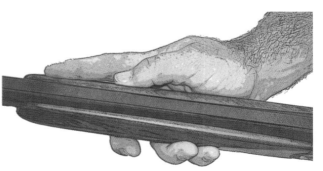

The extended forefinger extenuates your natural ability to point

Try this experiment to find the amount of pressure that works best for you. Grip the gun one hundred per cent, than back off to fifty per cent – how does that feel? Try a little more, then a little less until you find the amount of pressure that offers support and control without tension.

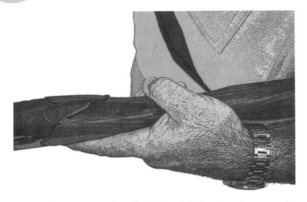

Correct rear hand grip is with the thumb wrapped over not left resting on the safety

Another way to get a feel for the right amount of pressure is to imagine holding two raw eggs in your left hand. You want to hold them with enough pressure so you can turn them over and not drop them, but not so much that you crush them.

Correct Head Position

Your head position on the gun during the act of shooting has more of an effect on the successful outcome of a shot than almost any other factor. I have always found it somewhat amazing that more has not been written on this subject, given its pivotal role in consistently shooting good scores.

To emphasise the importance, I would ask you to carry out this experiment. Take up the correct foot position and posture, but with your arms hanging comfortably at your sides. Look across the room and pick out an object or mark. Using your leading arm (the one that grips the fore-end), bring the arm up, forefinger extended, and point at the object.

Right on the button! Try it again and again. Always the same result. Through the gift of hand and eye coordination, you will always be able to point accurately at any object you can see. This ability is what allows us to catch a ball or a shoot a clay pigeon.

Now, I would like you to try the same experiment again, only this time, as your finger comes to the point, move your head, dip it down gently. Missed over the top? Try it again, lifting your head, or turning it left and right just as the finger reaches the mark. The result will always be the same – *you will always be off the mark*!

From this experiment you should plainly see how head movement impacts your shooting. Even with the correct style, a well-fitted gun, mounted one hundred per cent perfectly every time and laser-like focus on the target, if you move your head, deliberately or involuntary, during the shot, you *will* miss!

Poor head position is the result of many missed shots

The head is a considerable amount of our total body weight. In addition to holding our 'on-board computer', it is also the chassis for our eyes. We are pre-programmed to follow the head's lead. For example, when you negotiate a bend in the road while riding a bike, your eyes look for the next exit. The head follows the path of the eyes and the body follows the head. You lean the bike the necessary amount to counter the centrifugal pull and ride through the bend without crashing. If you looked at the front wheel or to the right or left, you would fall off. We can all remember learning to ride and the all-too-frequent falls until we mastered balance by looking where we wanted to go.

Every sport or activity that we take part in is likewise dependent on the control of the head. Take the gymnast on the high beam – she will look straight ahead as she balances –if she glanced at her feet, she would trip and fall.

In shooting, head movement negates gun fit and makes even the best-honed skills go awry. Great emphasis should be placed on the rigid maintenance of correct head position during a shot.

There is yet another factor that causes head movement while shooting. We sometimes forget that we are basically animals – sophisticated, yes – but, nonetheless, animals. The survival traits ingrained in our gene pool, oft forgotten, are always there. One that has a major impact on us while shooting is the 'alert reaction'.

Consider the first thing you do when you hear a loud or unexpected noise. The crunch of metal from a car crash, the tinkle of breaking glass and more important to the shooter, the slap of the trap arm releasing… you *lift your head*! Why? Because that is what nature has pre-programmed us to do.

In any stress or danger situation, you will always first lift your head and then more often than not, turn it from side to side. This allows you to hear, see and smell better to be prepared to flee or fight, according to how you perceive that danger. To see this alert instinct in action, look at any animal in the wild – a deer is a good example – it will lift its head every time it hears any unusual sound.

'Trouble with doubles' can usually find the root of the problem in head movement, rather than gun mount. It is the alert instinct that is to blame. One of the very best pieces of advice ever given to me was, see the first bird of a pair break before moving the gun to the second. After the incomplete gun mount, lifting the head to look for the second target before the first is broken, is the most frequent cause of missing the pair. How often have you had this scenario on a station? *Missed and hit – hit and missed – missed the pair.* This is more often caused by head movement than poor technique.

On the first bird you hear the slam of the trap arm and you lift your head to get a better look at the target. You start to move the gun before you have seen the target. Your eyes then pick up the target and coordination kicks in. You begin to swing the gun back towards the target. The target and barrels converge and the shot is made with your head off the stock. Then with the head still *off* the stock, the second bird is also cleanly missed. This is a classic over-reaction to the alert instinct.

Another cause of head movement is an incomplete gun mount. This occurs when the comb of the gun, instead of being fully mounted into the cheek, stops on the jaw bone. So, to obtain correct eye-rib alignment, the head is subconsciously lowered to the comb. The result is you lose visual contact with the target for a split-second.

The domino effect begins: to re-establish focus on the target, you have to find and focus on the target twice during the taking of the shot. On a slow target presentation there may be time for you to recover focus on the target and make a successful shot. However, on the faster targets and particularly, the second bird of a pair, nine times out of ten, the miss-mount will result in a miss.

If you combine poor gun mount with the bad timing induced by your head-lifting alert instinct, your score cards will really begin to take on Picasso-like configuration of noughts and crosses, rather than the unbroken line of success we wish to see. The great advice 'Eye on the Rock – Head on the Stock' really sums it up. Learn to stay in the gun shot to shot for better success at doubles.

How do we control this urge to get a better look at the bird? Like every other aspect of the game, you need to spend some time programming the brain to suppress this natural instinct and keep the head *still* during the shot. This is learned in the same manner as all the fundamentals: by repetition. It is essential to teach the brain to feel the comb of the stock firmly and correctly cheeked, on the completion of the gun mount and throughout the shot until the target explodes into dust. Work at head position in your shooting practice and you will definitely see better scores and cleaner breaks.

Correct head position is similar to a boxer's

Good Head Position is achieved through the following:

1. Adopt a good stance and posture.
2. Check that your gun is well-fitted.
3. Practice your gun mount.
4. Maintain proper weight distribution on the shots conducive to head lifting.
5. Reinforce head position by creating an anchor of the cheek bone.
6. Create the 'trigger' of a repeated promise to 'Stay in the Gun' throughout the shot.

Ready position

The most common denominator among the leading competitors is: *the head is always in the correct position on the stock*. This correct head position starts with the correct footwork and posture, and finishes with the head on the stock, in the right place to receive the well-mounted gun.

Let us look at a step-by-step approach to achieving a good gun mount.

Components of a good gun mount

1. Feet Position
2. Stance
3. Posture
4. Head
5. Start
6. End
7. Forend Hand Position
8. Hands Working Together

Parallel mount

Achieving a good gun mount

To repeat any act consistently, there must be some established constants: a *beginning* and an *end*. A good gun mount begins with the heel of the stock held level with the armpit. If you cock your right arm and feel with your opposite hand, you will detect a tendon just under your arm. This is where the gun stock should always be held to begin practicing your gun mount. The muzzle of the gun should be on and just under the gun hold on the target's line of flight, with your eyes looking directly over the barrel.

The *end*, or completion, of the gun mount is in the cheek After 11,000,000 years of evolution, the only purpose for the human cheek bone is as an anchor for the comb of the stock to ensure proper eye-rib alignment when mounting and shooting a shot gun.

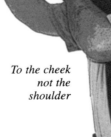

To the cheek not the shoulder

Take a second to reach up with your fingers and feel the part of your face where your teeth meet. Place your finger right under the cheekbone or the Zycomatic Process – this is where the stock arrives to finish a good gun mount

– where the gun is brought correctly into position on the face without any head move-ment. When you have arrived at this position, pause for three seconds to let the 'Subconscious Feel It'.

When you feel confident that the gun is being placed in the same place every time, you can begin to combine this exercise with a moving mount on a straight line. The emphasis must always be on feeling the comb of the stock firmly cheeked throughout the exercise and a three second pause before repeating. This way you will grove the sub-conscious to maintain that all-crucial spot-weld of cheek to comb throughout the shot.

Correct gun mount benefit

A defined beginning and end to an action creates consistency. Having put these fundamentals in place, there is the simple action of lifting the gun from the ready position to the cheek. It is here that the eighty per cent of misses occur.

Gun mount faults

There are many reasons this simple lifting action goes awry:

1. Poor Starting Position: The gun is held too low or too far out from the body.

2. Flying the Elbow: I see this more in the USA than in Europe and believe it stems from pre-mounting the gun in Skeet and Trap. When observed from behind, the elbows of a shooter with a well-mounted gun should form a forty-five degree angle to the body. By 'flying' or cocking the elbow of the trigger hand (I've seen it cocked up at ninety degrees or more) you close the shoulder pocket to the butt of the gun.

With the elbow cocked up, the deltoid muscle rolls over towards the face, blocking off the area of the clavicle where the gun should be mounted. This means that the gun is mounted onto the rotator cuff or the arm and the gun mount cannot be completed. Inevitably, the head will need to be repositioned by dropping it to the stock to complete the mount. The result? A miss over and behind the target. If you suffer from sore arms or bruising after shooting, you need to fix your gun mount.

3. The See-Saw Mount: The gun barrels, while being lifted to the face, rock and roll above and below the target line.

Incorrect – weight on the back foot, head erect, gun too low...   *... causes gun to be pulled into the shoulder creating see-sawing of the barrels under the target line...*

... the barrels to be brought back onto the line of the target...

... and the head to drop

4. **The Incomplete Mount:** The gun stops short of the cheek.

5. **The Pull-Back Mount:** The gun is pulled *back* into the shoulder pocket, rather than lifted *up* to the cheek and *out* to the target.

6. **The Mount-Then-Swing**

7. **The Rushed Mount**

Gun mount corrections

How do we cure these problems? First we need to re-educate the hands as to their proper role in the gun mount.

Consider some of your everyday actions: eating, using the telephone or moving the computer mouse. You will inevitably use your right, or dominant, hand. Therefore, when mounting the shotgun, you are pre-disposed to lifting the gun with the right hand. This strong use of the right or dominant hand causes all of the above faults and makes the mount go wrong.

The following exercises will go a long way to re-training your hands to work together and improve your gun mount.

Exercise 1

The place to practise this is in your home or garage, not the shooting grounds. Find a place where you can safely and comfortably mount the gun. Double-check that it is unloaded and safe.

Adopt good stance, posture, hands and ready position (be sure to wear your usual shooting attire, including gloves, glasses and ear protection). Now, in the initial training, all of the exercises are performed very slowly in the same manner that the martial arts student learns his kata.

To the brain there is no difference in the muscle memory of an act whether it is performed slowly or quickly, but it learns these muscle memories far better when performed in slow motion. So just as the martial artist learns the punch slowly before attempting to break a board at full power, you need to learn the gun mount in the same manner, by slow repetition until you are able to introduce it into your practice at the shooting grounds.

Exercise 2

Imagine that the part of the gun between your two hands is made of rubber. Apply gentle pressure to it by pulling the hands apart, almost as if trying to stretch the gun at this point. Now, begin your gun mount with the emphasis being on the front hand. You will find that because of the resistance created in the stretching exercise both hands will now work together, as a unit.

The left hand points and swings the gun to the target, in effect driving the gun, and the right hand mimics this action and pulls the trigger. If both hands are working in unison, the resulting gun mount will be smooth and correct.

Exercise 3

When you have mastered the first two drills, you can progress to a moving mount. Place a small Maglite in the end of your barrel and as you mount the gun, slowly trace up the vertical seam in the corner where two walls meet. Then, with the light, trace along the ceiling joint in one smooth motion. Repeat until you can do this to the left and to the right without any see-sawing or jerky movements. The light beam is a great aid, showing, by its path, just how smooth your mount is becoming. (There are also laser devices available specifically designed for this practice.)

Both hands should work together as a unit

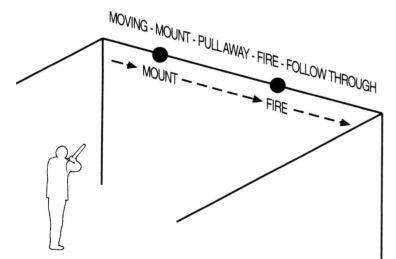

Gun mount and snap cap drills

Find a room where a gun can be safely mounted and swung. Along one wall at the join of the ceiling, fix two aiming marks one third from each corner (bluetack is ideal for this purpose). Standing on the opposite side to the room take up your stance to break the second of the marks, address your muzzles to the corner of the room gun down and proceed to mount, making sure muzzles stay on line throughout without any see-sawing or dip – both hands work in unison to achieve this. Maintain the line of the ceiling with gun coming into the shoulder as the muzzles reach the first target; pull away to the second target, fire and follow through smoothly to the corner. Repeat this three or four times in each direction. Great emphasis should be put on target line, a smooth mount and that the trigger pull and follow through are one flowing action (snap caps are used so as to be able to fire the gun without damaging the firing pins).

Exercise 4

As you develop these new motor skills, introduce a snap cap to the Maglite exercise and dry-fire the gun on completion of the mount. Use markers on the wall to replicate visual holds, gun holds and break points so you can better set up and execute each practice correctly.

You will very soon be able to take your new gun mounting skills to the range. Do not rush! Remember, the first rule of gun mounting is 'Rushing Ruins Rhythm'. Choose targets that allow you ample time to complete a good, smooth gun mount on every shot. With proper practice, you will soon reap the benefit of better scores!

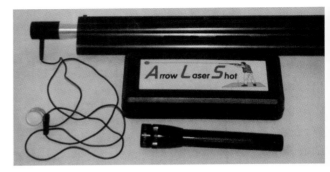

The Maglite or laser make excellent training aids

Gun Up or Gun Down

It is recognised that eighty per cent of all misses are caused by a poor or incorrect gun mount. So why, you might ask, does anyone shoot gun down at all? After all, there is nothing in the rule books with the exception of FITASC and International Skeet that says we have to call for targets with an unmounted gun.

If you took the top twenty performers in Sporting Clays from around the world, the majority, usually the winners, prefer to start shooting with the gun out of the shoulder for most targets. So, if starting with the gun down or out of the shoulder can cause misses, why do so many of the Master Class shooters choose to use what must be a flawed technique? Could they not shoot even better scores shooting all targets with a pre-mounted gun? The answer is complex and for every argument of 'no' you could find one for 'yes'.

I am going to put the facts as I see them for both gun up or gun down, and I will leave you to make your own decision.

The Dead Gun Effect

Let's begin with an experiment. Take your gun, check to make absolutely sure it is unloaded, then mount it completely, pointing at a corner of the room at the junction of wall and ceiling. Swing the gun smoothly, keeping the muzzles on the line of the junction until you reach the far corner of the wall. Try it again, maintaining an emphasis on smoothness and control.

Now, stop and consider what your first action needed to be. Try it again. Yes, you have discovered that there is no, or very little, arm movement available when shooting gun up. You are required to overcome the inertia, or dead gun effect, by using the rotation of the body. The heavier the gun, the more effort is required to overcome this inertia. This more often leads to the gun starting with a jerk, which can result in 'jumping' the target, causing you to lose the line or stopping to let the target catch up.

As you continue to swing the gun, you quickly begin to run out of turn or rotation. The arms cannot help...they are locked through the gun to the body, leaving only body rotation to keep the gun moving. Because you used up a considerable amount of available rotation getting the gun started, you will find that, two-thirds into the swing, you have run out of available movement.

If you attempted to push past this point, maintaining muzzle-target line alignment, you would fall over. But your subconscious will not allow this to happen. It sends a command to transfer weight from one foot to the other. This subconscious transference of weight results in the shoulders dropping or rolling and causes the muzzles to come off the target line.

Negatives of Shooting Pre-Mounted

1. Difficult to start the gun to overcome the dead gun effect smoothly.
2. Little if any arm movement available.

3. Involuntary transference of body weight and loss of balance.
4. Only body rotation to drive the swing.
5. Can result in aiming or gun watching.

Positives of Shooting Pre-Mounted
1. Removes the inconsistency created by an inability to mount the gun in sync with taking the shot.
2. Well-suited for short window and quartering targets.
3. Removes the necessity for a well-fitted gun as 'near enough is good enough' shooting pre mounted.

Skeet and Trap

I am sure by now you are wondering, 'What about the stars of Skeet and Trap? Why do they choose to shoot gun up if it is such a negative to consistent shooting?'

It is simply a matter of: 'Maximum Efficiency for Minimum Effort.'

Both Skeet and Trap are games of constants, their targets flying set distances, angles and heights. These can be, and usually are, learned by rote. It is therefore possible, with practice, to put in place the muscle memory for every shot. This includes the amount of effort required to overcome the inertia of a dead gun and perfect the timing of the swing.

The fundamentals of any pre-shot routine of visual hold, gun hold and break points are easily learned, as is the positioning of the body and the amount of effort needed to start the gun and smoothly shoot the target.

The ability to apply a 'robotic' approach to both Skeet and Trap has created a situation where perfect scores are common. Now, to make it more competitive, small gauge events in Skeet and handicap yardage in Trap have been introduced. With the necessity to shoot straights just to get into the shoot-offs, any variable that can have an impact on perfect scores is removed.

In either of these disciplines, it is rare to see any competitor call for a target with the gun out of the shoulder. I believe that both of these disciplines could be made more challenging, exciting and fun to watch if the gun down rule were introduced.

Sporting Clays

The origins of the sport were to practice for wing shooting. The early British shooting schools were built specifically for this. It was a good while before competitions shooting at inanimate objects became a regular event. However, once this occurred, particularly after the Second World War and into the 1950s, the sport developed rapidly. With more targets being shot, especially in a competitive environment, it was inevitable that skills would improve. This improvement has never stopped.

I remember shooting my first British Open at the West London Shooting Grounds in the early 1970s and, if memory serves me right, it was won with a score in the low eighties. The once-undreamed of scores of ninety-plus in Sporting Clays are now being shot quite regularly and the unimaginable score of one hundred straight in major competition has happened on several occasions. I believe with the very high standards of marksmanship being shown today, combined with better ballistics and guns, that the one hundred straight in Sporting Clays will no longer be so rare.

Course Setting

As a result of this increase in shooting ability, course builders have had to move away from targets that simply replicate game shooting scenarios. The modern course designer now looks for ways to 'beat the gun' using a variety of tools: landscape, angle, distance and trajectory, along with modern electric traps that throw the battue, looper and chondel. It is no wonder that we have witnessed such rapid growth in Sporting Clays. It is becoming more challenging, interesting and fun to shoot 'Golf with a Shotgun'. However, as *The Eagles'* song goes, '…every form of refuge has its price…'.

Consider a hundred bird tournament, consisting of fourteen stations and twenty-eight varying target presentations, each with an individual flight line, distance and angle. Each target requires a different approach, even before we consider the variables created by true, following and report pairs. These variables are further compounded by the fact that no two courses or designers are the same.

The greater variety in targets requires a matching variety in technique and the gun mount is not exempt from this. You will witness many individual styles on the shooting circuit. With the gun mount, as in any aspect of the sport, there are different techniques and approaches to it. There will always be advocates for one method over another. I, however, am a great believer in flexibility and using the best technique to maximise your scores.

I would compare the gun mount to the different shots and clubs in golf. If you are using the driver for a long shot, you open your stance and take a slow, big swing. If you need a short shot using a sand wedge, you take a small, quick swing. In the same way, your gun mount should be matched to the target's speed and angle. For those quartering targets, the short-window or trap-like shots, keep the gun mount short. For the long crosser and high driven targets where you have plenty of time, make a longer gun mount.

Small window shots, keep the gun mount small

The majority of top performers shooting both FITASC and English Sporting make the transition from pre-mounted shooting to gun down without conscious thought, because they use exactly the same gun mounting action at both disciplines, choosing to use a minimal gun mount movement where the rules will allow it.

To summarise:

1. For those short window quartering or trap-like shots, keep the gun mount short.
2. For the long crosser and high-driven targets with plenty of time, take a longer mount.

An easy rule of thumb is, the longer you can see the target, the longer the mount. The shorter time you can see it, the shorter your mount. Just apply the golf professionals' rule of the right stroke and swing for the shot.

Large window shots, take a bigger gun mount

That said, what successful Sporting Clays shooting requires is a far more flexible approach than that afforded by the pre-mounted gun. Putting aside for a moment the discussion of the appropriate techniques to apply, I will say that I consider shooting gun down is ultimately far more efficient and effective than shooting pre-mounted for the majority of Sporting Clays shots.

Negatives of Shooting Gun Down
1. A poor mount often results in a missed target.
2. Requires diligent practice.
3. Gun fit is far more important.
4. Fragile when put under pressure by short window or quartering shots.

Positives of Shooting Gun Down
1. A shotgun is a dynamic weapon of movement and the gun mount maximises this advantage.
2. Cures gun watching or aiming.
3. Helps maintain balance throughout the shot.
4. At its best on high and crossing targets.

Looking at the mechanics of what makes a consistent gun mount, it is simply the ability to take the gun from a relaxed ready position, with the gun out of your shoulder, and bring it to the face in alignment with the eye. The final position is ultimately the same, whether shooting gun up or gun down. I believe that you will begin to shoot better scores when you can, with the confidence achieved by practice, call for the target gun down.

Chapter 8
Gun Fit

It Has to Fit to Hit

T he act of shooting is one of synchronised hand and eye coordination with the eyes totally focused on the target throughout the shot. To hit the target accurately, the gun needs to point where the eyes are focused. If you have to adapt yourself to the gun to get the proper eye-rib relationship, it breaks your connection with the target, ruins your natural rhythm and timing and causes a miss. The gun should fit your build, style and discipline because in the process of taking your shot, there just isn't time to adjust yourself to the wrong dimensions.

In the highly competitive world of clay shooting, the margin between winning and losing is very small. The difference between being a champion or an also-ran is often just one target. A proper gun fit can get you that one extra target.

When Near Enough is Good Enough

With the exception of ladies and youths, unless you are extremely tall or short, when starting out you can usually get along quite well with a gun in its original factory dimensions: 'Near enough is good enough'. Temporary alterations can be made with pads, comb raisers or moleskin to get a comfortable fit while you practise and perfect your gun mount. However, as you improve, there is no doubt that a well-fitted gun can make a dramatic and positive difference in your shooting performance.

You will be told time and again that the top competitors could all win a tournament with a gun, new, out of the box. Yes, they could, but I can guarantee that they are all shooting a custom-fitted gun. Sporting Clays, in particular, is so instinctual that any distraction that breaks the visual connection with the target will compromise a shooter's style and technique, and a poorly-fitted gun will do this.

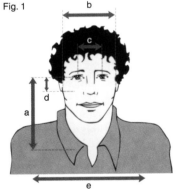

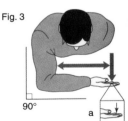

There are as many differences in gun stocks as there are in individuals

Individual Requirements

We are all built very differently. Take your first actions when getting into a new or strange car. First you move the seat and controls to fit so you can reach the pedals and operate the vehicle safely. You make adjustments for height, length of both legs and arms – mirrors are tilted to fit your natural eye alignment.

All of these personal alterations enable us to drive the car both comfortably and safely, giving our full attention to the road, without conscious thought given to the car's operation. This can be compared to gun-fitting, which, done correctly, allows us to concentrate on the target without checking our swing or adjusting our eye alignment.

Getting a Gunfit

You have decided to get a custom gunfit. Bring your eye and ear protection, a hat and the clothing you most typically wear when you shoot. If you do a lot of cold weather shooting, bring the jacket or vest you would use. The thickness of the material could make a difference in your dimensions. You may also want to bring several of your favourite guns, the ones you shoot the best, or want to shoot better.

Every gun fitting should begin with the analysis of eye dominance and the determination of the Master Eye. Any necessary correction for cross dominance should be made at this time. The next step is to mount the gun. *You need a good and accurate gun mount to get a good and accurate gunfit!* Beginner or winner; you need to bring the sound fundamentals of stance, posture and a proper gun mount to the pattern plate. If not, it is all gunfit guess-work.

There are several key places where the gun must fit to you.

Zycomatic Buttress

The first essential measurement is the distance at 'the face'. This is the place on the stock where, when the gun is correctly mounted, the cheek should be *spot-welded* on every shot. This is the point at which height and width between the eye and the rib at 'face' are measured. A correct dimension here ensures that the gun will shoot to 'point of aim'. This 'ledge' on the face is known as the 'Zycomatic Buttress'.

This measurement at 'face' is achieved by the combination of the drop at comb and heel. You can have several combinations which will give the same measurement. The comb should be of

Zycomatic Buttress –the cheek bone just below the eye

such a shape that it presents a parallel and level surface for an inch or more at the face so when the gun moves back under the force of recoil, it does not rise up into the cheek bone. Also it makes allowance for the different head positions used when taking the various shots called for on a Sporting Clays course.

When taking shots below foot level, such as a rabbit, your head will naturally creep back. When taking an overhead or passing shot, your head will tend to move forward. When shooting at eye level, the head will be in the middle position on the stock. So, having a parallel measurement at 'face' creates a single sight picture on every shot made.

Eye Alignment

Much is made of the 'eye to rib' relationship, with different measurements touted for the different disciplines and the guns used to shoot them. These can only be a guide and allowances should always be made for impact, barrel regulation and pattern placement. Furthermore, for those who have to wear glasses requiring bifocal, trifocal or Varilux lenses, the refraction created by such glasses can dramatically alter the wearer's sight pictures.

Another facet of eye alignment is consideration for an individual's cache of sight pictures built over many years of shooting with a gun that might not have fit. They may have physically adapted to the gun to hit the target, perhaps shooting several inches under and to one side of the target. When given a gun that fits and shoots to 'point of aim', they are now required to relearn all of their sight pictures to be able to hit the targets.

The variety of angles and distances in Sporting Clays and Skeet requires a gun that shoots a pattern sixty per cent above and forty per cent below the horizontal of the rib. This allows the target to be kept in view throughout the shot by 'floating it' on the rib. In Trap, however, the target is rising and going away on the first barrel, so the Trap gun is better set up to shoot a pattern seventy per cent above–thirty per cent below the horizontal of the rib. In this instance, because of the high comb-high rib configuration, a piece of daylight should be visible between the rib and the target.

There is a third school of thought that says because the majority of targets in Sporting Clays are dropping, a gun should be set up to shoot a pattern fifty per cent above–fifty per cent below the rib-target alignment. I personally believe a fifty–fifty set up increases head lifting and, in some situations, can result in cross dominance problems.

The preferred eye-rib alignments for guns in the three disciplines are illustrated here.

Sporting – 60/40%

Skeet – 60/40%

Trap – 70/30%

When the gunfitter is ready to begin the fitting process, he will be using an assortment of tools to take the seven dimensions required to fit your gun.

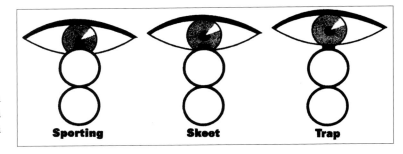

The Gunfitter's Measurements

1. **Length of Pull:** This is the measurement taken from the trigger (the front trigger on a double triggered gun) to the end of the stock at heel, middle and toe. Length of Pull should always be the first consideration, with an allowance made for each individual's shooting stance and style. When the gun is correctly mounted there should be a space of between one and a quarter and one and three-quarter inches between the trigger hand and the nose. This should place the eye between two to three inches from the comb or two-thirds of the distance from the end of butt.

    There are various opinions when it comes to the preferred amount of length. The British have traditionally favoured longer Length of Pull than most American shooters. A longer length has the advantages of increased recoil control, both perceived and mechanical.

    It is critical to find the correct length for an individual. Too long a stock is difficult to mount and will often check half-way up the shoulder or, more painfully, be mounted onto the bicep or upper arm. A too-low mount causes the head to drop and the gun to shoot high. If the mount finishes on the arm instead of the shoulder, the gun will shoot to the side, left for the right-handed, right for the left-handed. Too short a stock creates an inconsistent gun mount, the incorrect extension of the arms and dramatically increases felt-recoil. Bruising the second finger of the trigger hand and the collision of the trigger hand and nose are also caused by a too-short stock.

2. **Drop:** This measurement is taken from a parallel line from the rib of the gun to the stock at the comb, face and heel. This line determines the height at which the gun will place its pattern. Too little drop and the gun will shoot high, too much drop and the gun will shoot low, cause head lifting, or worse, cross dominance. Between the two, the higher relationship of the eye to the rib is always preferable.

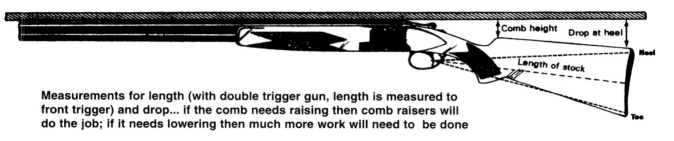

Measurements for length (with double trigger gun, length is measured to front trigger) and drop... if the comb needs raising then comb raisers will do the job; if it needs lowering then much more work will need to be done

3. **Cast:** A vertical line is run through the centre of the heel of the stock and measured against a straight edge from the rib, at the heel and the toe. A special tool called a banjo is usually used for this important measurement. The proper cast ensures the correct alignment of the eye, directly along the rib. This is achieved by the shaping or bending of the stock to fit left or right handed shots.

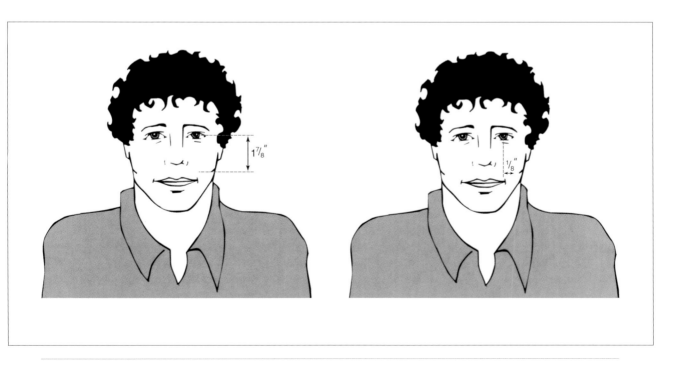

4. **Pitch:** This is the angle created by the butt of the stock and the rib of the gun. Pitch affects the 'standout' of the gun or how high or low it shoots. This measurement is often neglected and the amount of 'stand out' needs to be balanced against the necessity of placing the maximum area of the butt in contact with the shoulder pocket, which is essential to dispersing felt-recoil.

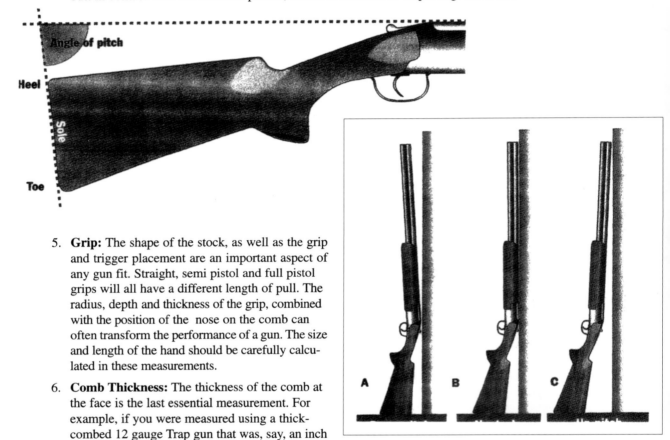

5. **Grip:** The shape of the stock, as well as the grip and trigger placement are an important aspect of any gun fit. Straight, semi pistol and full pistol grips will all have a different length of pull. The radius, depth and thickness of the grip, combined with the position of the nose on the comb can often transform the performance of a gun. The size and length of the hand should be carefully calculated in these measurements.

6. **Comb Thickness:** The thickness of the comb at the face is the last essential measurement. For example, if you were measured using a thick-combed 12 gauge Trap gun that was, say, an inch and a half thick at the face, it could require a quarter inch of cast. If you then purchased a 20 gauge field gun, with a comb that was one inch thick at the face, you would require a reduced amount of cast to compensate for the thinner stock.

7. **Barrel Flip and Impact:** Before any alteration is done, the gun should be checked for its point of impact, to ensure both barrels shoot in the same place, and, particularly in the case of small bore guns, for the degree of barrel flip.

The Try Gun

The first try gun was invented by W.P.Jones in the nineteenth century. It is built with a fully-articulated stock, which can be adjusted for length, cast, drop and pitch. When the measurements are set up and it is shot at the pattern plate, the fitter can see where the adjustments need to be made to achieve perfect fit.

It is always essential to fire the try gun, to make allowance for the effects of recoil which can be a large factor in gun fit, in both comfort and second barrel target acquisition. Once the try gun fit is obtained at the pattern plate it can be proven on moving targets, and comfort and accuracy can be double-checked.

Measurements

When the accurate measurements are taken from the try gun, this 'prescription' can be used to order your new custom gun or make alterations to the guns you already own. A competent gunsmith can bend the gunstock up, down or sideways to achieve the desired shape, as well as adjust the length of the stock by adding or removing wood and fitting the appropriate pad.

The first part of your gun fit may take place away from the pattern plate. Your guns may be measured and then you will proceed to the next step.

A variety of tools are required for precise adjustments and accurate measurements

The try gun must articulate for length, drop and cast

Dry Fit

Using the try gun, the gun fitter will set about doing the initial fit; referred to as a 'Dry Fit'. During this session the fundamentals of straight shooting and consistent gun mounting are checked. If you are unable to consistently mount the gun, it is difficult, if not impossible, to ensure an accurate gun fitting.

Starting with length of pull, followed by alterations to the drop, cast and pitch, the fitter works to achieve a gun that is smooth to mount and that has the correct eye to gun rib relationship for the discipline being shot. I like to use a laser device at this stage to confirm my initial fitting. The laser light, shot at various points, allows me to double check both the fit and the probable impact.

Initial fittings can accurately be confirmed using laser light technology

Finally, the fit needs to be confirmed with live firing on the pattern plate and at clay targets. Here the fit is really proven, for, when live firing, there are many movements both muscular and mechanical that are not apparent during the dry fitting and with the laser.

Pattern Plate

The pattern plate is used to check the point of impact of the shot pattern – the pellet distribution and position. The gun is fired at the steel plate from sixteen or thirty-two yards away.

The eye is, on average, three feet or one yard from the end of the barrel. If the plate is shot from the sixteen yard marker, the mathematics are: three feet into sixteen yards is a sixteen-to-one ratio. This translates to: two inches on the plate is an eighth of an inch adjustment on the gun. Thus, if you are a right-hander shooting four inches to the left of the aiming mark, you would require a quarter-inch cast-off to align the gun to your eye. This formula applies equally at thirty-two yards but here, four inches at the plate equals an eighth of an inch on the try gun.

The final fit is proved at the pattern plate

Groups of shots are made, usually four to six at the same mark. This allows for the inevitable flinch or bad gun mount that can happen when shooting a static target where both noise and recoil are greater than when shooting a moving target. From the placement of the pellets, the gun fitter can make the necessary adjustments to the try gun…'dialing' it in to 'point of aim' and achieve a perfect gun fit.

Factory Fitting

A good gun fit cannot be done in the shop, no matter the experience of the gun fitter. Accurate results can only be achieved by watching the person actually shoot. The reason for this is simple: the way a gun is dry mounted in the shop is very different from the way it would be mounted when live firing at a moving target.

Furthermore, fitting a gun by measuring the length of forearm, chest and shoulder width is inaccurate and has little bearing on where the gun will actually shoot. Barrel flip, recoil and impact cannot be measured nor can the individual's personal style and technique be taken into account.

Do it Yourself or Trial and Error Fitting

You can, to some degree, achieve a reasonably good fit by personal trial and error. Use your club's pattern plate or make a temporary one out of cardboard. Enlist the help of an experienced friend. This is key, as most people who shoot well at Skeet and Trap or in the mid-eighties and higher at Sporting Clays, have more than enough understanding of gun fit and its requirements to assist and help you.

If your gun is too long and too high, try using a shotgun that is too short, has a good deal of drop and a neutral or straight cast. By using extension pads, comb raisers, blue tack and mole skin you can add and remove to the various dimensions. Double check your handiwork at the pattern plate until you are happy with the fit and comfort of the gun.

The cast requirement needs to be analysed from the pattern placement on the plate. Using the sixteen-to-one ratio, work out the amount of cast required.

Next, you should shoot a few targets. This is where the input of your experienced friend is invaluable. He will be able to recognise, if you miss, whether it is gun fit or operator error. Once that is determined, you can correct your errors and proceed to the final step of measuring the gun. This can be done with a straight edge, a protractor, a ruler and a piece of string.

Use these measurements on your gun for awhile. You can see if the measurements need a tweak or two before settling on the final dimensions. This method is often the choice of the top competitors. Finally, you can use the measurements to order a new gun or have your gun altered to them. The nice thing is, if your gun is bent, lengthened or shortened it can always be re-done if you did not get it one hundred per cent right the first time. In any case, you will have learned a lot about how you shoot and what you need and want in the size and shape of a gun that you can use to shoot to your best ability.

The basic equipment needed for a 'do-it-yourself' fitting

Chapter 9
The Basics of Straight Shooting

Winning scores are directly proportional to your mastery of the fundamentals, (Chapter 7) which must be consistently applied through Set Up and Technique. The failure to learn the fundamentals and understand their importance can prevent a competitor from ever reaching his full potential.

Time Management

The shooting action is in two distinct parts, the actions *before* you call for the target, where you are in charge of time and *after*, where the target's speed controls time. It is essential to take full advantage of the time given you *before* you call for the target to properly prepare for the shot. This is referred to as the **Set Up** and maximises the time you have to apply the **Technique** to shoot the target.

Preparing for Action

You begin by *reading the target*. Everything that flies defines a line and, somewhere on that line, the target, for an instant, will appear sharper and slower. This is referred to as the 'sweet spot' – the optimum place to break the target. Establishing this point is the hinge pin around which every successful shot is made.

The Set Up

A good set up is required to place your body in the correct position to rotate smoothly to the target. This *principle of proper alignment to the target* is critical to straight shooting.

The principle of alignment can best be pictured this way: imagine a set of railway tracks leading from the station to the target break point. Now, adopt the correct foot position to point your gun along that track.

Establishing the Break Point

No matter the discipline, there will always be an optimum place to break the target. The ability to determine the target's break point is an essential skill in your pre-shot preparation. Get it wrong and you will miss. To shoot well consistently, you need to learn how to get the break point right every time. Establishing the break point requires careful observation of the target, not just looking at it from one angle, but studying it from several perspectives:

The Line + Visual Hold + Gun Hold = Break Point

This is a simple routine for finding the break point:

Hold the Line

This is all important! Misses can occur 360 degrees around the target; you can miss above, below, in front or behind. But if you can maintain the muzzles on the target line throughout the shooting action, you cut your chances of missing by half! By reducing misses to *missed behind* or *missed in front*, it is then easier to recognise the fault, analyse the cause and implement the correction.

Gun Hold

Think of a strip of 8 mm cine-film…the human eye sees movement at the equivalent of sixteen frames per second, while clay targets leave the trap arm (house) at the equivalent of thirty-two frames per second. So at first, the target is seen only every other frame, and appears in a strobe effect or a blur. But as the target slows, it transitions from thirty-two to sixteen frames per second, and is transformed from a blur to a solid target. This transition point is the gun hold. The muzzles should be held at this transition point, fractionally under the target flight line.

Visual Hold

Once you have determined the gun hold, look halfway back between the muzzles and the trap house. This is your visual hold. Do not look into, or too close to, the trap. The target will be leaving the trap at such speed that you will instinctively react to the movement rather than the target, resulting in a 'poke and hope' shot.

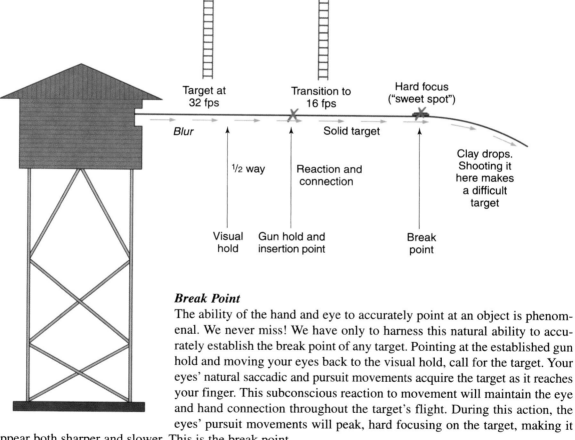

Break Point

The ability of the hand and eye to accurately point at an object is phenomenal. We never miss! We have only to harness this natural ability to accurately establish the break point of any target. Pointing at the established gun hold and moving your eyes back to the visual hold, call for the target. Your eyes' natural saccadic and pursuit movements acquire the target as it reaches your finger. This subconscious reaction to movement will maintain the eye and hand connection throughout the target's flight. During this action, the eyes' pursuit movements will peak, hard focusing on the target, making it appear both sharper and slower. This is the break point.

Address

Address this point with both stance and muzzles, placing the break point in the centre of your swing. Then simply turn back along the target line, taking the muzzles along the line towards the trap house to the gun hold and moving your eyes to the visual hold.

Note: Proper set up allows a controlled swing, rotating through 180 degrees, like a tank turret. However at the outer limits, the swing begins to slow, effectively restricting the arc to 120 degrees .This is why it is essential to set up with the break point at the centre of your swing arc.

The fundamentals of good footwork, stance, and posture together with good head position, will ensure that the muzzles stay on the line throughout the shot. Maintaining this balance throughout the shot is essential.

Start right and you will finish right.

You are now ready to call for the target.
1. Address the target, not the trap. You call 'Pull' and as the target appears, you begin your move to it in one continuous, smooth movement. It should all be a seamless flow.
2. Your eyes see the target and guide your hands to it, setting up a chain reaction of timing and tempo.
3. Once you get the big muscles in your body turning, the gun mount is smooth and unhurried, everything turning together, muzzles moving with and locked onto the target.
4. As the stock comes into the cheek, the shoulder rolls forward to complete the mount.
5. Forward allowance (lead) is seen and the trigger is smoothly pulled.

This is the complete and correct sequence in which to make a successful shot.

Tailoring your Technique

We are all distinctly individual. Just glance up and look around you at the difference in people's height, size, and weight. These differences also exist in the hidden internal workings of our personal coordination, reaction time and visual acuity.

The game of golf is, in many ways, comparable to shooting a round of Sporting Clays. Using golf as an analogy, an individual is required to negotiate a golf course in the least number of shots. The competitor is allowed fourteen clubs in his bag. This allows him to choose the right club to best tackle the variety of shots he will encounter during the game. No golfer would dream of starting a competition without the full complement of clubs. He will also have practised with and be able to use each and every one of them.

In the same way, the clay competitor requires a similar 'bag of clubs' or variety of techniques: Swing Through, Pull Away, Maintained, Instinctive, and Spot Shooting. This 'bag of techniques' allows him to choose the best one for the target presentations he encounters. When the golfer begins the sport, he is shown the basics of stance, posture, head position and swing. He starts with a short swing, usually a seven iron. As the fundamentals are grooved and his skills increase, the

Swing-through

Pull-away

Maintained-lead

Insertion point according to technique

rest of the clubs are introduced. Each club is designed for a specific shot, angle and distance and each requires a subtle difference in the swing used to play well with them.

The learning curve in the Shotgun Sports is exactly the same. As the beginner grooves the fundamentals, the various techniques are taught. The CPSA and NSCA quite sensibly encourage beginners to learn using the CPSA–NSCA Method. It is a sound technique and provides the perfect platform on which to start a shooting career. It is straight forward, easy to digest and delivers a good understanding of what is required in order to break a target.

But to be successful and 'play the game' to a high standard, it may be necessary to apply *all* of the techniques; to be able to recognise specific target's angles and distances and learn the best technique to adopt in different circumstances. As in golf, each target requires subtle differences in the swing used to shoot well with them.

Watching a champion, it is not always easy to see precisely how they achieve such a high level of performance and consistency. All have developed such an effortless way of shooting it is difficult to pinpoint just why they are so good and exactly what technique they are using. However, certain fundamentals are always present – the difference between one and the other is the technique being used.

Many top competitors are adamant that they shoot the same technique, regardless of the target presentation. Watch many top performers in various disciplines, yes, they do use one technique most of the time, but, whether they aware of it or not, all change, adapt and modify their first-choice technique on some target presentations. In fact, this micro-managing or adjusting of techniques occurs on every target they shoot. This can be best be seen when they miss (rarely), chip or are late on one of a pair of targets.

These adjustment actions are very subtle and probably totally unconscious (Unconsciously Competent). Their highly-programmed 'onboard computer' reacts to every target shot and alterations to technique and swing speed are adjusted constantly.

'I never worry about how I get the muzzles in front of the target; I just pull the trigger when the picture is right'.

Getting the Picture

The important part of this quote '*is when the picture is right*'. In any occupation, enough years of experience will help you learn from your mistakes and, hopefully, ensure you do not repeat them or, if you do so, not too often.

Once you have mastered the fundamentals and acquired a basic sound technique, the next step is to learn to blend the techniques to suit your own personal coordination, reaction time and visual acuity. Once you have established this 'personal blend', you will be able to 'pull the trigger when the picture is right'.

What is the sole purpose of a technique? To be able to *get the muzzles in front of and on the target line consistently*. Your technique will enable you to harness instinct and coordination into a sequence of pre-planned movements *to* and *in front* of the target.

All techniques need to deliver three things: Line, Speed of Flight and Gun Momentum. In a round of Sporting Clays, you may have only one or two stands that let you down. It could be that one target on each of these stands could make the difference of eight or ten targets to your score. Would you like to score eighty-five or seventy-five? A trick or two up your sleeve could make it possible.

Your Bag of Tricks

There are three mainstream methods: Swing Through, Pull Away and Maintained Lead. All achieve the essential requirement of placing the barrels in front of the target. However, some achieve this more easily and consistently than others. Some are more easily learned and applied, particularly by beginners. But each has an advantage on a particular target presentation. Just as the golfer has a favourite club, we all will have a favourite method, but you should be able to break targets using all of them. The following will explain the technique, its origins, strengths and weaknesses, together with the targets it is applied to most effectively. The basic target structures are constant – the only differences in each technique are in the muzzle hold points and insertion points.

Set Up: Visual Hold – Gun Hold – Break Point

Making the Shot: Gun Mount – Insertion Point – Forward Allowance

Swing Through or Follow Through
Method
The muzzles are inserted on the line of flight, just behind the target. The gun is than consciously accelerated through and past the target before pulling the trigger. It is this accelerating passage past the target that results in sufficient forward allowance to break the target.

Disadvantages
Achieving forward allowance by muzzle speed alone creates its own pitfalls. If the swing is too fast you will miss in front, too slow and you will miss behind. And that is presuming you are on the target's line and speed of flight. If the speed is misjudged, you need to rush to catch up and rushing results in loss of control. A swing too far in front will make you stop and attempt to ambush the target. Too slow a swing and you are unable to establish sufficient forward allowance. If the line is errant, then on a dropping target, you swing through the target and miss high and in front.

Swing-through

Strengths
Its greatest strength is in wing shooting. With the unpredictability of bird shooting, there can be no prior preparation for line, speed or lead and for movement to the bird and swinging-through, this is, by far, the most popular and successful field technique.

History
This is one of the oldest shooting techniques. Gun maker Charles Lancaster wrote on the subject in the 1800s and it was taught by the legendry coach and champion shot, Percy Stanbury. Swing Through is still taught today at the West London Shooting School.

Pull Away
Method
The muzzles are held on the line of flight and the target is never allowed to pass the muzzles. The gun is pointed at the leading edge of the target until the gun reaches the cheek. When the gun is fully-mounted, the muzzles should be on line and on the front edge of the target. It is then accelerated away from the target and the trigger is pulled. As in Swing-Through, it is this acceleration that achieves the forward allowance required to break the target. This technique falls half-way between Swing Through and Maintained Lead.

Disadvantages
The most common faults in Pull Away are letting the target past the muzzles and reverting to Swing Through, and looking at the gun and 'measuring' to try to establish the forward allowance, which results in stopping the gun.

Strengths

Its advantages are that it gives both speed and line of flight and no other technique does this. It is a great technique for beginners and I would compare it to the golf pro's use of the seven iron to establish a smooth swing and groove sound fundamentals.

History

Clarrie Wilson of the British Clay Pigeon Shooting Association pioneered the Pull Away technique in the 1960s and it is still the technique of choice for this organisation.

Maintained Lead
Method

The muzzles are, first, held on the line of flight. The muzzles are then inserted in front of and stay in front of the target at the perceived correct amount of forward allowance, from the moment it is seen. The muzzles maintain this gap in front until the gun reaches the cheek. When the gun is fully-mounted, the muzzles should still be the same distance in front of the target when the trigger is pulled.

Disadvantages

It is a technique dependent on very good hand and eye coordination to establish both line of flight and speed of target. Too far in front or checking the forward allowance will stop or slow the swing and result in a miss behind.

Maintained-lead

Strengths

In Maintained Lead, the gun is in front of the target throughout the shot. This means that the gun moves at the same speed as the target, which, psychologically, makes you feel in control and a smoother movement results.

History

The origins of Maintained Lead are in match and flintlock guns, where the slow percussion of black powder required a technique that kept the gun in front and on line while the combustion took place, after the trigger was pulled.

Instinctive or Churchill
Method

Robert Churchill's Instinctive Shooting method requires that the muzzles be held on the line of flight. By hard focusing on the target and moving the hands and body with it, the gun progresses to the cheek. When the mount is completed, the trigger is pulled. With the muzzles always pointed directly at the target, forward allowance is achieved from the speed of the target – the movement of the hands and eyes, coordinated by the target speed, automatically arrive in the correct position. The lapse between the time the trigger is pulled and the time that the shot leaves the barrel ensures that the muzzles are in front of the target when the shot leaves the barrel, though, if asked, the shooter would swear he shot directly at the target.

Disadvantages

The Instinctive Technique depends entirely on gun speed, consistent and accurate gun mount and complete trust in your hands and eyes. There are no mental pictures based on previous trial and error for the brain to store where instinct can be moulded by previous successes. So, each and every shot at each and every target is a new challenge to your reactions.

Strengths

This is the one technique where you will definitely not check your swing or stop the gun. After all, you are shooting directly at the target, exactly where your subconscious wants you to shoot.

History

The Instinctive Technique, invented and pioneered by Robert Churchill, combined with his XXV short-barreled shotgun to create a revolution in British game shooting in the 1930s. His controversial position that there was no requirement to visually see daylight in front of a target to hit it, is still being argued today.

Move, Mount, Shoot
Method

A combination of Churchill Instinctive and Maintained Lead, this technique allows the sportsman to maintain the correct lead and line on a target using hand and eye coordination. The muzzles are on the line of flight and hard focus is used to synchronise the body and hands, placing the gun correctly in front of the target, and maintaining that position until the shot is taken.

Disadvantages

Exactly the same as in Maintained Lead, judgement of line and lead is totally dependent on very good eye and hand coordination. Get the forward allowance wrong and a miss behind is certain, either from incorrect lead or stopping the gun.

Strengths

It is a technique used by many top shooters. With the muzzles in front of the target throughout the shot, there is the opportunity for control and smooth shooting. The element of Churchill, where the hands and body pace and mirror the target throughout the shot, give it a definite advantage over the majority of sustained lead techniques.

History

Three times World FITASC Sporting Champion John Bidwell developed this technique to spectacular effect during his shooting career. In 1990 he wrote a book of the same title: *Move, Mount and Shoot*.

Spot or Ambush
Method

It is possible to spot-shoot a target. This technique requires you to anticipate speed and line of flight, estimate the target's arrival at a specific point, insert the gun and precisely time the shot and 'spot-shoot' or 'ambush' the target at that point.

Disadvantages

This is a technique that is used very little. I know of no top competitor who uses this method unless forced to by poor target presentations. The ultimate test of hand and eye co-ordination, spot-shooting might better be called 'poke and hope'.

Strengths

There is one and only one strength. It can be used as a last ditch effort, where the target pick up was incorrect or visual contact is lost, i.e., a target passing in front of the sun, behind obstacles or the second of a pair – and there is no time to apply a more controlled technique.

History

The technique of early wing shooters, a combination of rifling and sustained lead.

Technique to Target

Ask any Skeet shooter 'what technique do you use?' and they will instantly reply 'Maintained Lead'. If you then ask, 'On every target?' The answer from the majority will be an affirmative. 'What about the second target of a pair?' Another affirmative.

Yet it is impossible to shoot the Maintained Lead technique for both targets for pairs in Skeet! You can maintain the lead on the first target, but you are forced to use swing-through on the second target of the pair. Because of the predetermined speed, angles and distances in the game, many learn the trick of spot-shooting or ambushing the second target. To the shooter, this may look and feel as if they maintained the lead on the second target, but it is simply an optical illusion.

I make use of video analysis a great deal in my instruction, mainly to analyse flaws in the fundamentals and swing. But often it demonstrates exactly what technique a client is really using, not what they think they are. In frame-by-frame analysis they are often amazed to find that they jump the target and do so to such a degree that they need to slow or stop the gun and ambush the target when they judge the picture is correct. I will ask them which technique they used, and rarely, indeed, is it the one they think they are using.

One Man's Lead...

It is possible to work out the theoretical forward allowance for targets at various ranges; but, it is nearly impossible to apply these distances in practice. After all, one man's three feet is another man's five. While it may be impossible to judge a particular number of feet in front of the target mathematically, by practice, trial and error you can learn the 'gap' that works for you on any target at any given yardage.

This ability can be compared to the golfer who, after learning to hit the ball straight, learns to fade and drift the ball according to the obstacles on the course. He does not 'measure' but he has learned how much to open or close the face of the club and how much swing speed he needs to put the ball where he wants it.

Reactive Shooting

Where is this going? I believe that each and every one of us uses a variety of techniques while shooting, whether at Sporting Clays or wing shooting. We are often unaware of doing so and it is an unconscious decision as to which one we use, target to target.

It is a simple synapse in the brain where the information from the target, gathered by the eyes, guides and controls the body's movement to the target. The technique we use is entirely dependent on the target presentation and our individual reactions and visual acuity. This automatic response is what I consider 'reactive shooting'; the unconscious adjustment of technique, target to target. If you practise shooting each and every target presentation with all three of the major techniques, you will achieve two things.

First, you will discover which technique best suits your individual style and timing for each target.

Secondly, you will pre-programme your subconscious with muscle memory so when making a shot, you can do so with no conscious reference to method or technique. During this practice you will discover there is little difference in the techniques, simply differences in the gun insertion points.

Practical Application

How to apply this to your shooting? First, ask yourself another question, 'Which do I consider the single most important part of the shooting equation?' For me, it is the *line*.

Misses can occur 360 degrees around the target. You can miss above or below, in front or behind. If you can keep the muzzles on the line throughout the shot, you limit your misses to in front or behind. You instantly achieve a fifty per cent reduction in missing. You also gain a significant second benefit. As a competitor, if you miss, you need to know the fault or the cause and understand the correction. If you can stay on the line, it becomes easier to recognise the fault. You miss either in front or behind, now you can analyse the cause and apply the correction.

You can improve the odds even more. You can make sure that if you do miss, it is in front of the target. Consider this: if you miss behind, even by a micro-second, you can never hit the target because the target is flying away from the shot string. If you miss in front, even by a mile, there is always a chance that the target and shot string will connect as the target flies towards the pattern. *'They don't fly backwards.'* This simple fact has been recognised since the first attempts were made to shoot birds on the wing.

So, how best can you attempt to be on line and in front on the majority of shots? By learning to establish the line and speed of flight of the target. Programmed with this data, our 'on-board computer' can make the computation required to ensure target and shot string collide.

On Line and On Time

The core requirement of any shooting technique is to establish speed and line of flight. However, this cannot be achieved just by the application of the technique itself. Its success is dependent on several factors. These can be broken down into two parts.

1. **Ballistic:** Before the bird flushes or you call 'pull'.
2. **Instinctive:** After the flush or call for the bird.

The Ballistic part of the equation is made up of:

A: Reading the Line
B: Angle/Speed/Distance
C: Visual Hold/Gun Hold/BreakPoint
D: Foot Work/Stance/Posture/Head Position

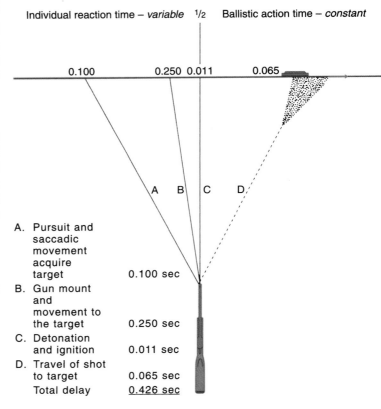

Individual reaction time – *variable*   ½   Ballistic action time – *constant*

0.100		0.250	0.011	0.065
	A	B	C	D

A.	Pursuit and saccadic movement acquire target	0.100 sec
B.	Gun mount and movement to the target	0.250 sec
C.	Detonation and ignition	0.011 sec
D.	Travel of shot to target	0.065 sec
	Total delay	0.426 sec

The need to 'lead' a target is because of the lag in pulling the trigger and ballistics of the shotgun

The Instinctive part includes:

A: Hard Focus
B: Gun Mount
C: Swing
D: Muzzle Insertion

Ballistic
A. Reading the Line
Where is the target first visible after launch? Try to pick out a feature such as a leaf, bush or branch.

1. Does the target appear instantly or after a short delay? If the latter, count to time it... One thousand and one, One thousand and two.
2. What type of target? Standard, Midi, Mini or Battue.
3. Is it rising or falling? Where in its flight is it most level and stable?
4. Does it pass any obstructions to interfere with sight or pattern?
5. Is the wind or landscape affecting its flight trajectory?
6. If one of a pair, where will the second bird be when you break the first?
7. Which target disappears or hits the ground first?

Reading targets is an acquired skill and you must constantly work on it to improve it. The top shots put as much time into this aspect of the game as they do the shooting.

B. Angle/Speed/Distance
The angle created by the intersection of the shot string and target line is the best indicator of the forward allowance the target will require. Remember, the smaller the angle, the smaller the lead, the larger the angle, the larger the lead.

The target's speed and distance will add to the amount of forward allowance required. Always try to ascertain the size of the target being thrown, is it a standard (110) or a midi (90)? The size of the target will affect its speed and the amount of lead it needs.

Judging distance is a skill that is easily learned. When you are next outside, be it walking the dog or just in town, pick out an object and guess its yardage. Now count the number of paces it takes to reach that object, with one stride counting as one yard. Within a short period of time you will be able to accurately gauge distances. Computing the distance with the speed and angle of a target will help the subconscious apply the correct forward allowance.

C. and D. are covered earlier in this Chapter.

Instinctive
A. Hard Focus
Beginning with the eyes, you need to capture and maintain hard focus on the target from beginning to end of the shot. A good tip to achieve this is to learn to open your eyes wide to allow the maximum amount of light in.

Look beyond the line at the Visual Hold, soft focusing into infinity. As the muscles in the eyes are more efficient at coming down and in to an object than up and out, this focal point allows a faster and better acquisition of the target. Always attempt to maintain hard focus throughout the shot. Quitting the target is one of the major causes of missing. After all, we shoot them with our eyes.

B. and C. are covered earlier in this Chapter.

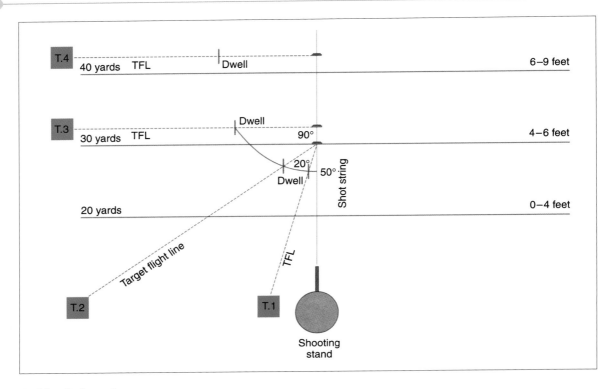

D. Muzzle Insertion

The gun insertion point on the target determines the technique applied. Insert behind and you will Swing-Through; on it and you will Pull Away; in front and you will Maintain the Lead.

The biggest mistake that I see is the complete lack of connection between the gun and target at this crucial 'make or break' point in the shooting technique. The gun is often mounted, then swung, in two separate movements, and all relationship to the target is lost for a moment. The result is a chase to re-establish contact with the target and the technique used becomes a lottery.

The swing and *the mount* should be *one smooth motion*…to wax lyrical, it should be 'a synergy of muscle, steel and walnut' linked and directed by the eyes to the target. The muzzles should never be inserted more than one or two inches in front or behind the target, regardless of the technique you use. When you insert the gun, it must be on, or close to, the target to establish and maintain those essential requirements of speed and line of flight.

Putting them Together

In your practice you should be able to demonstrate all of these techniques and apply the one that best suits you and the target presentation being shot. From this you will quickly discover a personal technique that is both simple and uncluttered. The signals received from the target should translate into a smooth sequence of muscular responses, allowing your body to coordinate with the target so the shot can be made with maximum effectiveness and

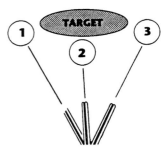

1 - Swing Through - muzzle inserted behind the target, then swept through as shot is fired.

2 - Pull Away - insert is on the target, then pulled in front as shot is fired.

3 - Sustained Lead - muzzle is inserted in front of target and lead is maintained as the shot is fired.

control. You are, in effect, programming a bodily response to the target that can be relied on presentation-to-presentation, achieving that elusive consistency we so desire and which wins tournaments.

The Blend

Those of you who imbibe the odd wee dram will be familiar with single malt whiskies. These are products of distilleries throughout the Highlands of Scotland. All have their own distinctive taste, some so strong they need to be diluted with a little spring water to make them more acceptable to the palate. Another method of softening the strong taste of peat and iodine is to age the whisky in old port and sherry barrels, adding both to their colour and taste. There is a third method where several single malts are blended together to create a smoother drink.

In this same way, I have blended together elements from several techniques to create a Blend Technique, designed to make a smoother shot. This combines the elements of several methods:

1. It emphasises hard focus on the target.
2. It incorporates Churchill's use of body rotation and the leading hand in mounting and guiding the gun.
3. It uses the establishment of speed and line of flight of Clarrie Wilson's Pull Away
4. It stresses the target control of Maintained Lead.
5. It includes the combination of mount and swing and its application to the target.

This is not a one hundred per cent solution to every target presentation, but the Blend Technique easily learned and applied, gives instant feedback in the result of a hit or a miss, the fault is readily identified and the required correction is simple to implement.

The Elements of Straight Shooting
Swing Speed

To ensure that forward allowance is maintained, the gun needs to be moving faster than the target when the trigger is pulled. If it is not, then in the momentary lag after detonation, the target will close the established gap and a miss behind will result. Speed is, indeed, lead and lead is speed.

Churchill made his controversial statement that there was no requirement for lead because of this. However, what worked for European-style driven wing shooting where a one-in-three average is considered good shooting, would win little in modern competition. That said there are components of the Churchill Technique that, when combined with a more modern approach, offer what I consider a solid Target Technique.

If you were to enter a race, would you prefer to be given a head start or to begin behind? I personally would choose the advantage of a head start, but you can make your own decision on this. When we are shooting, we are in a race with the target, so wouldn't the advantage of a head start work equally well? So, of the techniques we have examined, the one that gives us the most control and advantage must be Sustained Lead. But it does have one or two drawbacks, which, if corrected, could make it even better. On longer passing shots, the forward allowance that needs to be maintained can mean the loss of the all-important line, but the main disadvantage is sustaining the 'head start' gun speed.

Modified Churchill

Nash Buckingham used a combination of Churchill, Maintained Lead and Pull Away, referring to it as the 'Moving Spot Technique'. This utilised the strengths of the establishment of the line and flight from Churchill, the target control of Maintained Lead and the resulting gun speed gained from Pull Away. In the Moving Spot, you simply insert the gun a few inches in front of the target before opening the gap until your subconscious tells you the picture is right, then you pull the trigger. If the target is close, insert on the front of the target, at thirty yards, two feet in front and at forty yards, four feet in front.

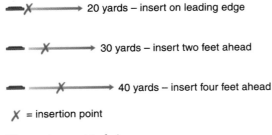

20 yards – insert on leading edge

30 yards – insert two feet ahead

40 yards – insert four feet ahead

X = insertion point

The moving spot technique

The visual relationships between target and muzzles will vary with the shooting technique. I find that this method is easily learned and can be adapted target to target and gives each and every shot direction and control.

There are certain targets and times, pairs being the best example, where the second bird could be better tackled with another technique. But the core of this blend works just as well when combined with Swing Through or Pull Away.

Due to the great variety of target presentations, the blend will not work on every shot, but the only aspect that needs to change is the insertion point on the target. Think of it as a structured approach, where the result will be smoother and more consistent shooting with more broken targets.

While learning these techniques and in any competition, recognition of where you missed and why is essential to discovering which of the techniques works best for you. When you are practising, think through why a miss occurred and if it could have been hit using a different technique.

An *instinctive shot* is one made without conscious thought as to the technique used. To me, it would better be described as a *reactive shot*. During any competition you will need to constantly adapt and correct your reactions to the various targets you encounter. This will result in your use of all of the techniques. So, the more they are grooved, the better you will apply them. The bulk of your shooting will be made with a method that suits your personal visual acuity and reaction times, but you will never be able to shoot to your full potential without mastering at least the three main techniques.

Forward Allowance

From the earliest attempts to shoot birds on the wing, it was quickly discovered that to hit a moving target it was necessary to place the gun in front of its path so that the shot string intercepted the target along its flight line. After all, **'they don't fly backwards'**, and, as yet, I have never seen a target that does. I consider the hardest-learned piece of the shooting jigsaw, to make a master class shot, is to educate the brain that you have **'to miss it, to hit it'**.

In life, being punctual and accurate are attributes that are highly regarded. We are often encouraged 'To Hit the Nail on the Head'. Well, to do so when clay target shooting is to ensure a miss behind. As an instructor, I witness many clients who struggle to apply forward allowance. Their conscious mind understands the concept, but their subconscious will not allow them to apply it. When shooting, they consistently miss behind.

I refer to this conflict between the conscious and subconscious minds as Separation Anxiety where the struggle between the two concepts vacillates between action and paralysis. Experience plays a big part in this and the brain is capable of storing the equivalent of a photo album of mental pictures based on previous trial and error.

The top competitor has control over his subconscious mind and can override its command to 'pull the trigger', until the barrel-target relationship is right. By insight, understanding and repeated successful practice, these dedicated shotgunners train their subconscious to **Miss It to Hit It**.

The Need for Lead

Why is it necessary to have to shoot in front of the target to connect with it? After all, modern cartridges produce muzzle velocities in excess of 1,200 feet per second, or more than 700 miles per hour. This is faster than 'Mach One', and, indeed, the bulk of the report heard on firing the gun is the shot mass breaking the Sound Barrier.

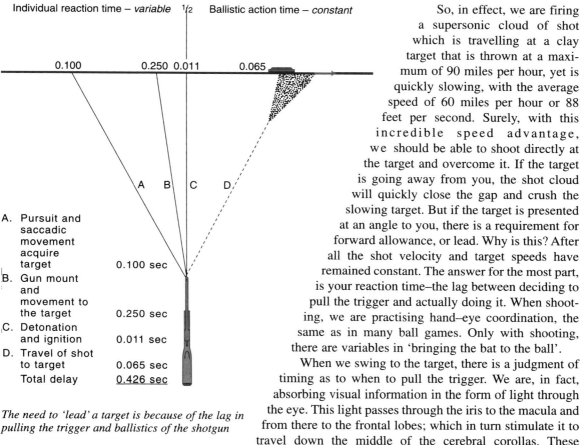

Individual reaction time – *variable*   ¹/₂   Ballistic action time – *constant*

0.100   0.250 0.011   0.065

A   B   C   D

A. Pursuit and saccadic movement acquire target   0.100 sec
B. Gun mount and movement to the target   0.250 sec
C. Detonation and ignition   0.011 sec
D. Travel of shot to target   0.065 sec
   Total delay   0.426 sec

The need to 'lead' a target is because of the lag in pulling the trigger and ballistics of the shotgun

So, in effect, we are firing a supersonic cloud of shot which is travelling at a clay target that is thrown at a maximum of 90 miles per hour, yet is quickly slowing, with the average speed of 60 miles per hour or 88 feet per second. Surely, with this incredible speed advantage, we should be able to shoot directly at the target and overcome it. If the target is going away from you, the shot cloud will quickly close the gap and crush the slowing target. But if the target is presented at an angle to you, there is a requirement for forward allowance, or lead. Why is this? After all the shot velocity and target speeds have remained constant. The answer for the most part, is your reaction time–the lag between deciding to pull the trigger and actually doing it. When shooting, we are practising hand–eye coordination, the same as in many ball games. Only with shooting, there are variables in 'bringing the bat to the ball'.

When we swing to the target, there is a judgment of timing as to when to pull the trigger. We are, in fact, absorbing visual information in the form of light through the eye. This light passes through the iris to the macula and from there to the frontal lobes; which in turn stimulate it to travel down the middle of the cerebral corollas. These produce the neuro-messages that make the muscles contract and react to coordinate our movements to the target, which finish with the trigger being pulled.

But then, after the trigger is pulled, still more time passes. The hammer falls, detonating the cartridge (lock time), after which the shot is propelled towards the target (ignition and powder burn, barrel and flight times). In all, this combined action takes an average of one tenth of a second. Hardly worth consideration, when we are talking about the shot cloud travelling at more than 700 miles per hour, right? Well, in that one tenth of second, a target leaving at 60 miles per hour (88 feet or about 30 yards per second) moves approximately three feet. The farther the shot travels, the more it slows down. And the greater the distance the greater the lead required. At forty yards, you need to place the shot nine to twelve feet in front of the crossing target to intercept it!

Timing is Everything

Time is the past, present and future regarded as a continuous whole. When attempting to shoot a moving target, we are, in fact, working against time in an effort to complete the shot in a limited period. It naturally follows that the core skill in our shooting is our timing – our ability to judge when to pull the trigger. The same applies to hitting a ball or playing an instrument in an orchestra. The top performers demonstrate an economy of movement, a *Maximum Efficiency for Minimum Effort*. When observed, they appear to have enhanced smoothness and more time to take their actions.

When well-honed timing and technique skills are demonstrated in shotgunning, onlookers will comment that that these fine shots are 'naturals'. To some extent they are correct. There will always be a small percentage of participants in any activity who are 'quicker on the uptake' than their neighbours. Lead is very personal to the individual shooter. You need to learn the different pictures for yourself and as your experience expands, so will your ability to judge distance, angle and speed and you will have the confidence to let your 'on-board computer' do the rest – *after* you have programmed in the correct information.

The Math of Gap Analysis

If we applied math to the question of lead, the formula would rely on the angle, distance and speed of the target, combined with the shooting technique used and the speed of the swing. But there are secondary factors that also affect lead, such as the velocity of the cartridge, the effect of choke on the pattern's width and density and a shooter's reaction time.

Such a formula could indicate the lead needed for a target that maintains a constant vertical or horizontal line. But many modern target presentations offer targets that are in transition, adding still another dimension to the equation: *multi-plane lead*, such as required on battues, chondels and even rabbits, all shot while transitioning between a horizontal and vertical line.

What the shooter needs is to be a *magician not a mathematician*. The latter would do his math and work out the precise lead required on any particular presentation, then attempt to apply it with slide rule precision. And he would fail. But if we apply a little mental magic and *trust* our 'on board computer', we will always put the gun in the right place, in front of the target.

It's Just a Matter of Trust

How do we achieve this trust? As usual, through practice. The learning curve has three stages.

1. **Unconsciously Incompetent** – When you depend entirely on your instructor, you are shown an exercise and then have to replicate it. At this stage, you are required to think about every move before it is made.
2. **Consciously Competent** – When the exercise has been repeated until it becomes muscle memory. The 'on board computer' is recognisably programmed.
3. **Unconsciously Competent** – Now you have grooved the mechanics to the point that you can make the moves as subconsciously as riding a bicycle…if you thought about how to ride it, you would lose balance and fall off.

Master class shooters are unconsciously competent. This leaves their conscious mind free to lock on to only one thing – the target. There is a fourth stage, which is where peak performance occurs. It is better known as being *'in the Zone'*.

You cannot hit targets consistently if you are thinking of the mechanics. The fundamentals must be practised and grooved to the point where they become autonomic and the movement to and in front of the target can be made without conscious thought.

The Autonomic Shot

To shoot your best, you need to concentrate totally on a single object: the target. The more intense the concentration, the better the outcome. With total autonomic concentration and focus on the target, you avoid destructive thoughts of mechanics or measured lead intruding into your consciousness.

You need to do more than just look at the whole target. You must single out the *leading edge*. Intense concentration on a small part of the target blocks out negative thoughts and, effectively, causes the target to appear to become larger and slower.

In Sporting Clays, one-third of lost targets are missed in front, two-thirds are missed behind. The competitors who miss out front are among the winners. My first rule to overcoming Separation Anxiety is to recognise that *'they don't fly backwards'*, so if you are going to miss, which is inevitable, *' miss it in front'*.

Blur that Barrel

Are the majority of targets missed behind due to lack of lead, poor mechanics or an ineffective choke or load? Perhaps so, in the very early stages of the learning curve. But after the shotgunner has achieved some experience, the cause of many shooters' problems is quitting the target and *looking at the gun.*

It is important to see both the target and the gun, but how they should be seen in relation to each other is rarely explained. This ability to perceive two objects in two different fields of vision, is what marries together the mechanics and the mind and allows us to shoot a moving object.

We have two eyes but only one receiver, our brain, which joins these two individual pictures seamlessly together, allowing us to see one clear, sharp image. But this clear single image can only be seen in one field of vision at a time, either up close or at a distance. So the fields of vision opposite our point of focus, the peripheral vision, will always be made up of two blurred or double images.

When we are shooting, if we hard focus on the target, the gun will be seen in the peripheral vision as a double blurred image of two gun barrels. If we attempt to place the bead at the end of the muzzle on the target, we are now looking at the gun, and the target is a blurred double image of two indistinct targets. Which one do we shoot?

To consistently shoot well, we must learn to maintain hard focus on the target throughout the shot. The more forward allowance or lead required, the more important it is to keep our vision firmly locked on the target. If at any time we quit the target and look back to the barrel of the gun, the target will double and blur and we will stop or

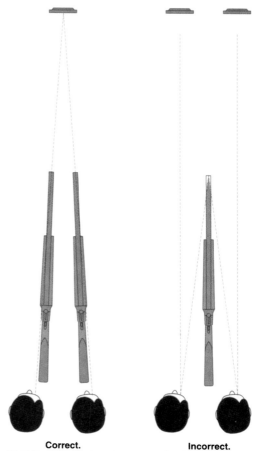

Correct.
Hard focus on the target.
Gun is a blurred double image in peripheral vision.

Incorrect.
Looking at the gun.
Target is a blurred double image.

slow our swing and miss behind. This is literally using a scattergun approach. We have all, at some point, experienced the following:

1. Inability to know where a target is missed.
2. A stop-start stuttering swing.
3. Your instructor or shooting partner is forever saying 'You missed behind', when you could have sworn you had plenty of daylight between the barrel and the target when you pulled the trigger.

Learn to recognise these symptoms and apply the cure: *reestablish hard focus on the target!*

Barrel Awareness

Any shooter must, of course, be *aware* of the gun and the gap between the muzzle and the target. But as individuals we all see things differently. This is well demonstrated by the fact that one person sees inches of lead at the barrels while another sees feet at the target. *Individual Lead* is the lead we see between barrels and target when we pull the trigger. This is less than the *True Lead* at the target. True Lead is actually greater; because of the delay in pulling the trigger.

For any shot to be successful, the barrels must be moving faster than the target – regardless of the technique used. We all have individual swing speeds and reaction times. If you asked several competitors exiting any Sporting Clays station 'How much lead did you give them?' one might tell you he gave the crosser, two feet, and the other shooter will say six feet.

This phenomenon is why Churchill was so insistent that you could shoot directly at a target without visible lead. If the swing is fast enough, the lag between the time the trigger is pulled to when the shot leaves the barrel, would be enough to place barrel and hence the shot string, several feet in front of the target. But if asked, the shooter would insist that he shot directly at the target.

Prime your Peripheral Vision

We all must amass the set of timing and lead pictures that works for us. How do we do this? The difference between the average shot and the good shot is that the good shot learns to shoot using peripheral vision to position the gun.

You use this peripheral vision every day of your life. When you drive your car, you do not aim the emblem on the bonnet at the bumper of the car in front of you. You drive looking ten or twenty car lengths ahead. But if something should unexpectedly happen to the car directly in front of you, you react instantly, braking or swerving to avoid the danger. *We are gifted with peripheral vision so we can see in two places at once.*

Another example: say you are serving in a tennis match – you toss the ball up to serve. If you then looked at your hand to check your grip on the racquet, the result would be a fluffed serve. Yet if you keep your eye firmly concentrated on the ball, you could hit it in the 'sweet spot' and serve an ace!

You drive a car and serve a tennis ball using both central and peripheral vision, *central* to look ahead and navigate or see the ball, *peripheral* to operate and control the car or see your racquet. It is exactly the same in shooting: you 'navigate' on the target with central vision and 'operate' the gun with peripheral. If you can see your barrels clearly, you have stopped the gun and missed behind.

To cure *Separation Anxiety*, you need to learn to drive or swing the gun with your peripheral vision, while remaining locked on the target with your central vision. You must develop *'Awareness of the Rib'* (Faint image in peripheral vision) along with *'Hard Focus on the Target'* (Leading edge in central vision).

Shooting straight requires sound fundamentals and a proper set up combined with hard focus and a sound technique.

Chapter 10
Sporting Solutions

History

S porting Clays, the most popular of the domestic disciplines, evolved in England as a means to practice for shooting driven game. In Skeet and Trap the speeds, distances and angles are fixed, and can even be challenged and checked before and during a tournament. Therefore, in both of those games, it is very easy to establish definite gun holds, focal points and break points, there being little, if any, difference between layouts.

Sporting Clays, however, is unique in its almost unlimited variety of target presentations. Course designers delight in setting targets to test your skills by presenting as many combinations of speeds, distances and angles as their terrain and traps will allow. As a result, a greater range of skills is required to match this variety and shoot competitively at this most testing of disciplines.

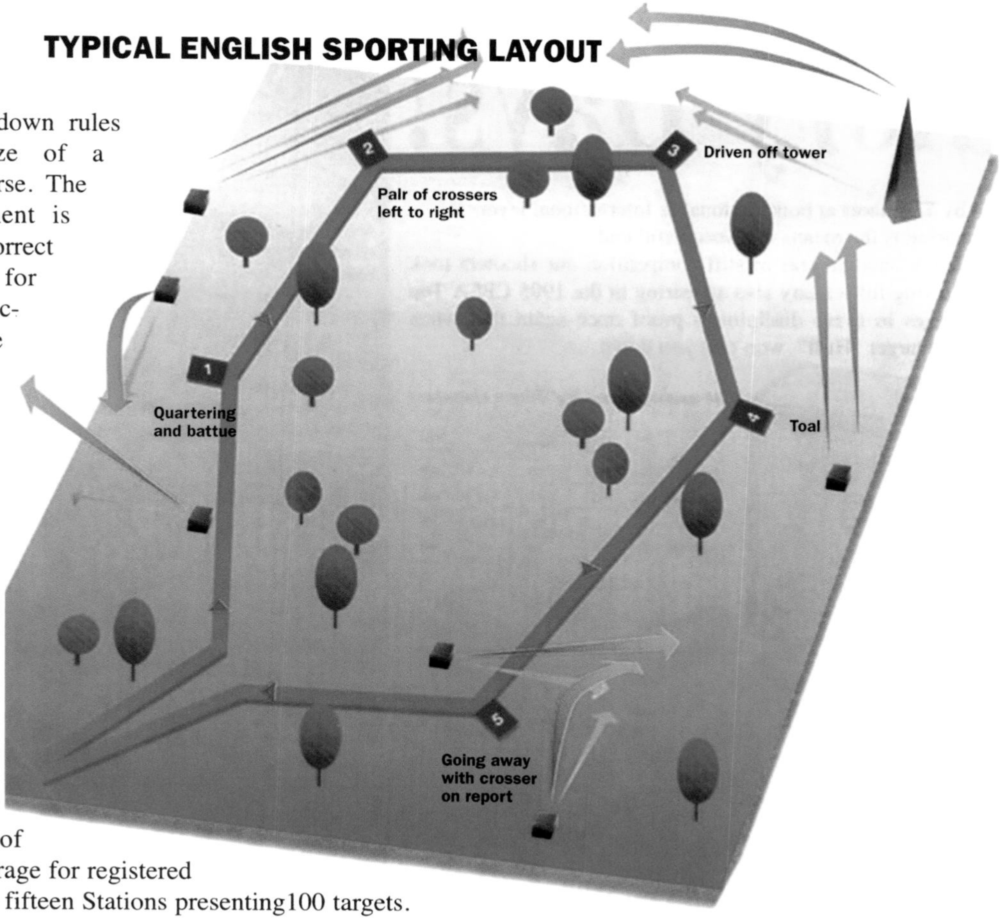

The Range

There are no laid down rules governing the size of a Sporting Clays course. The minimum requirement is that there be the correct safety allowance for shot fall in any direction shot. Unlike the regimented, manicured lines of Skeet and Trap fields, the ideal Sporting Clays course should offer a natural environment, haphazard and diverse in both vegetation and terrain, simulating the quarry's natural habitat. The course can consist of any number of Stations, but the average for registered competition is ten to fifteen Stations presenting100 targets.

TYPICAL ENGLISH SPORTING LAYOUT

Driven off tower

Pair of crossers left to right

Quartering and battue

Toal

Going away with crosser on report

FITASC - Sporting
International Sporting

5-Stand Compact Sporting

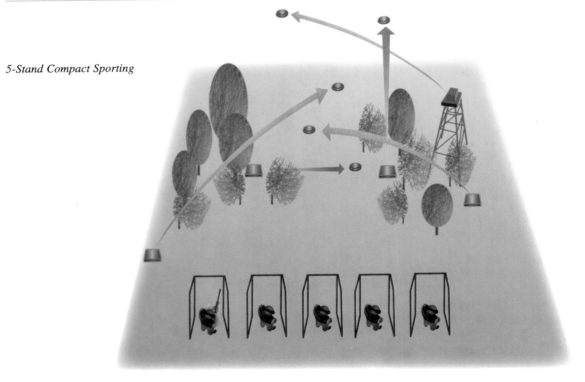

The Sporting Clays Gun

Because of the unlimited variety of target presentations, the Sporting gun must be more flexible than the dedicated Trap or Skeet gun. The Sporting gun of choice is the over and under, but many favour the fast-handling semi-automatic; and some competitors opt for a converted Trap gun. Multi-chokes and barrel selectors are essential and the gun should have enough weight to control recoil without sacrificing balance and handling.

The weight should be 7½ to 8 lbs, the barrel length between 30 and 34 inches. The pattern should be set up to print sixty per cent above and forty per cent below the horizontal of the rib. Lengthened forcing cones, back boring, long tapered chokes, regulated triggers and a quality recoil pad are performance enhancers worth considering.

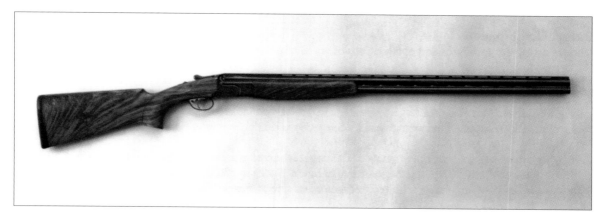

Choke and Cartridge

Cartridges for registered competition in the UK are 1 oz or 28 grams, loaded with shot no bigger than No. 6 – in the USA, an ounce and an eighth or 30 grams loaded with shot no bigger than No.7½. The target dictates the choke and cartridge combination. For example, No. 9s and true cylinder for close targets and No.7½s and modified for the distant targets.

The Rules of the Game

These basic rules are for UK Sporting Clays (see Appendix for other Governing Bodies):
1. When calling for the target, gun position is optional. The shooter may start with a low gun hold or a pre-mounted gun.
2. Only two shells may be loaded.
3. A visible piece of the target must be broken off the target for a score.
4. If the second target of a report pair is a 'no bird', the pair is repeated but the score from the first target is counted.
5. If a pair is broken with one shot, both are counted as dead.
6. Failure to remove the safety or load a shell is a lost target. In the case of a gun malfunction, the competitor should not open it, but remain in the station with the gun pointing down range until the referee examines the gun to determine the cause of the malfunction. If it is mechanical, and not 'operator error', the target can be retaken.
7. If an event is not shot in the squad format, a competitor can shoot the stations in any order. After handing in his card, he will be called to shoot in turn.
8. If there is no competitor in front of him, he is entitled to view a pair before shooting.

Targets

Shooting skills and equipment have improved significantly in the last twenty years and target presentations have had to change to match these improvements. There are no rules for target presentation in Sporting competitions. Targets can be thrown at any height, at any distance and in any combination of two. This can include any mixture of size and flight characteristics, the only requirement is that 'non standard' targets must not exceed thirty per cent of the total thrown.

Today, the course designer is truly only limited by his imagination and experience. The best ones try to set a course that will challenge the Master Class as well as the casual club shooter, with a mix of tough and interesting targets. He achieves this by making the target transition at *the exact point where you, ideally, would like to break it*. These target transition permutations are endless and you must learn to read and analyse these presentations if you are to make progress in Sporting Clays.

Target Combinations

The following are examples and explanations of some target tricks and combinations:

1. *Speed* – This is decided by the tension of the trap spring and the size of target. Take a following pair, consisting of a standard target off one trap with the spring backed off and a midi off a second trap with the spring wound on. The standard target appears first, but as you make your move to it, it is overtaken by the faster midi. This overtaking manoeuvre causes confusion and fatal hesitation between shooting the two targets.

2. *Type* – A minimum of seventy per cent of the targets thrown in a competition are standards, but it is easy to mistake one of the non-standard targets for a standard. For example, a rocket looks like a standard, but the difference in forward allowance required because of its size and speed can cause you to miss behind.

3. *Mixture* – With an on-report pair – the first target a midi at thirty yards with the spring backed off and the second a standard at forty yards with the spring wound on – they look the same but are completely different, requiring different leads and timing. This can cause a very discombobulating effect on your swing and forward allowance picture.

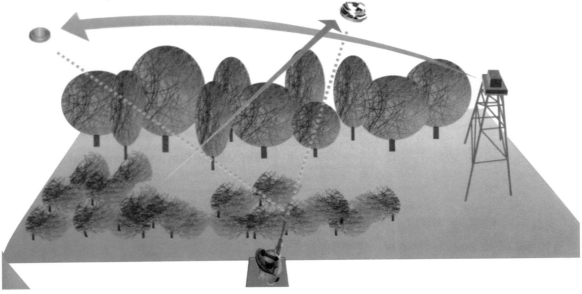

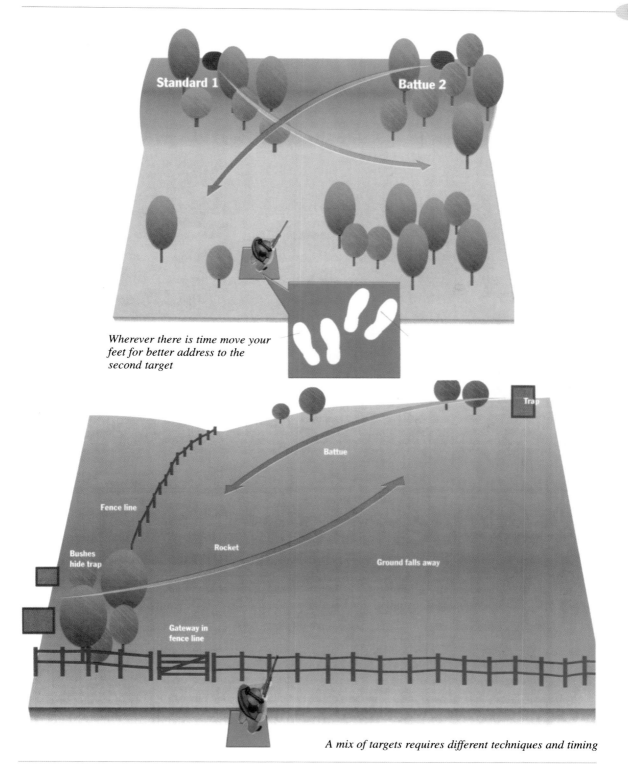

Standard 1

Battue 2

Wherever there is time move your feet for better address to the second target

Trap

Battue

Fence line

Rocket

Ground falls away

Bushes hide trap

Gateway in fence line

A mix of targets requires different techniques and timing

4. *Terrain* – A target thrown a long way, over ground that slopes away in the direction of flight, creates the optical illusion that the target stays level, when in reality, it is falling dramatically. This makes it very easy to miss over the top.

5. *Obstacles* – On an easy presentation, at the optimum place to break the target, it passes an obstacle. As a result it has to be shot earlier or later in its flight and requires a change in technique or method.

From behind the trap the target is not all that it appears ...

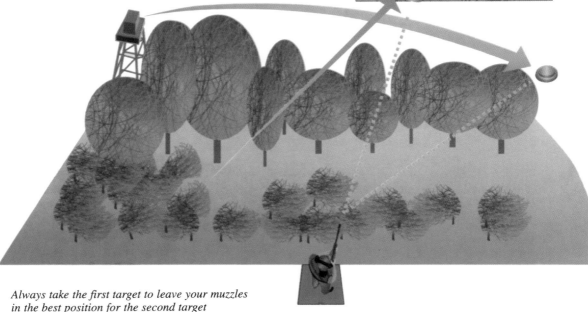

Always take the first target to leave your muzzles in the best position for the second target

6. *Colour* – Orange targets stand out better against certain backgrounds and can appear closer than they really are, especially when showing a little dome. When thrown in an on-report combination with a black target thrown first, the orange creates the optical illusion that the second target is closer, making it very easy to miss behind.

7. *Angle* – The clever use of angle can deceive you when you read the target. You analyse it as a crosser, but as it arrives at the break-point, it has transitioned into a straight-away and you over-lead and miss in front.

8. *Distance* – The combination of near and far catches even the best shots out. You need to change technique to hit the two targets at different distances.

9. *Sequence* – Two widely-angled targets create the need to move your feet through the shooting sequence.

The course designer has a very difficult job – he must walk the fine line between the challenging and the impossible: challenging enough to test the best, but not so impossible to beat the rest. There needs to be a balance between the two. If he gets it right he is a hero, if he gets it wrong he is chastised as a villain.

The correct numbers of left and right-handed targets together with the mix of standard and non-standard targets need to be factored into his design to make the course interesting and enjoyable for the mix of abilities shooting it. This often means combining a soft target with a hard one, to allow the beginner some success on each station but keeping the pressure on the top competitors to break them all. The true test of the course designer's success is the final scores. The game should be won with a score in the low 90s and each of the winning classes should be decided by scores on, or slightly above, the averages. The participants should feel challenged and intrigued by the targets, but happy with their score and the thought of 'if only I had not dropped…'

Target Characteristics

Standard clay targets are what Sporting shooters will face on most stations. The standard measures 4¼ inch or 110mm across and is 1⅛ inches thick. When shot up close, say, within 30 yards, a standard target can be broken with open chokes and small shot. Past 30 yards, especially when only the target's profile is visible, increase the amount of choke and use No.7½ shot.

Midi clay targets are 3½ inches (90mm) across, about ¾ inch less than a standard and are only ¾ inch in height. The midi can be mistaken for a standard by beginners, so always ask what type of target you are shooting before stepping onto the station. Midis are the most aerodynamic of the domed clays and maintain their velocity and flight path better than the standard. However, they do slow later in flight and it is better to shoot them when they have lost some of their speed.

Mini clay targets are the smallest of the clays. Often referred to as the 'flying aspirin', they are the same height as a midi – ¾ inch, but only 2⅜ inches (60mm) in diameter. Minis are easily broken with open chokes and small shot up to 30 yards, but it is best to choke-up past there. An on-edge mini can slip through an open-choked pattern at longer distances.

Rocket targets measure 4¼ inches in diameter, have a flatter profile, only about ⅝ in, or half the thickness of a standard. When thrown edge-on, the lower profile combined with its heavier weight make the rocket maintain its velocity longer into its flight. As a result, a good number are missed behind. For an edge-on rocket, choke-up and use No.7½ shot.

Battues are razor-thin and lack a dome, so they are aerodynamically unstable. A battue can also be thrown upside down, which makes its flight more consistent. As it reaches the zenith of its parabolic curve it rolls, showing its full face – this is the optimum time to break it. But remember, it is now accelerating into its descent, and on a windy day the position of the roll on its line of flight can be very inconsistent.

Rabbits can be traditionally presented or thrown as a chondel. Face-on they are easily broken with open chokes and No. 8 shot. For distance, maintain the shot size but choke-up. The outer rim of the rabbit is thick so it can withstand contact with the ground and is considerably tougher to break. If presented edge-on, use tight chokes and No. 7½ shot.

Target Sequences

The targets can be thrown is a variety of sequences. Learn to study the target from every possible angle it is safe to do so, not just from the shooting station. See what type and size the target is and, if you are not sure,

Targets come in all shapes, colours and sizes with flight characteristics to match

ask the referee. What is it *really* doing – is it *truly* straight, curling, rising or dropping? Consider the second target of a pair – it should be given equal scrutiny. Ask yourself the following target questions:

1. Where is it first visible after launch? Try to pick out a feature like a leaf, bush or branch to establish its line of flight.
2. Does it appear instantly or after a short delay. If there is a delay, count to time it… One thousand and one, One thousand and two …
3. What type of target is it? Standard, Midi, Mini or Battue etc.
4. Is it rising or falling? Where in its flight is it most level and stable?
5. Does it pass any obstructions that interfere with sight or have a pattern impact?
6. Is the wind or landscape affecting its perceived flight trajectory?
7. If one of a pair, where will the second bird be when you break the first? Do you need to move your feet?
8. What choke and cartridge combination do the targets demand?

Armed with this information, you can plan your strategy to best tackle the station. As always, begin with the fundamentals. Read the target, ascertaining gun hold, visual hold and break point. See where your muzzles should be to shoot the first target and be in the correct set up on the second and establish the correct holds and break points. Do you need to move your feet? Always practise a dry run of the shots to be taken. This rehearses the move to the target and pre-programmes mind and muscles for a smoother connection to the target.

Target Angles

The analysis and application of the correct amount of lead in Sporting Clays is essential to straight shooting. We have discussed the components of lead in Chapter 7 and broken it down into speed, angle and distance.

But it is the 'angle of dangle' that has the greatest impact on our perception of lead. You need to learn a simple and straightforward method of assessing the angle of a target.

Clay shooting is really a game of trigonometry – the amount of angle created by the interception of the shot string and target at the break-point is the best indicator of the amount of lead to apply.

Try to visualise a triangle in which the three corners consist of your firing

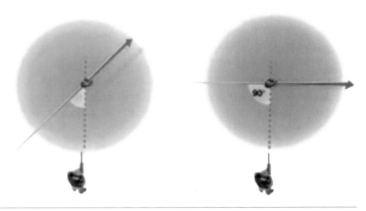

position, the trap and the target break-point. Now picture the shot string and its angle of intersection with the target break-point. If this angle is acute (narrow), you need little, if any, lead. If the angle is obtuse (wide), then lead is required.

To truly understand this, you need to conduct this exercise. On a Skeet range, shoot several targets from the Low House on Station 3. The angle at the interception of the shot string and the break-point is ninety degrees and the lead 3½ to 4 feet. Now shoot several targets from the Low House on Station 7. Same target, same distance, same speed but the angle at the interception of the shot string and the break-point is 0 – you need to shoot directly at it to break it. Work your way back to Station 3, shooting Station by Station, through Low House 6, 5 and 4. This will clearly show you that it is the angle that has the biggest impact on perceived lead.

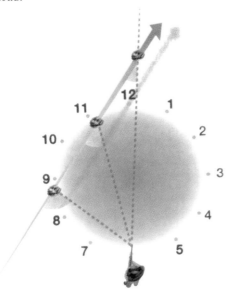

To establish the correct address to the target break-point, visualise yourself standing in the centre of a clock. (This visualisation of a clock face is also used for analysis of the targets' angles and transitions.)

To assess the angle (lead), use your imagination to over-lay the shooting field horizontally on a clock face, with the break-point centered over the pivot point of the hands and the Station at six o'clock. Now picture the target's flight across the clock face. For example, if it enters at nine o'clock and leaves at three o'clock, the angle created to the gun would be ninety degrees, requiring a good amount of lead. If it enters at nine o'clock and leaves at twelve o'clock, the angle would be less and less lead would be needed. *Taking the target earlier or later in its flight will change the angle and the lead required.*

Incoming targets present an optical illusion. As they fly towards the Station they are getting bigger and slower. Psychologically, this affects swing speed and lead assessment. But if you visualise the target entering the clock at eleven o'clock and leaving at five o'clock, you can see that the angle created is obtuse and the target needs more lead than you might have originally considered.

Target Transitions

To assess a target's transition, visualise the clock face, this time projecting it vertically onto the target itself. Once again, the break-point should be in the centre of the clock. Watch the target's flight through the clock face. If it enters at three o'clock and leaves at nine o'clock, it is a single plane target. But if it enters at three o'clock and leaves at seven o'clock, it is a multi-plane target and will require you to apply lead both in front and below.

Targets are at their maximum speed when launched, but the speed quickly bleeds off and the target peaks and begins gradually to descend. This is referred to as a parabolic arc. Whenever possible, the target should be broken as it reaches the peak of the parabolic arc, before it begins its descent.

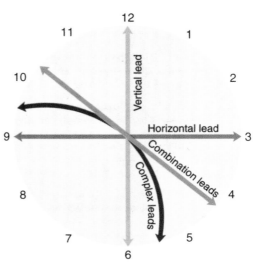

Single Plane Lead

Regardless of the name given to a target, if it is flying horizontally or vertically in one plane, there are only six presentations in Sporting Clays. All the other targets are variations of these six:

1. Outgoing
2. Incoming
3. Crossing
4. Quartering
5. Dropping
6. Rising

These targets are straightforward, and require lead in only one plane.

Multi-Plane Lead

Targets that are transitioning – moving from one plane (horizontal) to another (vertical) – require lead to be applied in two planes, to match their flight.

1. Battue
2. Chondel
3. Rabbit
4. Transitioning Targets
5. Looping Targets

Target Tactics

Pairs

Sporting Clays is a game of pairs. There are always two shots (with the exception of FITASC) and the targets are thrown in a variety of presentations and sequences.

1. True pair: both targets are launched simultaneously.
2. On-report pair: the second target is launched on the report of the shotgun shooting the first target.
3. Following pair: this can be presented in two different ways. From one trap, with the second target thrown from the same trap as quickly as it will cycle or from two traps, with a second trap in another location, and the second target thrown when the first is seen.

The course designer can use any and all combinations of different speeds and different targets thrown in different directions and can take any advantage to be had from terrain or natural obstacles to beat the competitor. He attempts to either create panic on the first shot or leave the gun out of position for the second. The following decisions need to be made on every presentation:

1. Which target to shoot first?
2. Where will the second target be when you have broken the first?
3. Is there enough time between the shots to move your feet?
4. Two targets means two visual holds, gun holds and break points – can you move the break point of the first target, to gain an advantage on the second shot?
5. Would a mixture of techniques work better?

Gather as many facts as possible: the target types, individual distances, trajectories, elevations and sequences. Take into account any obstructions. Determine which target will drop the quickest. This information will allow you to answer these questions and prepare your plan of attack.

Decide which target to shoot first

The best advice is to address the hardest target. If both are equally difficult, then a compromise position may need to be adopted. Can the second target be better addressed by moving your feet and does the presentation allow you time to do so? If not, you have a second decision, as to which target to favour.

On-Report and Following Pairs

An on-report pair from the same trap is the simplest presentation to shoot. But beware! The second target will be launched *on the report* of the shot and will be in at a different point along the flight line from the first, requiring a different gun and visual hold. If there is sufficient time, remount your gun between shots on a report pair. The second target of a following pair from the same trap requires similar adjustments to be made.

True Pairs

When targets are thrown as true

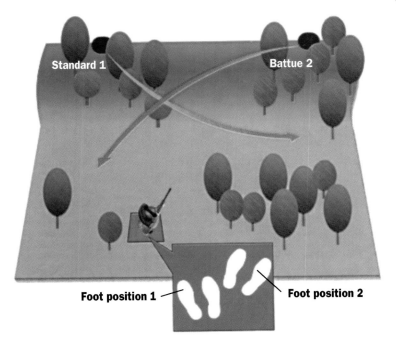

You should always move your feet but if the presentation doesn't allow always favour the more difficult target

pairs, where the presentation will allow, always take the lower target of a pair first. This reduces panic and allows a smoother move to the second target. This keeps them both in view and keeps the barrel from obstructing the second target, if the higher target is shot first.

Also take the trailing target first. This allows your swing to continue unchecked to the second target. If the leading target is taken first, the swing will have to be checked and restarted, often causing a miss behind.

The target that will disappear behind an obstruction, fly out of range or hit the ground first must always be the first target of a pair.

Be sure to see the first target break before moving to the second. If you miss the first shot, it is far better to stay with the same target for the second shot (unless it is an extremely difficult presentation).

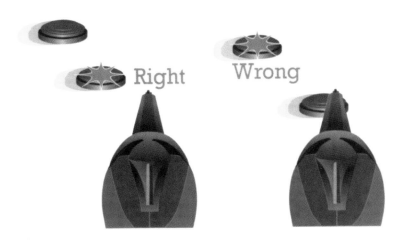

With true pairs composed of a straight-away and a quartering target, the sequence is to always shoot the straight-away one first, then move to the quartering target.

Driven pairs offer a very short window of time in which to shoot them. The first target should be taken well in front, creating more time for the second. Once again, always take the straight target first.

When establishing both break-

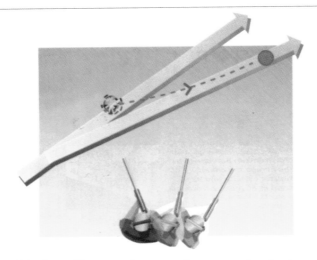

points, consider where your gun will be after breaking the first target. Decide whether taking the first target with a different technique or in a different place would help break the second.

On a true pair, the left-hander should shoot the left target first before moving to the second and the right-hander should shoot the right. When the first target is taken this way, it allows better target acquisition of the second and helps prevent head lifting. Be prepared to move your feet, if required, on a widely-split pair to avoid running out of movement and having to check your swing.

Take the trailing target first to continue a smooth swing to the second target

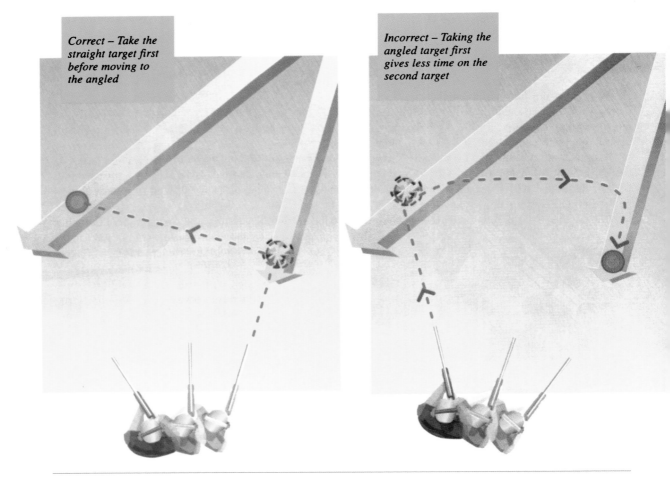

Correct – Take the straight target first before moving to the angled

Incorrect – Taking the angled target first gives less time on the second target

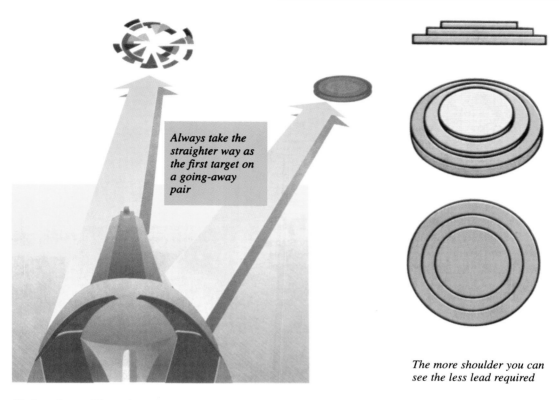

Always take the straighter way as the first target on a going-away pair

The more shoulder you can see the less lead required

Going Away Targets

Rising Away In Front

In its simplest form, this is a straight, gently rising target requiring no lead. At the other end of the spectrum, it is a 100-foot high tower throwing a midi, which needs several feet of lead.

A target rising and going away is one of the most straightforward presentations to hit, but is just as easily missed. It is first seen edge-on which always makes a target look farther away. Under full power, with its continual movement away, the quickly-reducing size is emphasised, and can create a rushed and panicked reaction.

Rushing translates into unwanted gun movement and can cause the gun to jump over the target. Remember, a couple of inches at the gun is a couple of feet at the target! Poor gun control can turn a straight-away target into a nightmare.

Minimal movement is required for a rising-away target, very similar to a trap shot. Take a trap-like approach – pre-mount the gun and swing through smoothly. Lead is applied by moving the gun to and through the target, in a bayoneting-action. This counters the tendency to miss over. The shot should be taken sooner rather than later, to avoid the tendency to aim on this presentation.

Passing Overhead From Behind

When the target comes from behind, keep your weight on your back foot and look for the target, leaning back slightly, tilting your head as far back as is comfortable. If you wait until it is over you to see it, you will panic and poke at it.

The gun hold should be with eyes looking straight up and the muzzles on the line of flight, where you expect the target to pass overhead. This position takes a little experimentation to get it right, but it allows you to see the target sooner. This gives you a greater opportunity to accurately estimate the speed and angle of the target. And when you can see it longer, the target will appear slower as it passes overhead.

As the target appears in your vision, you will begin a natural transfer of weight from your back to your leading foot, inserting and maintaining the gun in front of the target and firing without hesitation. If you are consistently behind or over this target, you will find that more emphasis on the front foot as the shot is taken can be a cure-all.

Do not fall into the habit of turning back to the trap! Trying to mount the gun while turning *and* establishing the line and target angle it is too complex a move with such a fast target. Maintained Lead or Pull-Away are the applicable techniques for

Weight on your back foot, tilting your head as far back as comforable, allows you to see the target sooner

It is a mistake to look back to the trap. Turning while mounting the gun is too complex a move

these targets. A strong extension of the left arm is essential to avoid see-sawing the gun mount.

On overhead pairs, take the first target as soon as possible! The longer you wait, the more difficult they are to break. Remember, as they fly directly over head, showing the maximum amount of 'soft under-belly', is when they are the most vulnerable to the shot charge. The farther the target gets away, the smaller the surface area becomes, leaving just the edge to shoot.

If one of the pair is straight and one is quartering, take the straight-away first. Similarly, the quick-dropper should always be the priority. If presented with a trailing pair, be sure to take the rear target first and follow-through to the second. The second shot requires an increase in choke and shot size.

Incoming Targets
High Driven, Passing Overhead
If you have two targets, one that passes over the Station and one that falls short of the firing line, take them in order of presentation. The advantage of the target that passes over the Station is, it is still at speed and your only consideration is the lead required.

The ultimate incomer is, of course, the High Tower, especially when in excess of 100 feet. This is a target that has special requirements. Once you have read the target and established its speed and line of flight, you need to adjust your stance. If the clay is driven straight, the normal stance, facing forty-five degrees to the line of flight, is right. If driven to the left, then close or turn your stance to the left. If driven to the right, then open or turn to the right. The correct stance will allow you to keep your muzzles accurately on the target line and keep you from checking your swing, dropping your shoulder and coming off the line ('windscreen wiping').

In wing shooting, this shot was taught two ways: the Stanbury method, by stepping into the line of the target and maintaining the weight on the front foot throughout the shot, or the Churchill method, by lifting the heel opposite the target flight and transferring weight from one foot to the other. On straight driven targets, the weight is maintained on the back foot.

The arguments for and against Stanbury and Churchill have raged for over half a century. A point to note is that Stansbury was a tall bean-pole of a man whereas Churchill was short and squat. I, personally, think that their physical characteristics had a great bearing on their individual approach to the same problem. As for which method is the best, I will leave you to discover that for yourself.

When clay shooting, we know the target's line and adjust our stance and body weight according to our method of choice. But, if there is time to move your feet, do so. I recommend taking the lower driven target early, with the weight firmly on the front foot, then taking the high target late, just short of vertical, transferring the weight to the back foot.

As always, your gun mount needs to be consistent; a low mount with the eye and muzzle in alignment on the line of the target. Start right, and you will inevitably finish right. The technique should be Pull-Away or Swing-Through, as both of these methods establish the line on every shot. There is no place for Maintained Lead on the High Tower. At 120 feet up, the wind can pull a target off line and, if you are to be consistent, there is a real need to lock *on the line, every shot*.

A word of caution on the Swing-Through technique: many people think that you let the target get well ahead of your barrels and then 'swing through'. This is a faulty approach that will lead to an inconsistent swing speed, a fault comparable to the wrong gun hold point on a teal target. The gun should be inserted on the rear of the target, followed by a gentle acceleration of the gun through and along the target line to establish forward allowance. This will give you more accuracy and control.

Stanbury off the front foot

Churchill off the back foot

A low mount with the eye and muzzle in alignment with the target

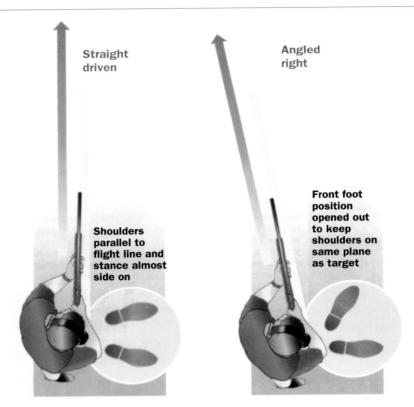

Straight driven

Shoulders parallel to flight line and stance almost side on

Angled right

Front foot position opened out to keep shoulders on same plane as target

Angled left

Stance slightly closed

Targets against the sky will always appear farther away than those of the same distance against a background. The ability to judge range is a good skill to acquire for high-driven and long-crossing presentations. The target is at its most vulnerable and closest directly overhead and, ideally, should be broken at eighty to ninety degrees.

The position of your hand on the fore-end can cause you to pull off the target line. Practise mounting and swinging an empty gun, tracing a direct line across the ceiling. You will quickly see the importance of the leading hand to holding a straight line. There is a tendency to drift off the line to the left (for the right-handed, right for the left-handed). To counter this, hold the muzzles on the right (or left – see above) edge of the target. This gives a better move to the target and counters this tendency to drift off the line on overhead shots.

If the target quarters to the left or right of centre, you will need to deliberately roll your shoulder opposite the line of flight, placing the barrels flat on the line to match the target's angle, to avoid shooting low and behind.

The one-eyed shooter experiences the most difficulty with the direct-driven target. He loses the target behind the barrel, causing the gun to stop and miss. If the target is high enough and allows enough time, shoot it as a crosser. Be sure to turn onto the line so the gun is being *pulled into* the face, not *pushed away* (right to left for a right-hander).

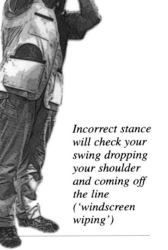

Incorrect stance will check your swing dropping your shoulder and coming off the line ('windscreen wiping')

Some shooters swing alongside the target, applying the lead before swerving onto the line as the shot is taken, in the same manner as overtaking a car on the motorway. Others learn to keep the gun moving even when the barrel has blocked the target from sight. The great strength of the Swing-Through technique is, the target is always in view until the move is made to shoot.

Low Driven, Passing Overhead

The first in a pair of low driven targets needs to be taken well out in front. Its low trajectory and angle to the Station do not give you time to shoot both in the optimum position overhead. The first target needs to be attacked and Swing-Through is the method of choice. Insert on the back edge of the clay and brush through it. As the target is obscured, fire and follow through, continuing the move to the second target which will be shot overhead.

Pick up from just behind target

swing

Driven targets create a tendency to lift your head to keep eye contact with the target especially if it gets obscured by the barrels. Moving the head and leaving the gun behind is a miss behind! Accentuate keeping your head firmly 'spot-welded' to the stock on incomers and always take the straight bird first.

Wrong. Too far behind creates much work to catch up.

Stalling Incomer, Falling Short of the Firing Line

The target that stalls short of the firing line is slowing and falling and it therefore needs lead in two planes.

Wherever the presentation allows, be bold! Take the target while it is still under power and maintaining a steady flight line. Do not rush, have patience, time the shot to break the target just before or at the peak of its flight. A low gun hold will prevent mounting the gun too soon and tracking the target, which leads to aiming.

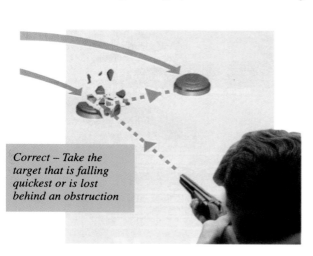

Correct – Take the target that is falling quickest or is lost behind an obstruction

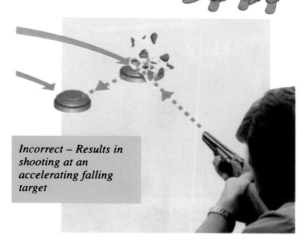

Incorrect – Results in shooting at an accelerating falling target

When the target can only be shot on its descent, you need a different approach. Read the target, visualise the line and flight in regard to its falling trajectory. Use the clock technique, determine the numeral the target enters by (i.e., two o'clock), and the numeral it leaves by (i.e., seven o'clock). From this, establish a juxtaposition of the barrel-to-target relationship; figure what the lead should be below and in front, taking into account that the farther a target falls, the faster it falls. When the target is accelerating, never let it drop beneath your barrels! Maintained Lead is the technique, keeping the target in view and gun movement to a minimum.

As always, when presented with true pairs, take the bird that is falling quickest or being lost behind obstacles or background first. If timing allows, take the rear target first to enable you to swing smoothly onto the second target.

Floating targets are often missed behind. Because of the illusion of target pace, they look slow, so you swing slowly. But a forty-yard slow target still needs a considerable amount lead, and really, not much less than a fast one.

Rabbits

The only predictable thing about the rabbit target is their unpredictability. No two targets are the same. As the target is bowled along the ground, every stone, dip and hollow has an impact on its course and trajectory, causing it to move and bounce this way and that. This erratic behaviour is further compounded by debris left from successfully broken targets and the shot string as it tears up the target's path.

The targets scurry along, bouncing and bobbing against the solid background, creating an optical illusion of speed. Rabbits look much quicker than they really are. As a result, they are often missed in front. A second optical illusion occurs when the slap of the shot on the ground is misinterpreted as a miss behind. The rabbit rolls over the bouncing shot, making it look like more lead needs to be applied, causing a miss in front.

A Sporting shotgun is set up to shoot sixty per cent above and forty per cent below the horizontal of the rib. If you shoot at the body of the target, two-thirds of your shot load is wasted. Keep the clay rabbit sitting on the rib of the gun! This way, you strike the target with the majority of the pattern, with the added benefit that the lower third strikes the ground, ricocheting up, lifting debris into the pattern, and helping to break the target.

To take this shot, the muzzles must be kept under the target line, keeping the target in view at all times. This means you can break the target on the ground or, if it bounces, a simple lift of the muzzles will allow it

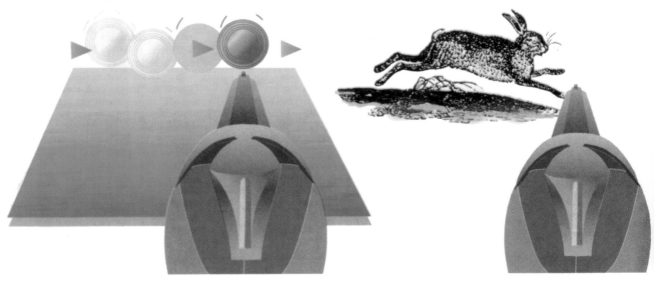

to be broken in the air. Do not anticipate a bounce that may not happen, however, make best use of a bounce when it does occur. This is the point at which the rabbit is most predictable and vulnerable.

When a rabbit target is presented beneath your feet, accentuate the hold beneath the line. With any target thrown beneath your feet, there is a tendency to miss over it; the reverse of the tendency shooters have to miss below on a high target.

Imagine the target is a real rabbit. Adopt a low gun mount where the muzzle, eye and line-of-run are one. As the rabbit appears, extend your leading hand and place the barrels on its 'feet'. Pull away to the 'front paw' as it stretches in its run, and fire without hesitation! On a left-to-right rabbit, imagine it is in the centre

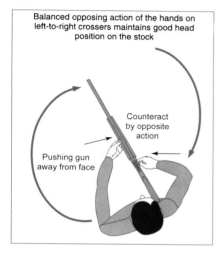

Balanced opposing action of the hands on left-to-right crossers maintains good head position on the stock

Counteract by opposite action

Pushing gun away from face

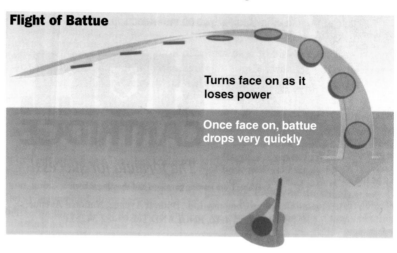

Flight of Battue

Turns face on as it loses power

Once face on, battue drops very quickly

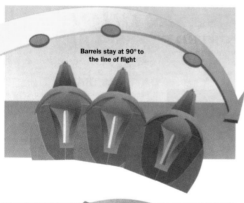

Barrels stay at 90° to the line of flight

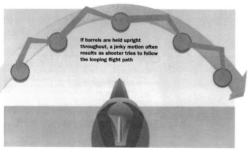

If barrels are held upright throughout, a jerky motion often results as shooter tries to follow the looping flight path

of the clock. Your muzzles should be at four o'clock.

Pull-Away or Swing-Through are the techniques for rabbit targets. They don't need much lead, but if the presentation is at thirty yards or more, take it late. Where the rabbit is slowing down, it will be more predictable. Just remember to expect the unexpected and shoot every rabbit as a single and individual target.

Battues

The secret to consistency with the battue is to remember that they fly faster by half than a standard target. It is the failure to recognise or acknowledge their speed that causes battues to be missed behind.

This speed is most apparent in the first half of their flight. The slim profile and extra speed makes them hard to see, hard to hit and hard to break. Edge-on, they are so thin they can slip through the shot pattern. However, as they slow, their poor aerodynamics and unstable flight cause them to roll over, presenting their full face to the gun. At this point they are easy to see, easy to hit and easy to break.

While the standard target is shot at the mid point of its flight, the battue is shot later, during the roll and presentation of its face. But once this roll has occurred, the target accelerates into its descent, requiring lead in two planes – in front and under.

Once again, visualise the target in the centre of a clock and see what time it entered. If it came in at eleven o'clock and will leave at five o'clock, this will give you a sense of how far in front and below you need to be. The technique to use is Pull-Away – the momentary contact of muzzle and target will account for any deviation in the target's flight path.

Because of their shape and light weight, battues are very susceptible to wind and are easily blown off course. A looping, wind-blown battue is not flying on a consistent line and Swing-Through won't work. Remember, the battue is much faster than the standard target. What you would consider the correct amount of lead on a standard, on a battue, you need to add half again as much. Battues are easily broken, and cylinder or Skeet chokes with No. 9 shot is the best combination.

The analysis of lead and technique for battues applies equally to chondels and loopers, but they do not have the speed or flight characteristics of the battue. They show their full face to the gun throughout their flight, so the break point can be established sooner.

Rockets

Rockets are a rarely encountered target. They are the same size as a standard, but with a shallower dome of solid construction. Its denser, slimmer profile gives a rocket increased velocity. This is sustained for considerably longer than a standard, but it slows and drops quickly at the end of its flight. The slim profile creates the optical illusion that it is further away and flying more slowly than it really is. A competitor who has never encountered this type of target before can be forgiven for missing behind.

Rockets are easily mistaken for a standard target and missed even further behind. If there is ever any doubt as to the type of target being thrown, consult the referee. He will be more than pleased to

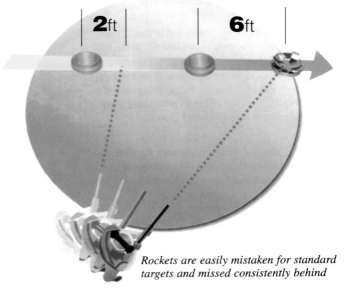

Rockets are easily mistaken for standard targets and missed consistently behind

advise you on the size and type of target being presented. This information is often displayed at the stand or in the course layout.

Once you know the target is a rocket, you can properly prepare to come to terms with it. Its extra speed means adjusting your gun and visual holds to match. Maintained Lead is the best technique for shooting the rocket and it must be exactly that. At no point can you allow the target to close the gap between itself and the gun.

The amount of lead will be more than you would expect because of this target's increased speed and illusion of slowness. Be prepared to add half again as much as you think might be correct. This target is rarely missed in front and needs to be attacked. Use No. 7½ shot, with a degree more choke than you would for a standard at the same distance.

Crossing Targets

I consider the crossing presentation to be the most straightforward of all the Sporting Clays targets. It is easy

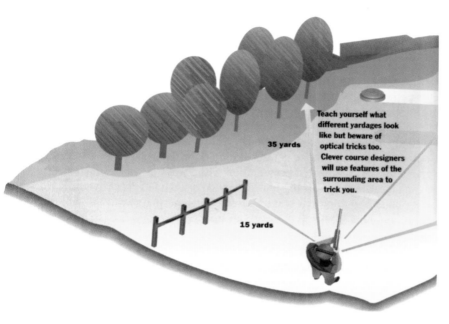

35 yards

Teach yourself what different yardages look like but beware of optical tricks too. Clever course designers will use features of the surrounding area to trick you.

15 yards

to read and any technique can be used to break it. The ninety degree angle created by the axis of the target line and the shot string readily indicates that it will require lead, how much depends on how far and how fast it is thrown.

Distance judgement is a valuable tool in the competitor's tool box. The correct 'guesstimate' of a target's range dictates technique, choke and cartridge choice, as well as which lead and how much to apply. The ability to analyse distances is a learned skill. One way to sharpen this skill is, when out walking, pick out a

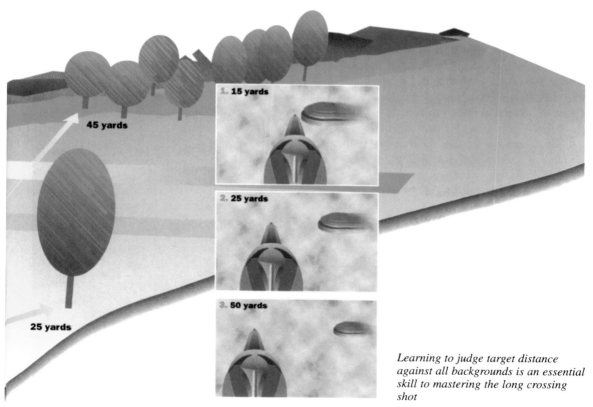

45 yards

25 yards

1. 15 yards

2. 25 yards

3. 50 yards

Learning to judge target distance against all backgrounds is an essential skill to mastering the long crossing shot

marker – a tree, lamppost, whatever – then walk towards it, mentally counting off the paces. You will learn quickly to judge accurately distances of target presentations. This will allow you to make the first analysis: how far away the target is at the optimum break point.

How fast the crosser is flying is ascertained from previous experience, target type and presentation, whether it is it edge-on or showing some dome, and the quality of your 'on-board computer'. This will tell you how fast the target is and, factoring in the distance, should give you a good idea of the lead required.

A close target can be broken by gun speed alone and here the Swing-Through technique would work well. But a target at a distance will need visible lead and Pull-Away would work better.

The amount of time available on long crossers offers many choices as to where to pull the trigger and it can be difficult for beginners and experienced shots alike to get this timing right. This choice of lead can be further complicated by the target's direction. A right-to-left presentation will always be an easier shot for a right hander, with less lead required than the same target going left-to-right. When the target is travelling *with* the natural swing rotation, the leading hand is pulling the gun to the left, keeping the gun in the face and ensuring the correct head and eye position on the stock.

When a target is going to the right, against the right-hander's natural rotation, the gun is being pushed off the face. Pushing the gun is far less efficient than pulling it, like having a horse push a cart from behind, rather than pulling it from the front. This means that, for the right hander, left-to-right targets require more lead than right-to-left targets.

When it comes to distance, what works at 25 yards will not work past 35 yards. To consistently break the long shots, everything has to be that little bit tighter, sharper and more focused. You can be off-line or miss-time your swing at closer targets and the shot string might 'save your bacon', but you will not get away with it at a distance. The need to see daylight between the target and the gun can cause a shooter to 'measure', looking from the muzzle to the target, trying to get the right amount of lead. This results in slowing or stopping the gun. Instead, hard focus on the target, keeping the barrels in your peripheral vision.

Proper address to the break point is essential. If you run out of rotation and shift your weight from one foot to the other, your shoulder will drop in the direction of rotation and you will 'windscreen wipe' the muzzles off the target line. The correct address and the Pull-Away technique will let you turn the target's flight and direction into your line and swing. This process starts with the eyes guiding the hands moving to the target, establishing the lead and making the shot without pause or hesitation.

Long crossers require half-choke or more, with No. 7½ shot. Just remember that you miss in feet and choke only gives you inches. Finding and holding the target line is the secret to breaking long crossers.

Quartering Targets

Targets that are neither crossing nor straight are referred to as quartering. This term covers many target presentations and the majority of targets in a competition could be placed in the quartering category. The amount of lead required on these targets can be difficult to recognise and careful assessment is required.

The quartering target can create optical illusions. For example, you read the target and assess the holds and break point. Where you visually pick up the target, the flight line tells you

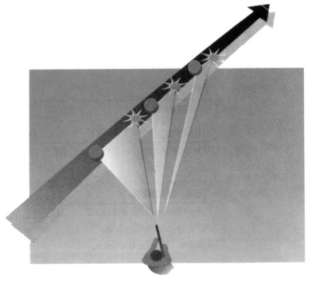

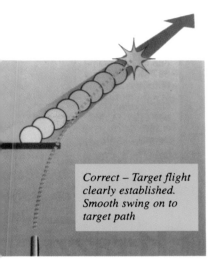

Correct – Target flight clearly established. Smooth swing on to target path

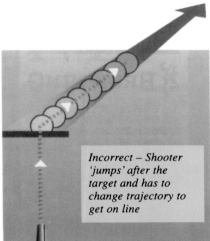

Incorrect – Shooter 'jumps' after the target and has to change trajectory to get on line

it's a crosser. Then as the shot develops, at the break point its angle has changed to a going-away target. But you are already committed to the lead and miss in front. Vice versa, the target that visually sets off as a straight-away shot is actually crossing at the break point. This would require more lead than you planned for and the result is a miss behind.

Problems with quartering targets are caused by several factors: distance and angles, both in elevation and to the shooting station, as well as speed and size. They are particularly hard to read for beginners and average shots who tend to overestimate the required lead, have too much gun movement and take the target too late in its flight.

The quartering target requires little gun movement. The farther away, the less the gun should move. The angle created by the shot string and the target is very acute and requires hardly any lead. Unlike the crossing or driven target, the required lead by the quartering target does not significantly increase with distance.

The gun hold should be moved further along the line towards the break point to help control and minimise gun movement and the target should be taken as soon as reactions will allow. 'To wait is to miss' on the quartering target.

Chokes should be appropriate to distance and, combined with No. 7½ shot, will give you the edge on quartering targets every time.

Teal

First, as always, read the target. Observe it not only from the front, but from the side, whenever possible, to establish if it is flying straight or at an angle. A true vertical teal will require lead in exactly the same way a driven or crossing bird does.

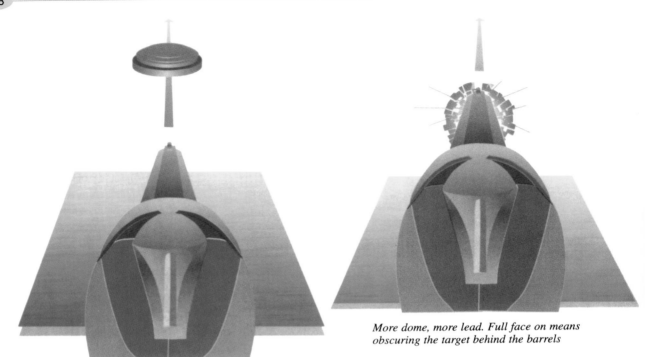

More dome, more lead. Full face on means obscuring the target behind the barrels

The only technique to use on a teal is Swing-Through, which allows the target to be kept in view while the shot is taken. The gun hold is half to two-thirds of the way along the target flight line; your visual hold is at the side of the barrels. Hold just to the right side of the target (for the right hander). As you watch the target roll up the side of the barrel, you time your move to it, and when the target comes on to the end of your barrel, you smoothly swing through the line, pulling the trigger just as your muzzles cover the target...like knocking an imaginary hat off the target.

The most common fault in shooting teal is adopting too low a gun hold, some shooters even hold on the trap house. At this hold point, the target streaks past your barrel, your subconscious kicks in and you chase after it in a rushed swing, with little control. Then the fast-moving gun catches and passes the now slowing target, the swing doesn't match the target speed and the shot powers past the target, missing above.

The too-low gun hold also causes head-lifting which compounds the missing-over-the-target problem. A too-high gun hold is equally bad, resulting in poking or stabbing and missing below.

With edge-on targets, establish angle and line of flight, but also consider the amount of the clay you can see. The more rim the less lead it will require – it becomes, in effect, a trap bird – and you can shoot directly at it and through it. The gun hold and technique remain the same as with a face-on target.

Avoid the dropping target! Wherever possible, shoot it on the rise or just as it peaks The dropping target is badly affected by wind and is accelerating and falling much quicker than it appears. The dropping target causes aiming and stopping the gun or 'spot-shooting' and should be avoided.

With true pairs, take the first target under power, firing as you blot it out, passing through it and smoothly moving to the second target, shooting its bottom edge just as it peaks. Once again, consider obstructions and think about which target will fall first. Where smaller targets are used, especially the midi, more lead is required than with the standard. Look out for combination pairs, like standards and rockets.

Edge-on targets need half choke and No. 7½ shot. With face-on teal, choke should be Skeet and No. 8 or 9 shot. You will need to adjust choke and cartridge combinations to match target distances.

Below the Feet

Many targets are thrown beneath your feet. These presentations require some changes to the basic set up to counter the tendency to miss over low targets. The best way to tackle a low target is to transfer more weight to the leading leg and bend forward from the hips. This will help keep the barrels under the line of the target, particularly on the crossing target, where the miss over the top is most pronounced. With the low, going-away target, the tendency to shoot high works to your advantage, building in lead on that shot.

Head Movement

Taking targets at different elevations can cause the head to move on the stock. If the target is high, the head tends to move forward. If the target is low, the head will inch back. The comb of the stock should, ideally, be parallel for about an inch at the face to allow for this movement. This will maintain the correct eye-rib alignment.

Summary

1. Start your shooting movement with the leading hand.
2. Keep your head still.
3. Keep your eye on the target.
4. Move to your own timing and pace.

Take Time Out to Sharpen Your 'Axe'

Unless there is a system to your practice, you will fail to improve your skills and cause more harm than good. Practice can become mind-numbingly boring and end up a waste of time, money and energy.

Time spent working on the basics at home, however, is never wasted. Gun mounting and swinging drills are a must, and visual and mental rehearsals are also good practice techniques that can be honed at home. A combination of practices works to establish and reinforce muscle strength and memory. I like to practise using a small maglite inserted in the barrel of the gun. Used as a pointer, the beam is a visual reference and check. You can practise and perfect your gun mount and swing by using the maglite's beam to trace along the join of wall and ceiling as if it were a target's flight path.

When it comes to live firing on the range, most shots consider practice to be simply shooting a fifty or a hundred bird round at their local club. The local club is where the bulk of their shooting takes place and they are familiar with the target presentations as the targets change very little visit to visit. Regardless of how they are shooting, they will top this off with a round of Skeet or 5-stand, perhaps even a second go-round the course. In effect, all they are achieving by this is subjecting themselves to a large dose of recoil with little, if any, learning content or improvement. Let me qualify this by saying that if you are going out to shoot for the enjoyment of it, then that is fine! After all, shooting is a hobby and you *should* do it simply for the pleasure it gives you. However, please do not confuse shooting round after round with meaningful practice.

There are three accepted practice formats for you to consider.

The Basic Score Builder

1. Choose a particular target – it can be anything you like – a rabbit, teal, incomer or crosser.
2. Address the target some 20 yards away and attempt to break it half a dozen times straight.
3. If successful, move back 5 yards and carry out the same exercise.
4. With success, add an extra 5 yards and continue to push the envelope of your shooting until you fail to shoot five in a row.
5. If you should miss at any time, you have to start over at the 20 yard mark.

This drill teaches you to focus and concentrate on every shot. It is particularly effective when practised with a friend where a wager can introduce some pressure to your practice.

The full use of a skeet or trap field is perfect for this and one or two boxes of shells are a perfect number to practise with. The emphasis should be on crushing one bird at a time back to the 40 yard mark

The Intermediate Score Builder

1. Once again select a suitable target, preferably one that you struggle with, let's say a rabbit directly cross ing at about 25 to 30 yards. First, just shoot it in your usual style.
2. When you are breaking half a dozen straight consistently, you should attempt to shoot the target with a different technique. If you are a Swing-Through shooter, try Pull-Away, if a Maintained Lead shot, then, Swing-Through.

You should be prepared to miss when you first attempt this. However, with practice over a few weeks, you will soon be able to tackle any target presentation with the best technique for a better score. This improved flexibility in your shooting will gain you extra targets.

Once again, one or two boxes of shells are all that is required once a week and the skeet range is great for this kind of shooting skills practice. I do not know of any top shooter who, when called on to do so by the target presentation, cannot shoot all three of the techniques, regardless of his chosen favourite. They read the targets, choose the technique and, as if changing gears, apply it.

I would like to comment that *the only difference in technique is where the gun muzzle is inserted on the target*. Insert behind, and you will shoot Swing-Through, on it and you will shoot Pull-Away, in front and the result will be Maintained Lead. The basics are the same, regardless of technique chosen.

The Advanced Score Builder: The Winning Edge

1. Choke up! Yes, in your practice put full choke in both barrels. If you do not have full, then use the tightest choke available to you.
2. Now you can shoot the hundred birder at your local course, a round of Skeet or 5-Stand and get some real benefit from it. Don't think about the distance from a target, be it 15 or 50 yards, just trust your ability.
3. Don't rely on the mechanical safety net of open chokes. Don't fall into the trap of thinking how tight your pattern is; just shoot your normal game.

Learn to trust your hand and eye co-ordination. Remember, *the best shots in the world shoot tight chokes on every target*. This practice develops a belief in your own ability and gives you more confidence.

Once you have established a good foundation of the basics, good shooting is really a game of confidence. Even though your scores will suffer at first, the sight of clays being reduced to balls of smoke will do wonders for your confidence, *especially when you open your chokes back up for your next competition!*

If you want to improve your shooting, you really do need to put some time into the dry mounting drills at home and give one of these three practices a try. What have you got to lose?

I would like to recount a short story that might put practice into perspective. Every year in Canada there is the lumberjack tree-felling championships. The contestants enter the forest with nothing but an axe and, for over six hours, attempt to fell more trees than their competitors. The sponsorship within the industry is great and the prizes attract entrants from all over the world, in just the same manner as Sporting Clays.

A whistle is blown to start the event and, once again, after six hours, to end it. On this occasion, the whistle blew and the contestants thundered into the forest and the thunk of metal on wood reverberated throughout the woods.

The judges were most surprised when, after an hour or so, one of the lumberjacks, Henry, emerged from the woods and sat down. His fellow competitors continued to chop away furiously. After ten minutes, the lumberjack arose and re-entered the woods. This anomaly continued to happen every hour on the hour throughout the day.

When the six hours were up, the whistle was blown. The judges marked and counted the fallen timber and the contestants waited in a huddled group for the results. When the winner was announced, there was a stunned silence, both on the part of the judges and the contestants.

The winner was Henry! None other than the lumberjack who, throughout the day, insisted on taking ten-minute rests, every hour on the hour. The judges congratulated him, but felt duty-bound to ask how it was that he had won, even though he had rested for sixty minutes, in effect, only chopping wood for five hours instead of six, while the others kept on chopping.

What had he been doing during those ten-minute breaks?

His reply was simple, 'I was sharpening my axe'.

Practice is simply that: sharpening your skills and abilities to break more targets than your competitors.

Chapter 11
Simplifying Skeet

Skeet

T he game of Skeet is one of the big three of Trap, Skeet and Sporting Clays. It began as practice for wing shooting and quickly evolved into one of the most popular disciplines. Shot worldwide, there are three distinct versions: English, American and Olympic. Once again, each discipline could fill a book in its own right so I have chosen to concentrate on the English version.

English Skeet is very close to the American discipline. The only exception is in the American version the pair on station four is replaced by shooting two singles on station eight. All other aspects of the field set-up and the game are the same.

Skeet challenges the competitor with its great variety of target speed, angle and distance. Though the target's flight path and distance are constants, the progression through the shooting positions from stations one to seven constantly changes the competitor's angle to and perception of the target. Therefore a systematic approach to learning the fundamentals of Skeet is required. You learn your address to the target, your gun and visual holds together with the correct break points and lead pictures. This approach will enable you to shoot straight with greater success.

Range

Where possible, a Skeet field should be built facing north-east, to keep the sun behind the competitors' backs. The field consists of two houses, each containing one trap. One trap is set low, three feet from the ground and one is set 10 feet high.

There are seven stations, (eight in American Skeet) arranged around segments of a twenty-one-yard circle. The base chord between the houses is exactly 40 yards and 9 inches. The stations are three-feet square and place the shooter 22 yards from the centre position between the two houses.

Each trap is set to throw a target 65 yards. At the centre point it must pass through a three-foot diameter hoop, placed at the centre point between the two houses, 15 feet above the ground.

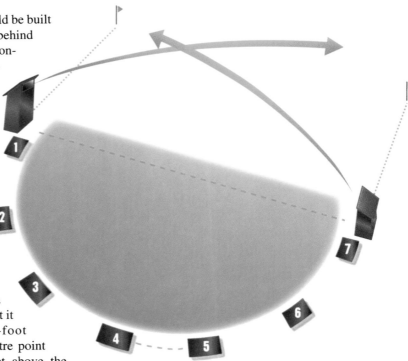

English Skeet

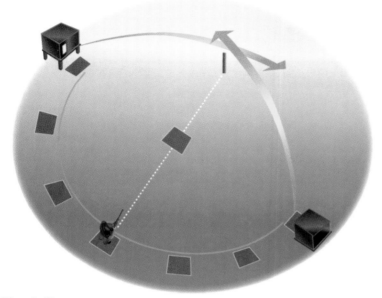

Olympic Skeet

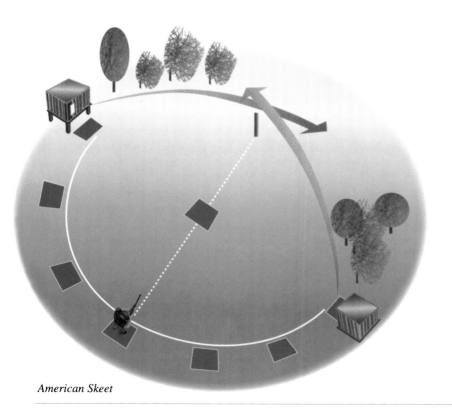
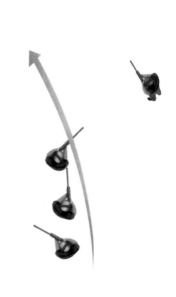

American Skeet

The Skeet Gun

The best choice would be either an over and under or a semi-automatic, with a barrel length of 28 to 32 inches. It should weigh about 7½ to 8 lbs. Because of the great variety of angles and distances shot in the game, the Skeet gun must have a combination of liveliness and steadiness, aiding a smooth swing. But it should not be so lively that it causes loss of control.

The weight should be well-balanced, with the moment of inertia between the hands for swift handling but dependable control. There are several pairs in a round of Skeet and second-phase recoil control is a must for good second barrel acquisition. A recoil pad and the weight of the gun should combine to achieve this. Trigger pulls should be crisp with no drag and set at 3½ and 4 lbs.

With the exception of the Olympic discipline, a 'Sporting' shotgun with open chokes is perfect for Skeet. The sixty per cent above/forty per cent below sight picture allows the target to be kept in view throughout the shot but places its pattern exactly where the eye is looking.

Chokes and Cartridges

Though some top performers opt to use tighter chokes, an ideal Skeet gun should be choked Skeet 2 (eight thou) or Improved Cylinder (ten thou) in both barrels. If the gun is to be used solely for Skeet, there is little point in fitting it with a multi-choke system, though most new guns are set up that way. Fixed chokes, properly regulated and combined with lengthened and polished forcing cones, not only improve patterns but control and reduce recoil.

Rules

In Skeet, targets are released in a combination of singles and doubles from the High and Low trap houses on fixed trajectories and speeds. The targets add up to a total of twenty-five per round.

Squads made up of five competitors shoot in order at the seven Stations in the following sequence.

Station one Two singles high/low and a double, High house first.
Station two Two singles high/low and a double, High house first.
Station three Two singles high/low.
Station four Two singles high/low and a double, with the competitor nominating which target he intends to take first. (In American Skeet there are only the two singles at station four with two singles shot at station eight instead.)
Station five Two singles high/low.
Station six Two singles high/low and a double, Low house first.
Station seven Two singles low/high and a double, Low house first.

The first single target shot on stations one through six will be the target from the High house, but on station seven, for safety reasons, the, Low house is shot first.

The first target shot in the doubles on stations one and two will be the High house and on stations six and seven, it will be the Low house target. On station four, the competitor nominates the target he will shoot first.

Every shooter will complete his shooting on each stand before leaving that stand. No one in the squad moves to the next stand before all those on the squad have completed the sequence on that stand.

The target or targets should be launched the instant they are called for.

If you hit every target in the round on stations one through seven, you have an 'option' – a single target shot from either the Low or the High house. Otherwise, the first target missed will be repeated and the outcome will be recorded as the twenty-fifth shot.

Two shells must be loaded for the singles on every station, with the exception of the 'option'.

Gun mount is optional in the UK. Many competitors shoot both Sporting Clays and Skeet, so there is a mixture of pre-mounted and gun down approaches to the targets, while in the USA most shoot with a pre-mounted gun.

Fundamentals

Feet and failure both begin with an F! Your set-up governs your swing. Poor foot position creates an imbalance

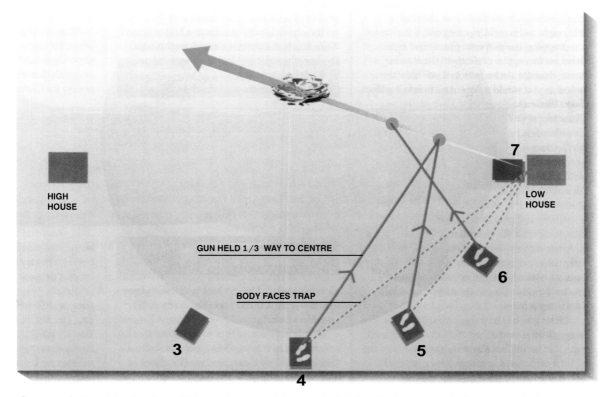

Correct – foot position for the right-handed shot would mean the belt buckle facing into the low house window

and impairs your ability to pivot through the target break point, without slowing or stopping. When the feet are truly misaligned to the target break point, you create sway and that transfer of weight results in dropping the shoulder, rolling the muzzles off the line and eradicates a smooth swing and follow-through.

The correct position is as follows: stand in the front and centre of the station. Address the break point of the clay, by pointing your belt buckle towards it. With your feet shoulder-width apart, take a quarter turn to the right.

You will find your gun pointed at the intended target break point and you will feel relaxed and comfortable. Picture an imaginary line running directly from the station to the break-point of the target. If your feet are correctly positioned, this line would pass through the heel of your rear foot and the big toe of your front foot out to the break point.

You will find this position promotes smoothness and consistency in your swing, and more targets will be broken. Another excellent rule of thumb is when you have adopted this address position to the target on stations one through six, your belt buckle will be pointing into the Low House window for the right-handed shooter and vice versa for the left-handed.

Posture

The correct posture should begin with your weight evenly distributed between your feet. Upon completion of your gun mount, whether pre-mounted or gun down, seventy per cent of your weight should be on the ball of your front foot. This balance promotes good head position, and enables you to make good forward movement towards the target. Positive aggression is needed in attacking the targets, particularly the doubles, which need a very positive approach. Other benefits of correct posture are improved rotation (pivot) over the front foot and assistance in keeping the head firmly on the stock.

The correct posture, stance and head position ensures a good gun mount

Gun Holds

The tried and trusted formulas for breaking clays apply to your gun holds as well. You must watch the target to ascertain its transition point, when it changes from a blur to a solid object. This becomes your gun hold.

In Skeet, this transition point occurs one third of the way from the trap house towards the centre peg. Because of variations in our personal visual acuity and reaction times, individual adjustments will need to be made to this generic hold-point.

Take two stacks of fifteen to twenty clays and place them on the target flight line, each positioned one third of the way from the Trap houses towards the centre peg. By reference to the stacks of clays, you can establish the correct gun hold. You will soon make adjustments, learning your personal gun hold for each Station. Remember, your muzzles should be just under the line of flight for every target so that the clay can be better seen.

Visual Holds

The correct visual hold should be halfway between the muzzles and the Trap house. The eyes should be relaxed and holding a soft focus. Some individual experimentation is required to find your exact visual holds. Your eyes should achieve hard focus just as the target reaches the muzzles at the gun hold, making a seamless hand-eye connection to the target.

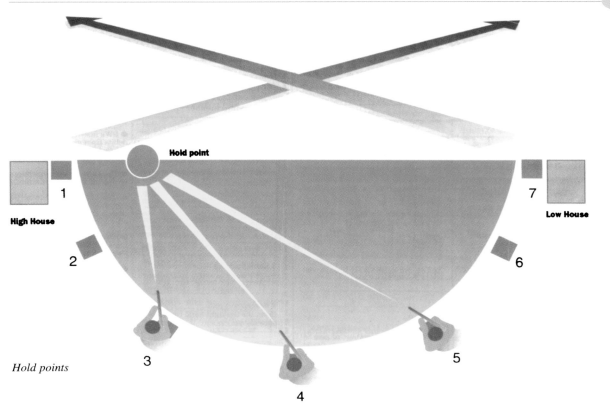

Hold points

Place two stacks of 15–20 clays on the target flight line, positioned one-third of the way from the trap house towards the centre peg

Place two stacks of 15–20 clays on the target flight line, positioned one-third of the way from the trap house towards the centre peg

Beware of looking directly into the Trap house window! The eyes seem to be magically drawn to the window, but focussing there will cause the target to blur past your visual hold, you will jump at the target, rushing and shooting too soon. Avoid this 'poke and hope' technique!

Place a stack of 15–20 clays on the centre point of the target's flight path. Then place two more stacks 40 inches on either side of the first stack, also on the target's flight path

Lead

Even though the target trajectories and distances in Skeet are constant, the angle to the shooter changes constantly as the squad progresses around the stations. Angle, more than any other aspect of the target presentation, dramatically changes our perception of lead.

For example, shooting the Low house from station three, you will need to give the target three to four-and-a-half feet of forward allowance. Now go to station seven and shoot the Low house. Here you will shoot directly at the target with no lead at all.

Lead, or forward allowance, is a very personal perception. One man's two feet is another man's four feet. Attempts have been made to lay down computed measurements of lead for Skeet, but there are so many variables: the technique used, the weight of the gun, the speed of swing, is the shooter left or right-handed, an individual's perception of lead – all require that each person learn and understand his own personal lead pictures.

The accepted leads for starting out at Skeet are as follows:

Station one: High house–0 lead, Low house–1 foot of lead

Station two: High house–0 lead, Low house–1 to 1½ feet of lead

Station three: High house–3 to 4½ feet of lead, Low house–3 to 4½ feet of lead

Station four: High house–3 to 4½ feet of lead, Low house–3 to 4½ feet of lead

Station five: High house–3 to 4½ feet of lead, Low house–3 to 4½ feet lead

Station six: High house–1 foot of lead, Low house–0 lead

Station seven: High house–4 to 8 inches of lead, Low house–0 lead

(In American Skeet **Station eight:** High house–0 lead, Low house–0 lead)

A quick and easy way to learn the lead pictures is to places a stack of fifteen to twenty clay targets on the centre point of the target's flight path. Then place two more stacks three feet, four inches to either side of the first stack along the target flight lines.

When practising on each station, you can reference these stacks of targets to get a visual awareness of what the approximate lead pictures should be. The lead for the Low house targets is the space between the centre stack and the stack on the Low house side of the field. The High house lead is the space between the centre stack and the stack on the High house side of the field.

Practical Skeet Practice

The first rule of successful Skeet shooting is to shoot the singles where you would shoot the doubles. This way, you only need to learn how to shoot fourteen targets, not twenty-five.

Begin at Station one and systematically shoot all of the incomers through Station seven, using the markers for your hold points and lead pictures. Do not move to the next station until you can shoot five straight. If you miss, go back to the previous station and start again.

Concentrate on being smooth and seeing the target clearly before moving. It may take several sessions before you can consistently break all of the soft targets. Do not rush, but concentrate on good fundamentals and building up your bank of lead pictures. When you have mastered the incomers, replicate the whole process with the going-away targets.

If you have applied the first rule, shooting the singles where you would the doubles, you will be in good shape to progress to the doubles.

The doubles create pressure and it is easy to lose the smoothness you have worked so hard to achieve with the singles. So when you first begin, shoot the doubles on report, i.e., instead of a true pair thrown simultaneously, the second target is released on the report of the first shot.

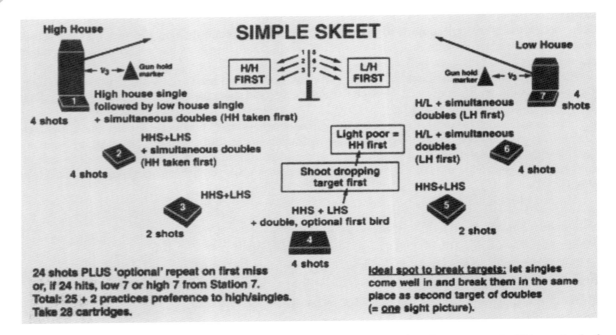

With practice, this delay can be gradually shortened until you are shooting a true pair. This method of practice encourages a smooth and successful progression from the singles to the doubles.

Start practising the doubles on station seven and station one. Then, as you succeed, move to stations two and six, then to stations three and five, and finally, to station four. This will take several sessions, so be patient. If you struggle with the pairs, consider the following solutions:

1. Good balance is essential–if you start right you will finish right.
2. The doubles present widely-angled targets…do not favour one target over another! Too much movement in one direction and there's no time to recover to shoot the second, more difficult target.
3. Be smooth: do not rush the first shot. On or just past the centre peg is the optimum place to take the target.
4. Create time by moving smoothly; remember *rushing ruins rhythm*. Do not 'poke and hope' at the second target. Make time to shoot it correctly.
5. Where the first target is taken impacts directly on the outcome of the second. If all of the above do not help, then experiment with taking the first target at different places.

The hard targets require accentuated concentration; this is where shooting straight happens. Here are a few tips and tricks that can help with the hard targets.

Station one
The High house can create difficulties, and there is nothing worse than missing the first bird at the beginning of a competition.

Create better visual pick up and time on this target by moving to the back of the station. By stepping back, you effectively see the bird three feet sooner! The gun hold should be just under the target line and a gentle push of the barrels into the departing target will see it broken over the centre peg.

Avoid the common mistake of holding high and allowing the bird to pass and disappear behind your barrels! This can cause you to slash down blindly to catch up, with a reflexive 'poke and hope', when it suddenly reappears.

Create better visual pick up at High house station one by moving to the back of the station

By standing at the front of the station, you see the target three feet later

Station two

The High house. Moving to the left back corner on this station will also give you more time and a better view of the target. This target screams 'crosser' at the pick-up point, but by the time the shot is taken, it has turned into a straight away!

Move your gun hold out a foot from the marker towards the centre peg and adjust your visual hold likewise. Also, you will find that this combination will work well if you just 'see bird–shoot bird'. A smooth swing *to* and *through* the target works every time on High house two.

Stations three, four and five

The lead required is the same for all three stations. Remember, if you are right-handed, the perceived lead on the High house targets is half again as much as on the Low house and vice versa for the left-handed. This is because the target is going *against* or *away from* the direction of your natural swing rotation. The stock is, in effect, being pushed *off* your face and your left hand is pushing instead of *pulling* the gun.

Like High house station one, moving to the back corner of High house station two will give you more time and a better view of the target.

Station four

The first target of the pair is nominated and can be shot in any order. However, there is a distinct advantage to shooting the High house target first.

The Low house target crosses the centre peg at the same height as the High house target. But then it flattens out and holds that line far better than the High target, offering a more constant second shot. If the wind is blowing or gusting, you may need to take the targets in reverse order. Shooting this pair in reverse order should be a part of your practice routine.

Station six

The Low house creates problems for some and is easily tamed if you adopt a gun hold ninety degrees to the base cord, flat on the line of the target. Do not look back for the target, but soft focus directly out past the gun to the target flight line. You will find that the bird will come into sharp focus as it passes the barrel and you will naturally pick it up and, with a smooth swing, shoot it in the same manner as the High house on station two.

Station eight

For the American Skeet shooter. Place the muzzles into the window of the Trap house. Point to the right side of the window and then to the top right hand corner, now move to the corner of the Trap house level with the top of the window.

Soft focus on the left side of the barrels and call for the target. Once again, 'see bird–shoot bird'. The lead is inches and your quick reaction to the speed of the target will create the lead, if hard visual contact is maintained throughout the shot. The Low house is shot with the same set up and technique.

Leading Techniques

Though Maintained Lead is the method of choice in much of Skeet, the second target of the doubles is shot using the Swing-Through method.

Shifting Positions

Many people like to adopt one foot position for the High house target and another for the Low house. Consider that by constantly changing your feet, you are introducing several variables to gun and visual holds, as well as different swing timing and characteristics.

When you shoot the doubles, you do not change stance for the different targets, it is far better to adopt a single, well-balanced stance which works well for both the singles and the doubles. This eliminates unnecessary cluttering of lead pictures and swing timing.

Consistency Counts

Skeet is a game of consistency. It requires great mental discipline to shoot straight. Consistency must be combined with flawless technique. The only way to achieve this is through structured practice.

You will never get past the doubles on station four or the 'bogie bird' of station two High house, by just shooting round after round! Keep a shooting log and record your performance in competitions. Look for patterns in any misses that occur and work to rectify these in your practice.

Chapter 12
Touching On Trap

Trap

Trap is the oldest of the Clay Shooting disciplines, the historical aspects of which are covered in Chapter One. There are many Trap shooting games, but the most popular is Down the Line, the one I will be describing in this Chapter.

In the USA, Single Barrel, Handicap, Back-up, Double Rise, Automatic Ball or Wobble Trap are some of the other variations of the Trap games. Universal Trench and Olympic Trap are even more challenging and complex and if the reader is interested, the details of these other versions can be found in the books recommended in the Bibliography.

The popularity of Down the Line Trap is due, in no small part, to the fact that the inexperienced shooter can achieve some initial success rather rapidly yet there is enough of an on-going challenge for the experienced shot to keep him coming back for more.

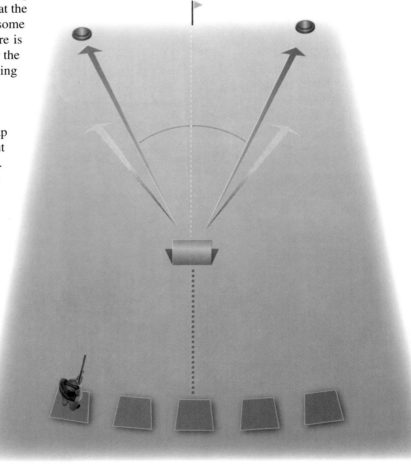

The Trap Range
Down the Line is shot over one trap machine that has a fixed elevation but random, constantly changing angles. The clay target is thrown away from the shooter and must travel between 50 and 55 yards. The height of the target is adjusted so that, at a distance of 10 yards from the trap, it will pass through a hoop at a height of between 8 and 10 feet.

The angle at which the target is thrown, to the left and right of the shooter, is constantly changing and appears random and unpredictable. The maximum target angle is set at 22½ degrees either side of the centre of the trap house. Shooting takes place from five stations, 3 feet by 3 feet square, placed in a semi-circle, 16 yards from the trap house.

Down the Line range

AUTOMATIC BALL TRAP (ABT) DOMESTIC/ INTERNATIONAL.

Single trap with varying angle and height but constant speed.

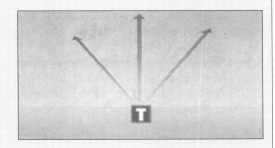

UNIVERSAL TRENCH (UT) INTERNATIONAL.

5 traps per layout all set at different speeds, angles and height.

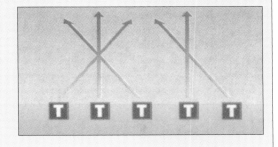

OLYMPIC TRAP (OT) INTERNATIONAL.

15 traps per layout (5 groups of 3) all at different speeds, angles and height.

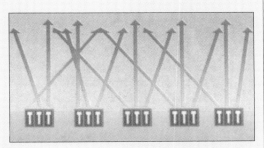

The variation is greatest in Olympic trap.
It is very much a game of speeds, combined with tough angles.

The Trap Gun

Trap is, without a doubt, shot at the quickest pace of all of the disciplines. As 100 cartridges are shot in swift succession, the ideal Trap gun should have enough weight to help absorb recoil. A gun weighing somewhere between 7¾ and 8¾ lbs is the accepted standard. It should also be well-balanced, with good handling and pointing capabilities.

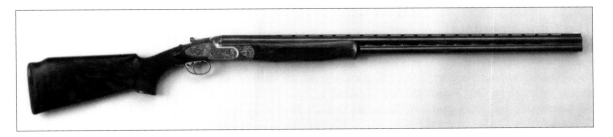

Because the target is consistently rising and going away, another important requirement in a Trap gun is that it be conducive to smooth, controlled movements. The longer-barrelled guns, from 32 to 34 inches, deliver on this point. A minimum half-inch, file-cut rib, ventilated both top and centre, is the best choice for Trap.

The stock of the gun is designed to place the pattern high so the shooter can clearly see the target throughout the shot. Adjust the stock so the pattern shoots seventy per cent above and thirty per cent below, this builds in lead and eliminates the need to shoot above the fast-rising target. This set-up prevents the target from being blocked by the barrels as the shot is taken, a frequent cause of head-lifting.

The Trap gun should always have a full pistol grip and, often, a palm swell. A fully-rounded fore-end, with or without finger grooves, provides better control as well as heat protection for the leading hand. A quality recoil pad or recoil reduction system, capable of spreading and dissipating the effects of recoil, is a necessity. A crisp, well-regulated trigger pull, set around three-and-a-half to four pounds, completes the ideal Trap gun.

Choke and Cartridge

There is little requirement for multi-choking a Trap gun. The targets are shot at known, fixed distances, so this allows the shooter to take full advantage of the inherent certainty of the pattern produced by fixed chokes. Half (Modified) and three-quarters (Improved Modified) are my personal recommendation. The choke choice should be complemented by lengthened forcing cones (three inches), back-bored barrels and long lead-in tapered chokes.

The interaction of choke and cartridge requires serious consideration. I recommend that, once you have made a decision on the size of choke and a particular brand of cartridge, you take the time to pattern the combination at yardages you favour for your first and second barrels.

With regard to shot size, a combination of 8s in the first barrel and 7½s in the second offer the best performance. A word on the care of cartridges: if you wish to obtain the best performance from them, store them at an ambient temperature of fifty-five to sixty-five degrees. If cartridges are allowed to get too cold, poor ignition and compression can result, causing reduced velocity. If allowed to get too hot, excessive pressures, increased recoil, more deformed pellets and inferior patterns can occur.

Rules

A round of Trap consists of twenty-five shots, with groups of five shots taken from five shooting positions. A maximum of five people, or squad, shoot per round. Each shooter on the squad shoots five shots from each of the five shooting positions.

The shooters take turns shooting in order: the first shooter will shoot one shot…the second shooter takes their shot, etc. until all five shooters have shot five times at the first station. The shooters then rotate right to the next shooting position and repeat the process until all five stations have been shot. The gun is pre-mounted and the targets should be released immediately on the competitor's call.

Most competitions consist of one hundred targets or four rounds. In the UK, two shots are allowed per station. A first barrel kill scores 3 points, a second barrel kill counts two. In the USA only one shot is allowed and a kill scores 1, a miss, 0.

The Fundamentals
Stance

Placement of the feet in Trap is less complicated than in Sporting Clays and Skeet. First, there are only five stations and the target is always travelling away from the shooter. As a result, the range of body motion is greatly reduced, as very little rotation is required.

Addressing the break point of the target doesn't work in Trap. Because of the random nature of the target, you don't know where the clay will be. So feet should be placed to favour the right hand target for the

right-handed, left for the left-handed, while still permitting suffi-cient motion to cover the other angles presented.

The proper stance for the right-handed shooter is achieved by looking at the extreme left-hand angle boundary marker and visu-alising a line running straight from the marker, through the centre of the trap house and crossing the station. Place both toes, with feet shoulder-width apart, on this visualised line. This position will handle the hard right-angle target, while giving ample move-ment for the other angles.

Because of the changing angles on stations one through five, you will always be in a position to turn the hard right-hander into a straight-away shot.

Posture

Your weight should be evenly distributed between your feet, so that when the gun is pre-mounted and you adopt your gun hold position, there will a natural transference of weight over the front foot. This creates a natural head posi-tion, enabling you to swing the gun with your whole body and stay in the gun. In the exaggerated weight-forward, bent-knee position, you are forced to make the swing with your arms, where the tendency is to come out of the gun. The pre-mounted gun can cause the head to lower to the stock. This unnatural position creates tension, so when the shot is taken, a smooth swing is hindered and head-lifting occurs. Learning to mount the gun to a natural head position is an essential part of good posture in Trap shooting.

Gun Holds

As a general rule of thumb, the basic gun holds are the following:

Station one Point at the front left corner of the Trap house.
Station two Hold halfway between the corner and the centre of the front edge of the Trap house.
Station three Point at the centre of the front edge of the Trap house.
Station four Hold halfway between the centre and right front corner of the Trap house.
Station five Point over the right hand corner of the Trap house.

Mount the gun to a natural head position. It avoids tension that results in head-lifting

A significant number of competitors find that these holds do not sufficiently favour the hard right-angle shot so they move their hold points out a little further to the right. Depending on your visual acuity and reaction time, you will need to experiment to find the best gun holds for you.

Using clay targets, you can place them on the Trap house to mark your gun holds for each station. With practice, you can find your correct hold points. Move the holds backward or forward of the recommended start positions, experimenting to improve personal smoothness and timing.

Use clay targets to mark your gun holds

After deciding on your horizontal holds, you need to give attention to your vertical holds, or the hold height. One-eyed shooters find it better to hold their muzzles along the front edge of the Trap house. This prevents the barrels from obscuring the target.

Those with binocular vision prefer to adopt the more popular high-hold, pointing one to two feet above the Trap house, minimising gun movement. The two-eyed shooter can do this because they have increased peripheral vision and can see the target emerging under their barrel. You can add or remove targets on your hold markers, building them to the height that works best for you.

Visual Holds

In every Clay target game, you need to ascertain the point in the target's flight off the trap arm where it transitions from a blur to a solid target. In Trap, as the target rises from the Trap house, you must look *up and out*, past the barrels, into the space where this occurs. Adopt a soft focus, not concentrating on anything in particular. Allow your eyes to relax and maintain focus soft in the transition zone. When you visually acquire the target, let your eyes guide your hands to the target and take the shot without conscious thought... See 'bird–shoot bird'.

Lead Pictures and Practices

Trap, with its narrow angles and fast targets, makes it difficult to 'blue print' the application of lead. Try to and you are guaranteed to stop the gun and miss behind. Good visual target acquisition and hard focus, combined with a smooth move to the target, will give you enough gun speed to apply the appropriate forward allowance.

Apply the basic rules of breaking clays, practise these exercises and you will quickly learn the correct lead pictures.

1. Start by locking off the trap oscillator so the trap throws a straight-away bird. Begin shooting from station three. When you can consistently hit this target, move to station two. This will change the angle and introduce lead. Repeat this process at station one, and repeat on stations four and five, adjusting your gun holds as you progress.
2. Practise shooting this target from all five stations for the next few sessions.
3. When you have become consistent on the locked-off target, have the oscillation turned back on, but set to minimum movement. Start again at station three, repeat the practice sequence. With success, work your way through all the stations.
4. Repeat this exercise with the trap set to full competition oscillation.
5. It may take several practice sessions to learn the leads required. When you are breaking the locked-off targets with consistency, turn the oscillator back on and shoot the random target presentations.

You should find your confidence and scores rising with every session. Finally, the oldest and still best tip for the Trap shooter is 'Keep Your Eye on the Rock and Your Head On the Stock'.

Chapter 13
Eyes and Vision

E yesight is the most essential part of shooting. Your hands are controlled by the brain which receives its instruction from the eyes. As you make a shot, the brain is required to manage over one hundred billion neurons – these neural paths are controlled by your vision which in turn controls your arms and body. These paths remain organised for a very short window of opportunity and the shot must be taken when this process is at its peak. This is referred to as eye and hand coordination, but it is simply the interaction of the eyes and the hands as a single unit.

You can't hit it if you can't see it.

In our day-to-day life we have very little cause to 'hard focus' and our normal vision setting is 'panoramic', with no single object in mind. This is because we have no real need for concentrated focusing, which is hard work for both the eyes and the brain.

Try a little experiment to demonstrate this: look up from this book and pick out an object on the opposite side of the room – the centre of a clock or the corner of a picture frame. Zero in on it and attempt to keep intense focus on it for the count of twenty. See? You have already quit and relaxed your vision!

It is extremely hard and sometimes uncomfortable to hold a 'hard focus' on an object for even a few seconds, yet this is the essential skill we need to master if we are to shoot clay targets with any consistency.

Concentration

It takes concentration to maintain focus on a moving target and 'hard focus' means keeping both eyes on the target without being distacted by background, peripheral images, shadows, colours or movement.This concentration is divided into two parts:

1. Saccadic which is the first visual reaction to a moving target; it locates the target by direction and speed.
2. Pursuit which is the second reaction: it centres in on the target.

Saccadic and Pursuit work independently. Saccadic cannot centre and Pursuit cannot locate , so it is a balance between the two that is essentail to straight shooting. Once the target is centred, if you let your Pursuit reaction lapse into the Saccadic mode, the target becomes lost in your peripheral vision and vice versa.

If we stare at the visual pick-up point of the target in an attempt to centre on it, we reduce our peripheral awarness and the target literally gets the jump on us. Learning how to look for and at the target properly is one of the critical fundamentals of shooting well.

The secret to centreing on a target is to know where to look and why.

Optical Illusions

The motion of a moving target is created by its passage against the background of trees or sky. From this, the eye gathers the information required to locate and centre on the target and the motion is always perceived to be behind the target. Until it has passed in front of a background or an object, the target is, in effect, stationary to the eye. The eyes are programmed to detect and react to movement–a defence mechanism–and therefore we naturally look at where the target has been, not where it is going.

Centreing

Earlier in the book I described how the shot column cloud disperses into a string stretching approximately five to eleven feet long. This shot-string is what gives us the margin for error in shooting a moving target. If our focus is on the rear of the target, this margin is considerably reduced because the target is moving *away* from the shot-string.

Even with the correct lead, you will always be hitting the back of the target. If we learn to centre on the leading edge of the target, we achieve two important benefits: first, the target will appear slower and second, it is now travelling *into* the shot-string, maximising our chances of success and increasing margin for error.

When you learn to concentrate on the *leading edge* of the target, you will feel more in charge, and you will feel that you have more time to take your shot. If you look at the back, or the 'wake' of the target, you will falter and fumble and miss behind.

Visual Hold

We are pedestrians and have pedestrian-paced vision. If you can, visualise an 8mm film projector – the human eye sees the equivalent of sixteen frames per second. A target thrown at sixty miles per hour is initially moving at thirty-two frames per second. If we look in the wrong place, the target is seen only every other frame or as a blur. The wrong visual hold defeats the Saccadic process and slows the Pursuit mechanism.

On every target presentation, regardless of the discipline being shot, you need to observe keenly the target's flight line. As the initial velocity decreases, the bird will transition from thirty-two frames per second to our natural visual rhythm of sixteen frames.

From this transition point, you need to look half-way back to the Trap house. This becomes your Visual Hold, the point at which you maximise your Saccadic reaction to the target and ensure swift Pursuit acquisition.

Do not attempt to look hard for the target–this restricts Saccadic movement. Instead, adopt a 'soft focus', looking at nothing in particular. Out past the visual pick-up, raise your eyebrows just before you call for the target. This simple action gives you a twenty per cent increase in light-gathering vision! Light reduction causes vision reduction and makes the target appear vague, fast flying with trailing comet-tails…the cause of many missed targets.

Opening your eyes wide as you call for the bird will result in a marked improvement in your shooting performance.

Eyesight Fitness

The eyesight standard of twenty/twenty is what we see – vision is the process of *reacting* to that which we see. When we are making a shot, the lens of the eye is flexing repeatedly (Accommodation) to maintain a sharp focus on the target and has to make many thousands of adjustments for depth, background and flight.

This is comparable to the lens on a motorised camera focussing back and forth to achieve a sharp picture. The eye is like any other muscle in the body and can be exercised to improve this skill. A few simple exercises each day can strengthen the lens' ability to flex so as to better locate and concentrate focus on a moving target, in the same manner you can increase the strength of your arms by exercising your biceps.

The muscles of the eyes can move the eye through 360 degree rotations – left to right, up and down. Though we may have become rather sophisticated animals, we are still, none the less, animals. We are omnivores or hunter-gatherers, in the main, gatherers. As such, our eyes are predisposed to look down and in.

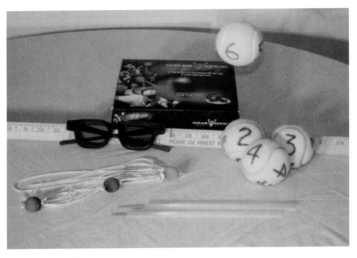

Aerobics for the eyes

Most of our everyday activities take place *below* the level of our eyes and the eye muscles for looking down and in are much stronger than those used for looking up and out.

Any activity that requires the eyes to look up and out for any length of time, is extremely fatiguing. Take, for example, driving a car. This activity uses very similar eye action as is used when shooting. The modern car is effortless to drive and extremely comfortable, yet if you drive for an hour or more you quickly become tired. This is due to the on-going contest between the stronger lower eye muscles and the weaker upper eye muscles.

Eye-Vision Exercises

These exercises are simple and the equipment needed is minimal. We begin with some stretching exercises for the eyes.

1. With your eyes closed but relaxed, start by rotating them up and around in a 360 degree circle, five full rotations, first to the right and then five full rotations to the left. Then with your eyes still shut, look up and down five times in each direction. Finally, roll your eyes five times fully left and right. At first you will find stretching exercises difficult to do, but with practice they become an excellent preliminary work out before further exercises or as a pre-match warm up.
2. Cord ball has long been an exercise in many hand and eye coordinated sports. You will need a ten feet length of butcher's string and three half-inch wooden balls of different colours (red, yellow and green) from a craft shop. Place the red ball in the middle of the cord, securing it with a knot. Tie the two remaining balls eight to ten inches from the ends of the cord in the same manner. You will need to secure one end to a wall so that when the cord is pulled taught it is fifteen inches above your line of sight. Place the loose end on the bridge of your nose and positon yourself so that the cord is pulled taut. Begin by focusing on the farthest ball. When you do so correctly, the string will form a 'Y' in your peripheral vision. Moving your point of focus back to the second ball will produce a 'X', and once again moving back to the third ball, will create another 'X'. At first this requires concentated focus but with practice, you can move your point of focus across the fields of vision at will. By altering the position of the balls on the string you can increase the range of your practice.
3. Take a straw and a toothpick and hold them horizontally at arm's length. Bring them together, inserting the toothpick into the straw. Do this twenty times, ten times holding the toothpick in your right hand, then ten times holding the toothpick in your left hand.
4. Thread a tennis ball on a piece of cord. Write four numbers on it with a black felt pen. Hang it from a beam or in a door frame. Take a yardstick or three feet dowel and start the ball in motion. Concentrate on one number and, with the stick at arm's length, touch it as it swings and rotates. You may have to start with just your finger and graduate to the stick as it is a lot more tricky than I have made it sound.
5. Take a pen and, holding it vertically at arm's length, look at and concentrate hard on an object aross the room. The pen will appear double in your near-sight (the pen and a ghost image). Now transfer your point

of focus to the pen, concentrate hard and the object across the room will double (the original and a ghost image). Repeat as often as you feel comfortable doing so. At first it will only be a few times, but, with practice, you will be able to increase and decrease the separation of the object and the pen and increase the number of times you can perform the exercise.

6. Using a yardstick, put a mark in the middle at the 18 inch mark. Now hold it at this point with one hand and move it out at arm's length. Keeping your head locked rigid, move your eyes to the left and right as far as you can, seeing how far out you can read the numbers on the yardstick. With practice you will increase the range of eye movement to be able to read almost to the ends.

7. Take a dozen tennis balls and mark each one with a black felt tip with a single digit number, one through nine. Practice with a friend or friends standing 10 to 15 yards apart. Toss the tennis balls, underarm, to each other, and try to look past the actual ball and read the number on it, calling it out during its flight.

8. There are computer games specifically designed to improve eye and hand coordination. One in particular is called the 'Visual Edge'. You receive a pair of 3D glasses, a cord ball and CD. By following the prompts you will progress through a series of exercises that will increase your visual dexterity.

9. Take a blaze-orange clay target and with a black felt-tip pen place a dot on the dome and at the twelve o'clock, nine, six, and three o'clock points on the edge of the clay. Keep it on your desk or work top and, when possible, take a minute to look at the clay. *Really* concentrate on the centre dot. Then relax your eyes and look at the whole clay before centreing on one of the dots on the edge. Repeat the exercise until you have hard focused on each dot in turn. At first you will find it hard to sustain this visual concentration for long, but with diligent practice your hard focusing ability will improve.

The emphasis of all these exercises is on flexible focus, both near and far. All will help improve **Accommodation, Focus and Centreing,** increasing your abilltiy to locate and shoot the target. We all have a given amount of eye and hand coordination – the better shots have, by natural acquisition or diligent practice, sharper visual acuity. The ability to focus sharply can be learned and mastered but it requires constant practice.

Visual Enhancement

Clay shooting takes place under varying light conditions and backgrounds. The target is in constant motion against this background and the fluctuating light and shadows make it difficult to maintain hard focus on the clay. This creates inaccurate information for the brain to process, and the result is often a missed target.

It has long been recognised that wearing shooting glass lenses in certain colours can enhance the target under specific light and background conditions. The right coloured lenses can make the difference between a hit and a miss. This is because the eye achieves better definition and depth perception when the pupil is constricted and maximum constriction is achieved by using the lightest colour lenses you have.

For example, vermillion-coloured lenses make orange targets stand out when thrown against a moderately bright background while yellow and orange tints work well in overcast or poor light. Brown tints in varying shades are very effective in bright sunshine. All tints offer enhanced contrast and definition, however, the choice is very subjective and often person-specific. Everyone has a degree of colour blindness and it is important to experiment to find the tints that work best for you in various light conditions and with different target colours.

The more light that enters the eye, the better the vison process and the better the hand coordination, as well. Any colour lenses that we use block some part of the light spectrum, actually reducing the amount of light available. You need to redress this by balancing any light loss with enhanced contrast, using the lightest tint possible.

Lenses for shooting glasses should be polarised for ultimate protection from ultraviolet radiation which contributes to the development of cataracts and has been shown to cause degeneration of the retinal pigment

ABOVE: *Always choose shooting glasses with interchangeable lenses*

LEFT: *Choose the lenses with the minimum tint for the light conditions, in a colour that gives the best target contrast*

epithelium. It has also been discovered that exposure to harmful UV rays can accelerate age-related macular degeneration.

Frames

Regular glasses are designed to place the lens centre directly in line with the pupil. When we lower our head into the correct shooting position, we end up looking off the optical centre of the ordinary spectacle lens. A further problem is that everyday glasses are designed for fashion and looks rather than function, this often means that the frame iterferes or, in the worst case, obscures the vision.

Properly-designed shooting glasses sit high up on the nose and have correctly placed optics so that when the head is lowered into the proper shooting position, the pupil is looking through the optical centre of the lens, slightly above the actual centre. Shooting glasses have lenses that are oversized and frameless, so there is no obstruction between the eyes and the target. The frame arms have padded,curved ear pieces and nose pads to stop the glasses from slipping or being knocked ajar by movement or recoil. This high fit means that they stand slightly off the face and air can freely flow between the lens and the eye, preventing fogging on wet and humid days. The lenses can also be polished with an anti-mist solution.

Eye Sight Correction

The choice of eyewear is very important. The type of lens, the frame design and fit all can contribute significantly to a shooter's performance. The lenses for shooting glasses are made from two materials, CR 39 plastic and polycarbonate. In terms of safety, polycarbonate is the best and most effective. The lenses are less than half the weight of glass lenses and polycarbonate has outstanding impact resistance. The polycarbonate lens requires careful processing and is prone to scratching when uncoated. It should always have an anti-scratch finish applied.

A clear lens will only allow ninety per cent of the available light to pass through to the eye, with ten per cent being lost in reflection. Anti-glare coatings allow more light to reach the eye and allow you to see better, especially in poor conditions.Polarised lenses offer the ultimate in UV protection but eliminate reflections and glare.

The best shooting glasses should include a comfortable and durable frame, tinted and coated lenses, providing protection, increased visual acuity, better depth perception, improved vision and contrast and will help to control eye fatigue.

If you require corrective prescription lenses, have only single vision lenses fitted to your shooting glasses. Bi- and tri-focal lenses cause distortion and the graduated prescription or Varilux type cause even more visual problems: as the light passes through the lens it is bent or refracted when the head is in the correct shooting position.

Contact lenses offer distinct advantages compared to the prescription glasses. Contacts project a larger image on the back of the eye and eliminate spectacle distortion. This helps you see your targets sooner, sharper and bigger. Coated shooting glasses with appropriate coloured lenses further enhance your vision.

A growing number of people are choosing laser corrective surgery. When doing so they often opt to have one eye fixed for long sight and one for short, to eliminate the requirement for glasses entirely. This is also done with contact lenses. If you choose to go this route be sure that the eye for long sight matches the shoulder you are shooting from.

Target Taming Tips

On sunny days, black clays will reflect light. This reflected light will appear as white dots on the clay. If you use your new visual concentration to hard focus on these spots, the clays will disappear in a ball of smoke.

On dull days, focus on reading the maker's brand mark on the clay. If you can, see the dome, or look hard at the shoulder, or even at the rings and dimples on the shoulder of the target.

At times we can all listen and not hear, touch and not feel, look without seeing; you must learn to maximise your visual stimulus on every target.

The eyes control the body, they synchronise the motor-muscular movements to the target, decide the timing of when to pull the trigger.

Misses are a result of faulty visual perception caused by failure to centre on the target.

Learn to zero in and remain locked onto the point of impact – the primary zone – of the target throughout the shooting action.

The primary zone of the target is always changing direction, speed, angle and distance and needs to be learned with instruction and practice.

Chapter 14
The Mental Game

I am sure you have heard or read the following statement regarding the shooting learning curve. 'When you begin, it is ninety per cent mechanical and ten per cent mental, when you finish it is ten per cent mechanical and ninety per cent mental.'

Why do the majority of shooters tend to get just so good and no better? Well, it's more than muscles that make a champion. When we step out onto the field we each bring, not only our equipment and ability, but ourselves – our doubts, fears and frustrations – the internal conflicts that can destroy our 'concentration' and ultimately our game.

The word 'concentrate' as defined in the Oxford dictionary is 'to bring together at one point, the ability to employ one's full thoughts or efforts to increase strength'. To shoot straight, you need to develop your ability to 'concentrate' – to block out all distractions, both internal and external. Total concentration on each and every shot, as an entirely independent and all-important task, means breaking one target at a time until they are all broken. The ability to do this consistently is the major difference between the intermediate and the advanced shot.

Clay target shooting is different from other sports in that there is little physical activity to relieve stress build-up which increases incrementally as scores increase. How often have you flunked the first one or two stands in a competition and then shot straight? Or shot straight, only to throw it away on the last two stations? This is your way of relieving the stress caused by the pressure. There is no natural outlet such as the starter's gun for the sprinter where explosive action releases the built-up stress.

However, in a sport that requires smooth, controlled movement, stress can be destructive-it needs to be properly controlled. Too little stress will produce an indifferent performance – too much can cause one to choke. The top competitor finds the balance between the two extremes and manages and even uses performance stress to reach the height of his game.

Stress management is achieved through 'concentration' and its foundation starts in mastering the mechanical and visual skills. This chapter is not intended for the beginner, but for the B, A and AA-class competitor looking for that extra target or striving to move up in class.

Top competitors have learned to control unwanted brain activity that interferes with target focus

To get the most from this chapter, all of your mechanical skills should be well-grooved and practised, visual acuity should be understood and the setup of your shots well-demonstrated. You should have a gun that fits and you should have a good understanding of targets, chokes and cartridges.

With all of the above in place, you are ready to learn the mental game. I urge you to take a long and honest look at your shooting – refer to the list above and address any of the weak or missing elements before looking for a quick fix here. The mental side of the equation will not help if you are still struggling to master the basic physical techniques. The key to consistent straight shooting and high scores is in sound basics. The mechanics must be mastered first or you will find the following difficult to implement and get little from it.

Bob Rotellas in his book *Golf is not a Game of Perfect*, offers sound advice on the need to be mentally strong in sport. Mental control is, without a doubt, the final piece of the shooting jigsaw puzzle. The first step is to acknowledge that the mental skills must be learned and practised in just the same manner as the mechanical.

The mechanics are learned quicker than you think – once they are mastered, a miss is often not the result of a mechanical mistake, but a slip in 'concentration'. Try this exercise to determine if your missed targets are a result of mechanics or concentration:

1. When you are shooting at your best are you satisfied with your skill level?
    (The mental approach is not a substitute for poor mechanics.)
2. Are your misses random? Do they increase with pressure? Is there a predictable 'missing pattern'?
3. When missing, how do you feel? Are you confident or confused? Are you in control or rushing?
4. Is there more than one aspect of your shooting that results in missing? (Pressure creates stress that increases muscle tension and restricts movement which results in poor concentration and reduced visual acuity.)

If you answer yes to one or more of these questions, then you are ready to look at the mental approach to the game. You now need to learn:

Why do you choke when the pressure is on?
Why do you miss the easy shots so often?
Why do you make the same errors again and again?
How can you change all of this permanently?

Swedish psychologist, Lars-Eric Unestahl has developed a concept called the 'Ideal Performance State' or IPS. His athletes report that being in IPS is like an altered state of consciousness – they often refer to it as being 'The Zone'. The athlete is intensely focused on a limited number of tasks, and removed from everything except those tasks, almost like being in a bubble. In 'The Zone', targets appear to be moving in slow motion and action is effortless. In this state, very little of the mechanical action can be recalled.

Unestahl's training involves teaching the shooter how to:

1. Breathe and Relax
2. Control Anxiety and Arousal
3. Concentrate and Focus to Eliminate Distractions

These three skills, when learned, allow the shooter to enter 'The Zone' at will and produce the best performance of which they are capable.

1. Breath and Relax

Breathing and relaxing are often referred to in the martial arts as Centreing. This is a process used to create feelings of being grounded, calm and relaxed. This is the opposite of being anxious.

When you are centred, your muscles are loose and relaxed but ready for action. Your breathing is slow and deep, slower than normal. Foot position is your normal shooting stance with the legs relaxed, knees slightly flexed and the weight evenly distributed between your feet. This position results in a sense of being balanced, of being ready to move with purpose in any direction.

Learning to centre is the keystone to performing well. To achieve this, you need to establish key words or phrases that you associate with being centered. These words will become your 'trigger' to peak performing in competition.

One word or phrase must reflect *physiological* feelings, i.e., loose, relaxed balanced, strong, smooth. The other word or phrase should be perceptual and reflect a state of mind, i.e., controlled, powerful, calm and confident.

Physiological Trigger Words might be: 'Be smooth', 'Strong', 'OK' etc.

Perceptual Trigger Words might be: 'Can do', 'Still' 'See target' and so on.

2. Control Anxiety and Arousal

Anxiety and arousal are often confused and thought to be the same, but really, they are different aspects of similar reactions. Arousal is being up and ready. Anxiety is nervousness or distress. This leads to trying too hard, creates tension, tightens muscles and reduces performance. Anxiety causes attention to stray from the target to interior focus.

Nervousness is normal and is necessary to achieve the optimum arousal levels, but by balancing or controlling Anxiety and Arousal you can reach 'The Zone'.

3. Concentrate and Focus to Eliminate Distractions

When you are shooting you engage in four types of concentration:

1. Broad
2. Narrow
3. External
4. Internal

You use these in a combination of ways:

1. Broad internal, when you need to think, plan and analyse.
2. Broad external, to assess situations and conditions.
3. Narrow internal, to rehearse or visualise.
4. Narrow external, to react or perform.

During the shooting sequence, you are required frequently to shift back and forth among these four types of concentration.

Arriving at a competition, you use broad external to determine the background, the sun's position, wind and terrain to evaluate what effect they will have on the targets. Broad internal is then used to analyse this information and plan the shoot. For example, you may wish to shoot certain stands first to avoid those times when the sun would distract from the target, or to choose the correct lens colour for your shooting glasses.

Narrow internal is used to visualise your performance. Narrow external is for hard focus on the target and is used to actually perform.

In the stand, you will be mainly using external focus; broad for assessment between shots and shifting to narrow to actually shoot the target.

'The Zone' is achieved when you can control these shifts and maintain focus on the target. This action requires almost entirely narrow external. (Target, Target, Target.)

Visualisation and Imagery

These are two more aids to reaching the Improved Performance State.

Visualisation is a cheap way to practise on non-shooting days. There are no clays or cartridges to be paid for and it is a very productive practice because you never miss. Visualisation builds confidence and experience. Remember, the body cannot tell the difference between imagined and real events, so every target you visualise calling for, shooting and breaking becomes another successful memory.

Imagery is the simple previewing of the intended outcome of impending action in the moments prior to shooting. You imagine the target breaking as preparation to call for the target. It focuses the conscious mind on the action and so keeps irrelevant thoughts from intruding as you make your shot. Both Visualisation and Imagery are improved by practice.

The Training Programme

There are three levels of learning:

1. **Cognitive – Unconsciously Incompetent:** where you are entirely dependent on the instructor to break a target.
2. **Over Learning – Consciously Competent:** where you are capable of making a shot independently of an instructor's input.
3. **Autonomic – Unconsciously Competent:** where you can make a shot without conscious thought.

A training programme requires conscious planning and action, you are attempting to make things change and improve. By working through the three steps above, you are learning to think less and less and to remove task-irrelevant distractions from your thinking, replacing them with autonomic actions.

You start by breaking your concentration down into separate elements, practising and developing these elements, then putting them back together. Ultimately you will be able to perform the entire shooting sequence automatically and then you will have discovered 'The Zone'.

Clarify and identify your goals; they are the foundation for your shooting success.

1. Long term aims.
2. Shorter term objectives.
3. Intermediate goals.

These specific goals should be written down and your performance checked against them regularly. This exercise will ensure that you are on course and give you milestones of progress, encouraging you towards your ultimate goal.

'The Zone' is the next level and can only be achieved by practising to reach that point where you can respond automatically or unconsciously instead of thinking about all of the things you have to do. In 'The Zone' you are simply allowing the shot to happen.

The Zone Explained

You will all be familiar with the expression 'Being in the Zone'. This is simply a state of relaxed concentration during which peak performance can occur. In Andrew Cooper's book *Playing in the Zone*, 'The Zone' is variously described by elite athletes:

By Billie Jean King, women's tennis player 'Violent action taking place in an atmosphere of total tranquillity.'

By Bill Russell, NBA great 'Magical – profound joy, effortless action taking place in slow motion – self-transcendence.'

Mihaly Csikszentmihalyi and Susan Jackson in their book *Flow in Sports* define 'The Zone' as 'A state of consciousness where one becomes totally absorbed in what one is doing to the exclusion of all other thoughts and emotions.'

The words of importance in this quote are 'to the exclusion of all other thoughts and emotions'.

In my opening words, I state the ninety/ten per cent rule to optimum performance. After we have mastered the fundamentals, the next step is to learn to clear our mind of all of the self-doubt and clutter to allow our subconscious to make the perfect shot. This is the secret to the Mental Game. How do we achieve this? Well, read on.

How do the top competitors suppress these negative thoughts that we are all prone to? This is a question sports physiologists have been attempting to answer for years.

A major break-through in this area has been achieved through the results of research carried out by Christopher Janelle, Assistant Professor at the University of Florida's Department of Exercise and Sports Science and Charles Hillman in the Department of Kinesiology at the University of Illinois.

They discovered that top athletes in all major sports pause and dwell moments longer than the amateur when focusing on their target or visual cue. This 'pause and dwell' moment enables them to control and quiet the left side of their brain – the side which produces the analytical messages that interrupt deep concentration. In effect, they have learned to switch off the clutter.

This is a readily observable distinction between elite and novice shooters. The elite shooter is able to block out all outside influences and focus on the target or the appropriate visual cue for several seconds before initiating his shot.

Janelle and Hillman have also discovered that they can dramatically improve a performer's ability to respond accurately through coordinating a period of intense concentration on the target visual hold. This visual cue and the extended duration they fixate on it before response to its flight, results in better coordination to the target, actually making it appear slower and bigger.

Shooting is self-paced and the timing derives from focus on the target. In Clay Target shooting this can be improved by the One-Two Punch of Focusing and Pausing.

Janelle states 'This is not just about aiming; it's about giving yourself a better chance to respond correctly'. If you look and dwell at the visual hold longer, you can block out other mental reactions. This concept is referred to as the 'Quiet Eye Phenomenon'. It was introduced at the National Coaches College at the USA Olympic Training Centre in November of 2001.

Janelle found that the more successful shooters focus longer on their targets. The top performers had much higher levels of alpha waves of the right side of the brain – that the unwanted analytical thought process of the left had temporarily been suppressed. This allows top shots to better focus on and coordinate to the target.

Across the various sports that have been tested, top performers have traditionally used a longer 'Quiet Eye' period. It is only with this research that this practice has been shown to produce favourable brain-wave characteristics.

The inability to suppress left brain activity is what leads to 'choking'. This is a condition in which even the top competitor can fail to shoot to his full potential. Dr Debbie Crews of Arizona State University was recently commissioned by the PGA to test this phenomenon under controlled laboratory conditions.

Dr Crews found that it is not the level of anxiety that determines performance, but how the brain processes the increase in activity. She found that the main reason for competitors 'choking' was, when competition pressure increased, they had the left side of the brain doing most of the work. The successful competitor had comparable increases in the brain's activity but that activity was spread evenly through both sides of the brain.

Simply put, you need to increase the activity of the right side of the brain if you wish to avoid 'choking'. 'Imagery and target awareness are created in the right side of the brain', says Dr Crews.

When the left brain is dominant, the competitor becomes self-aware. 'What am I doing?' 'Do I have the right lead?' 'I always miss teal.' It is this kind of thinking that results in 'choking'.

Dr Crews has developed a concept referred to as 'The Balanced Brain'. Balancing brain activity is essential to a good performance as a competitor. This is not something you can develop overnight. You need to apply pressure during your practice. It does not have to be extreme, even something as simple as a small wager with another shooter is enough to significantly increase brain activity.

The following is Dr Crews' recommended pre-shot routine to help balance brain activity and avoid 'choking':

Start with a deep breath, always a simple but effective first step. One big inhale and exhale clears your mind and helps you to focus.

1. Visualise the shot/target. (Imagery)
2. Recall a favourite song. (Rhythm and Timing)
3. Imagine a feeling of 'YES'. (The trigger to 'Yes, I can')
4. Picture a sense of 'Success'. (Accomplishment.)

The following word cues do not work:

1. 'Don't' (instead 'Do' or 'Can')
2. 'Should' (instead think 'Want')
3. 'Just' (instead of 'Just do it', think 'Do it!')

The following pre-shot steps are proven to energise both hemispheres of the brain to enhance performance:

1. Take a second longer to stare at your visual hold when preparing to make a shot. This will allow time for your subconscious to gather everything you need to create the correct movement to the target – Quiet Eye Phenomenon. Do not do anything conscious during this look, simply put your eyes on the visual hold, 'pause and dwell'. Ensure that the focal point is stable and not drifting about. This initiates the Quiet Eye Phenomenon.
2. As you go through your pre-shot routine, check out each part with a 'YES'. The 'YES' signifies that the action is done and there is no need to go back and check. When there is nothing left to check, call for the target and commence your swing.
3. Complete your imagery. This means not only seeing the target in the air, but sensing it flying. Break it, but follow the pieces to the ground. This helps complete the programming of the brain.
4. If you become distracted or lose focus during your routine, START OVER. Do not try to fix it. Stop and start again from the beginning.

Of course, you cannot merely memorise these cues then hope to put them to use the next time you are under pressure. They must be practised to become automatic and that means creating pressure on the practice field. In reality, performing under pressure is just good stress management.

To achieve this, you need to find an exercise to reduce left brain analytical activity and increase right brain rhythm and motion. In effect, an ideal performance state is achieved when both hemispheres of the brain are in balance.

A simple exercise for achieving this is to utilise a balancing board. This is simply a board that has a pivot or ball in the centre that creates a see-saw. To get the board to remain steady and horizontal while standing on it requires a combination of both muscular and mental balance. This balance board exercise is well known in sports therapy and rehabilitation. It is now being utilised to great benefit to enhance specific sports training. All of the professional sports that are using this simple device in their training regimes find that the players become better coordinated, faster and fitter after using the balancing board on a regular basis.

If you would like to imitate the actions of the champions, to see the target better, bigger, slower, make a more coordinated smooth, controlled and powerful swing to the target, then get balanced, both physically and mentally.

The Quiet Eye and Balanced Brain Phenomenon is an extraordinary concept. Beyond well-practiced mechanics, these are the next steps to achieving your peak performance.

Any new skill takes practice. There is a need to develop muscle memory for the mechanical skills, allowing the subconscious to perform the act without input or conscious effort from ourselves. Learning to concentrate to the exclusion of all distractions is hard work. At this intensity, concentration can only be maintained for brief periods and you need to practise its management.

Find the correct sequence to move from broad to narrow focus in the same manner. This training must involve actual shooting. Concentration is an essential part of straight shooting but is only that – a part. It must be learned and built into the overall shooting action and practised until the moves are made unconsciously.

The three domestic disciplines are one hundred target competitions, but Trap and Skeet have a natural rhythm which assists in switching concentration on and off. When it is your shot, you take it and then there is a paced time until you shoot again. This allows you to develop a routine where turning concentration on and off is more easily managed.

Relax after your turn and then begin a gradual rebuilding of concentration. Watch the target immediately preceding your next shot. Your concentration should peak when your shot routine starts and relax once the shot has been taken.

Sporting Clays presents different challenges as there is little, if any, rhythm to the shooting. As stations are shot in multiple targets with the distance, speed and angle constantly changing, it is very easy to let your concentration drift from narrow to broad focus during the shooting.

If you treat a round as if it is a One Hundred–One Bird Competition, each one a separate tournament, you will find that this is the best way to manage your concentration in the haphazard rhythm of Sporting Clays. And, after all, you can only break the targets one at time. There are a few states of mind that get in the way of concentration:

Over confidence results in carelessness.
Superstition and rituals can be both negative and positive.
If being the first in a squad is lucky for you, and you find yourself number three, it will be negative. If you have faith in a particular brand of shell it will be positive for you – if you run out, negative. These are both distractions – try to build your game without them – just concentrate on each and every shot as an entirely independent and all-important task.

Develop a positive outlook and concentrate: expect to 'see the target–break the target' – every time you call for one.

There is only one thing to beat: that is the target. You do not have to beat the other competitors. Their success or failure does not affect your own score. Only you can win or lose a competition.

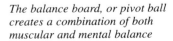

The balance board, or pivot ball creates a combination of both muscular and mental balance

Chapter 15
Competition

T he human being is by nature competitive. The shooter who is beginning starts out happy to break more clays than he misses, but this soon evolves into a desire to break them all! The next step in the progression is an awareness of scores and comparing them to those of friends and other squad members. The urge to compete finally increases to the point that it can only be satisfied by testing one's ability against that of others in open competition. If you have reached this stage, you are ready to take part in competition! Whether it is your first or your twenty-first, it is hard to describe the incredible buzz of being in a competition – the anticipation in the lead-up to the event, the preparation, the new edge to practice and the big day itself.

Clay Shooting is unique – there is no other sport where the amateur club player can compete alongside the professionals. There are no special rules, no favouritism – it's the same targets, with a class or handicap system in place, that ensures the level playing field. Your scores will be compared against others of the same level of skill. It is not uncommon for a squad to be made up of a mixture of abilities and for a novice to be shooting in the same squad as a National or International champion.

In Clay Shooting of all disciplines there are four levels of competition:

1. Club
2. Local (County or State)
3. National
4. International

And four Class Levels:

1. C
2. B
3. A
4. AA

In the USA they have a larger class system from E to AA including a Master Class. There are separate classes for Ladies, Veterans and Juniors.

There is a natural progression through the Class system. In the UK you start out unclassified, next you are placed in the Class appropriate to your annual averages. In the USA, progress is through a punch system. Winning or placing in your Class moves you up in Class and, as your skill increases, you progress through the ranks.

Rules and Regulations

There are many disciplines, each with a Governing Body that set the rules for each individual discipline. These rules vary from country to country and it would be too complex to try to describe all the rules and regulations of the numerous disciplines in this chapter. So, in the appendix you will find a list of the names and contact details of all of the relevant Governing Bodies.

Let The Competition Begin!

When competition is the motivation for your practice; it sets the bar of your ability and provides the

challenges to improvement. There are three requirements to win a competition:

1. Attitude
2. Ability
3. Equipment

Once the decision is made to enter a competition, to do your best you need to properly prepare. The Army uses the training motto of the 5 Ps: 'Prior Planning Prevents Poor Performance'. This should become your mantra on the lead up to all competitions. Nothing should be left to chance and everything should be double checked and in place. It is the only way you can concentrate on the real job at hand: breaking more targets than the next guy!

There is a natural sequence of events in the lead-up to a competition. The following is the sequence I recommend:

1. **Plan ahead.** Learn, and practise the Rules and regulations of your chosen discipline. You should know them as well, if not better than, the referee.
2. **Plan the annual events** you intend to compete in early. Book well in advance. The major competitions are usually over-subscribed and if you wait too late you will not get in. Can you imagine all that practice and hard work wasted?
3. **Plan your practice.** Work on your weaknesses (feedback from shooting log book) and be sure to include pressure situations (See Chapter 13).
4. **Seek help and advice** from more experienced friends and club members. It is amazing how much information they will have gleaned from competition. They may have shot the venue before and can advise you on travel and distances, accommodation, terrain, weather, the club facilities and share other valuable information.
5. **Have all necessary equipment** and make sure it is in good condition. If anything needs to be replaced, do so well before an event and use it in practice. Never introduce something new and untested on the day of a competition.
6. **Learn from every event** that you enter. Keep a log of the events you shoot, the conditions of the competition, your competitors and your scores. Experience and success will increase in proportion to the number of competitions entered.
7. **Prepare for any weather.** Cover every eventuality in clothing, footwear and accessories.
8. **Allow good time for travel.** Plan to arrive early and, if possible, walk the course. Shoot the side events. Relax and both loosen and sharpen up. Balance calmness and alertness to find your optimum performance state.

Controlling Competition Stress

There are two states of mind experienced in competition – anticipation and apprehension. Both are created by stress. The secret to successful competitive shooting is the ability to convert the 'stress negatives' into 'stress positives'.

There are techniques that can be learned to achieve this ability. These techniques are not unique to the top competitors – anyone can learn them. They can help control, choking, jitters, self-consciousness, anger, lack of confidence and all of the other emotions that can ruin a good performance.

You need to develop a 'Winning Attitude'. This is not simply an all-out determination to win… nine times out of ten the all-out attitude generates too much pressure and performances suffer. You will, naturally, be trying too hard.

You really need to learn to get out of your own way and let your training and preparation kick in and do the job for you. Too often we create unreasonable expectations for ourselves; this can crank up the pressure that causes stress. Learn there is only one person to compete against and that is: yourself!

A major competition attracts hundreds of entries. If you set your goal to win it all, that is applying unreasonable expectations and pressure. If your goal is to shoot to the best of your ability – to beat your best ever score – that would be reasonable! And, you never know… your best might be good enough to win it all.

I have seen friends and fellow-competitors create so much pressure for themselves with their unreasonable expectations, that on the first station they trembled so badly, they had trouble putting the shells in the gun! Pressure must be controlled and channeled – it is essential to 'getting us up'! It can actually sharpen our vision and reflexes. But this control only comes with experience. The more you compete, the better you become at controlling and channelling pressure. You should always attempt to complete a practice at a level above your ability. Your expectations will be less and the experience gained will be of immense benefit when you are in regular competition.

There is a fine line between anticipation and apprehension. Take, for example, a competitor who acts as if he doesn't care about the outcome – he even laughs when he misses. This is his way of deflecting or trying to remove the pressure of his fear of failure… and this causes him to lose.

The competitor who has learned to control pressure… to channel it, shoots with intent. He applies maximum effort on every shot, regardless of whether he is winning or losing. He never gives up! Each target is important – not his score or where he places. This attitude you should develop. Always shoot each target one at a time, station by station. By all means check your score card to ensure that the referee noted the correct score, but don't count the total as you go. Try to build the best personal score that you can, putting all thoughts of winning from your mind. Good scores are the direct result of the amount of effort you apply to your shooting. A mediocre effort will seldom win a competition whereas a gargantuan effort more often than not, will.

Everyone attempts to win, however, it is recognised that, at different times, the same amount of effort can have different results. Why is it that trying your best can sometimes not be enough? Simply put, you have to harness both the mechanical and mental to perform your best. This is a demanding and tiring task. We are only capable of concentrating for short bursts of time. A more frequent cause of lost concentration is, that we try to concentrate for too long a period of time. For example, while waiting your turn you attempt to concentrate on every target thrown. By the time your turn comes, you are mentally exhausted! Your mind wanders and a poor performance is the result.

You must learn to isolate the things worth concentrating on and be able to switch off and relax between these bouts of mental exertion. Keep your thoughts to a minimum up to the act of shooting. It is impossible to think of everything and still shoot well. Apply your concentration to just one specific part of your shooting. Selectively directing your concentration will help you sustain a good performance throughout a competition. The set sequences in Trap and Skeet offer a natural rhythm which is conducive to concentration management; Sporting Clays' more discombobulated rhythms, break up concentration. Because of the large number of targets shot at one time and the down-time between stations, it is easy to let your concentration drift.

For example, in the time it takes to shoot ten singles or five pairs, unwanted thoughts can break into your concentration. 'I will straight the stand if I shoot this last pair.' Next thing you know, you have missed the last target! Or, with two stations to go, you add up your score and realise 'If I can run the last two stations, I could win'. You might as well just tear up your score card! Your concentration is lost and so is the competition!

There are many other scenarios on this theme and I'm sure you recognise these lapses that cause a miss. It is only by competing and understanding how they happen, that you can learn to control them.

Focusing Techniques

Finding a technique or rhythm to help maintain your focus through a one hundred bird competition is as essential as acquiring a gun.

Divide and Conquer

The best advice I got a long time ago was to break the competition into smaller, equal parts: a one hundred-bird competition should be tackled as three thirty-bird shoots and a ten-bird Pool Shoot. Trap and Skeet should be shot as four twenty-five bird competitions.

This technique breaks the total into more psychology-manageable numbers for us to deal with. Consider how much easier it is to imagine shooting twenty-five straight, as opposed to one hundred straight. 'Divide and conquer' is one excellent way to maintain your concentration in competition.

The One-Bird Competition

My approach is, they are all one-bird competitions. You should take each target one at time. See the target – break the target. Concentrate on each shot as an independent and all-important target and forget about everything else…especially your score!

The One-Man Competition

You will miss. Accept it, and get over it. It is history. Nothing you can do will change the fact that you missed, but to dwell on it is to lose focus and miss again. Remember that what is happening to you is happening to everyone else. If the targets are tough, they are just as tough for them. If the wind is gusting and the rain pouring, they are standing in it too.

If you can learn to concentrate on your game, groove your routine. Work to develop a style where you relax between shots before you get ready for the next target. Give every shot your maximum attention. Regard each target as the first shot of the competition. Target by target is the secret to concentration.

Remember, there is only one person to beat, and that is you! You do not have to beat the other competitors. Their success or failure matters not a jot to your own score. The best shot in the world can do no more than break the next target in front of him. If you can learn to keep breaking the next thrown for you, there will be no one who can beat you. Adopt the mindset that your best score is your competitor, not the imaginary score of your opponent.

Beware of over confidence, it can result in carelessness!

The Fatigue Factor

Fatigue can have a major impact on your ability to concentrate. Several fatigue factors are:

1. Travel time to competition.
2. Accommodations.
3. Gun and equipment.
4. Fitness.
5. Course terrain and distance.
6. Waiting or standing time.
7. Weather conditions.

Conserve Energy

1. Be sure to wear loose cotton fabrics, layers are better than bulk.
2. Wear shoes or boots that offer good support and have good grip.
3. Carry your shells and equipment in a tote bag. Only put enough shells in your pocket to shoot the station (three or four extra for no-birds).
4. Place your gun in a rack or other safe location, whenever possible.
5. Stay hydrated, carry plenty of fluids.
6. Take along a couple of towels.
7. Rest when ever the opportunity present its self, particularly between stations.

Conserve your energy. Should you get in a shoot-off at the end of a long competition, it will pay great dividends.

Avoiding the 'Copy Cat' Syndrome

We are all prone to mimic or copy success. We imitate the leaders in any field of endeavour, hence the fashion trends in all aspects of our life from popular music, to clothing, cars or sports. The same is true in the shooting sports, but it is temptation to be avoided. You may copy the clothing or equipment of a top competitor, but when it comes to actually shooting the target, you copy them at your own risk. The visual acuity, timing and coordination of the shooting superstars are just that…super. You should trust your own instincts and shoot to your own best strengths.

1. Learn from the leader but do not just blindly follow. Work to your own game plan and strategy.
2. Break the target where it suits you, where you have chosen to break it in practice.
3. With pairs, consider the best sequence in which to take them.
4. Never ask, 'How much lead did you give that?' No two people will see the same lead picture.

Self-Analysis and Self-Correction

It is against the rules for a competitor to receive coaching or instruction while shooting in a competition. Therefore, it is important that, if you do miss, you know *where* you missed and why. It is essential to be able to self correct.

For example, if you missed high or over the top of the target: that is the FAULT. The CAUSE is coming out of the gun or head lifting. The CORRECTION is: remember to stay in the gun on the subsequent shots.

Watch the champions. If they miss, they do not curse their luck, the referee and the Gods of Shooting. No, they dig in, and reassess the target presentation, what went wrong, what to put right and then start again at the next target with a clean break.

Novice and club shooters just continue to shoot the station, missing the target in the same place every time, expecting a miracle to happen and the target to somehow break. Learning to self-analyse and self-correct is an essential competition skill. Learn this skill and when the inevitable miss happens, you can get yourself out of trouble.

Of course, there will be times when you just cannot work it out. When this happens, don't despair, learn from it, and work it out in practice. You will be able to get yourself out of trouble on that target the next time you see it in competition.

Analysing the Course

Target Irregularities

The targets thrown in Trap and Skeet are thrown to very rigid rules. Heights, angles and distances are established and must be adhered to exactly. To meet these requirements, the clay targets themselves must be manufactured to strict tolerances and consistent standards.

In Sporting Clays, there are guidelines for target size, but there are no rules for target presentations. They can be thrown at any speed, angle or distance. I personally believe that because of the randomness of the target presentations, clay manufacturers do not have to adhere to the same exacting standards demanded by the Trap and Skeet disciplines. This uneven quality often seen in Sporting Clay targets contributes to the randomness of trajectories and their occasional irregular flight paths.

The manual trap is quickly becoming obsolete. However, if a manual trap is operated by properly trained trappers, they can throw some excellent target presentations. If the trapper is inexperienced or rushed, they will sometimes fail to place the target against its stops and this can cause an irregular flight.

The automatic trap is not exempt from this problem either. Chipped or hairline-cracked targets or targets that have been incorrectly stored can all fly errant paths. Broken clay debris can mean that the target does not sit flush to the trap arm, further compounding the problem.

These irregular flight paths in Sporting Clays are often not recognised because of the non-conformity of target presentation. This is why each and every target path needs to be analysed and shot as a separate target. This can also explain the following situation: you are shooting well, on your way to straighting a station, you're into a groove…then one of these slightly 'off path and speed' targets gets thrown and you inexplicably miss! This is a scenario all-too-familiar to many competitors and one of the reasons why the perfect score of one hundred straight is so rare in major Sporting Clays competitions.

Reading the Course

With most competitions being shot over one hundred targets, you need to have a strategy to assist you in building a good score. It is not enough to just shoot the course station by station. If at all possible, walk the course before it is your time to shoot. Look at the position of traps and the stations…check the angles and distances of the targets to the gun at the break point.

Look for the target setter's tricks, like making the target transition right where you would like to shoot it. These can be subtle adjustments, from the use of the terrain or the tilting of the trap, these can fool you into thinking a target is doing one thing when it is actually doing something completely different. You can use your gun as a level or plumb line, holding it against the background, to see what a target is really doing.

Your Club versus their Club

You have shot at your local club for years. You know the type of targets thrown and the tricks the terrain can play. Here you can shoot consistently good scores, and now you feel you are shooting the kind of scores to win your class. You enter a major competition. Suddenly nothing seems to go right! You just cannot find your club form and you post a really poor score.

What occurred is not really a mystery. Consider your own course. It may be wooded with rolling hills and birds thrown at moderate ranges and you will have, unconsciously, adapted your technique to hit these target presentations. At the out-of-town competition, the course is set on a ground with little cover, as flat as a pancake, with targets at longer distances than you have ever shot.

Of course, you do not have the skills or the technique to tackle these targets. You have to learn to shoot all kinds of courses and all kinds of targets, in all kinds of weather if you are going to win your class at a major competition.

Competitors versus the Course

The top competitors have put in their time. They have travelled to competitions domestically and internationally. They have learned from every event, how to travel, rest, prepare and compete. They have kept a shooting log, in which they make notes and they refer to them in practice. The next time a particular venue hosts a major competition, they can refer to their log.

The top shots are constantly on the move, both at home and abroad, shooting all kinds of courses of all types of contours, shapes and descriptions. They encounter every variety of course design and learn all the tricks and tactics of distance, angle, transition or target mix they use in setting targets to beat the competitors. The top shots have years of experience and practice reading a course and adapting their technique to its requirements. It is not by accident or magical fairy dust that they are so good.

Reading the Stations

The game of competitive shooting is ten per cent physical and ninety per cent mental, from the shoulders up. You must learn to think your way through every competition, station by station. Read the course; get to know the targets and conditions that can affect your performance. You need to learn to think on every shot, not just automatically shoot the course station by station.

When you have the opportunity to watch a top competitor, try put yourself in his mind. Try to think *with* him…why has he chosen that choke, cartridge, set up, technique and method? Watch the order in which he breaks the targets. Don't just copy, blindly imitating, but learn from his approach. Adapt the ideas that can be learned to complement your own style and strengths.

Checks and Balances

A major competition is a complex mix of targets. The majority will be standards and midis. The specialty targets, the mini, battue, rocket, rabbit, chondel are used in the following combinations: on report and true pairs. These are set at a variety angles, speeds and distances.

Target presentations have now became a contest between the target setter and the top competitors and every Sporting Clays course will contain several targets designed to push shooting skills, both physical and ballistic, to the limit.

Realistically, the course builder has to find a balance in his design to accommodate the recreational and/or average competitor. So, an equal percentage of softer targets may be included with the tough ones, with the ideal course being won on, or just over, the class averages.

This should mean that not many targets are thrown farther than thirty yards. Twenty or twenty-five yards is more common; often there is a combination of targets thrown, with the softer bird as one of a pair. There will be another ten targets that are more difficult because of the target type and presentation, not because of the distance thrown. Once again, the tricky ones are usually combined with a more straight-forward target.

Bankers and Bonuses

In any competition, there is an average thirty/thirty-five hard target to sixty-five/seventy soft target distribution. The soft targets should be considered bankers and the hard targets, bonuses. You need to concentrate on breaking all of the soft targets. If there is a hard and soft target presentation and the soft target is the first of a pair, use both barrels to be sure you break the first target. Only move to the second target if you break the first with the first barrel.

Every hard target is a bonus, but the soft targets are where you build your score. It is all too easy to let your concentration slip on the soft targets. Believing they are so easy, you do not give them your full attention. You allow your mind to wander – to count scores, dream of winning or how 'so and so' is doing in your class.

We have to learn not to worry or pay so much attention to the long target that you end up missing what should have been a 'card-filler'. Failure to give the same attention to the banker shots that you would the hard targets, can cause an 'expensive' miss. Remember, your final score does not reflect the degree of the difficulty of the targets shot. One is just as valuable as another, point-wise, it was just easier to hit. Give these targets the same respect you would a forty-yard crosser…they are just as valuable.

Breaking more targets is accomplished through consistency and making sure you hit the soft targets. Don't lose focus trying to think your way through the hard ones. You can't forget about the hard shots, just consider them a bonus. They are set to separate the winners from the losers among the top competitors.

Until you reach Master Class, good averages and more punches are to be found in breaking the softer targets.

Straight the Station

This is a method that is very helpful in negotiating a Sporting Clays course. It works for every class of competitor, gives structure to each station and alleviates a great deal of the angst and pressure on the hard shots.

Considerer an 'A' class competitor: he needs to break a minimum of eighty targets to be in contention. By breaking the course down into the number of stations and dividing it into his desired total, on a ten station course he would need to break a minimum of eight targets per station to be in the running. He doesn't want to, but he could actually afford to miss two targets per station. Now, if he treats each station as a separate competition, he can work hard on shooting just one station straight.

Say at Station one he breaks nine targets. This means he has a one target credit on Station two. He could afford to miss three targets on Station two and still be on track for his desired minimum score. Then at Station two, he does straight the stand, now he can carry a credit of three targets to Station three, and so on. When he does come to a station that is particularly difficult, he hopefully has built up a sufficient number of credit points to make up for any shortcomings on the tough station.

This method of credits and debits removes a great deal of pressure, enabling you to confine your expectations to the far recesses of your mind, while systematically building a winning performance. Throughout the competition, you will be concentrating on hitting every soft target, building a credit to apply to the hard shots on the next station.

Competition Conclusions

Concentration is easily broken: no-birds, late pulls, delays while traps are filled, back-ups on stands, breakdowns, a dozen fellow-competitors watching…all these distractions, combined with the inevitable fatigue and anxiety inherent in any competition, can cause you to lose focus.

A one hundred bird competition in any discipline is extremely hard work…it can also be an exhilarating and rewarding endeavour. You can experience the satisfaction and enjoy the rewards that come from your steady improvement and growing confidence as a competitive clay shooter.

Remember, success is forged in the furnace of experience and practice.

Chapter 16
Fitness

'Fatigue Makes Cowards Of Us All'
Vincent Lombardi

What would you consider the greatest cause of missed targets? Wrong choke choice? Poor gun mount, lack of lead, off the line, choking in the shoot off? The list is endless and I am sure you can add your own excuses to it. Well, like the monkey puzzle, you would be right and wrong at the same time. In my opinion, one of the greatest reasons for missing is fatigue.

I have said many times that eighty per cent of all misses are caused by poor gun mount. Once the mechanics of the mount are learned and grooved, it is fatigue that is at the root of a poor gun mount. Fatigue can also be the source of many of the other causes of missing. I am not talking about the fatigue that arises from hard physical work or lack of sleep, but that creeping fatigue that, unnoticed, drains away the concentration and coordination that is a prerequisite to straight shooting. This gradual erosion of performance can be felt in:

1. Strength – muscular weakness.
2. Concentration – easily distracted.
3. Vision – unable to focus.
4. Hearing – prone to flinches.

Strength and Conditioning
Both our physical strength and our general conditioning affect our ability to maintain a correct stance and posture. The inability to maintain balance causes extra emphasis to be placed on the arms, with a corresponding sapping of strength. The arms get tired, and the gun mount, timing and reflexes all begin to suffer. Proper coordination comes from the ability of the hands to carry out the information transmitted from the eyes. The head is simply the chassis for the eyes (your cameras). If the neck is weak, the head will loll about. This, combined with impaired visual acuity, quickly makes it impossible to maintain hard focus on the target.

Concentration
With fatigue, a gradual decline in concentration will result in poor scores, this is most apparent when you travel to a competition.

Vision
Sharp eyesight is essential to good shooting. Fatigued eyes are a sure recipe for a poor performance. Be sure to give your eyes time to relax and recover , especially if you have to drive some distance to a competition.

Hearing
Fatigue can result in an increased sensitivity to loud noises. This can cause flinching and hesitancy, resulting in poor swing and timing. This problem can often be so subtle as to go unrecognised, with only unexplained poor scores to show for it.

Fit to Hit
In any squad of shooters of similar ability, those that are fit will out-shoot those who are not. Most top competitors consider a physical fitness regime to be a vital ingredient to their success. Next time you are at a

major competition, look at the physiques and physical conditioning of the Top Guns. You will soon notice that they are almost all, *Fit to Hit*.

Good physical conditioning is as important as gunfit, technique, mental strength, visual acuity, gun or cartridge selections. You will never shoot to your full potential until your physical condition is such that you can complete a major competition with enough 'gas in the tank' for the shoot-off.

Consider a major Sporting Clays championship contested over twelve to sixteen stations. It requires a piece of land some 150 acres to allow for safe shot fall-out zones and the adequate spacing of target presentations. The average competitor is required to walk at least one and a half miles, including walks to and from the car park and participation in the side events. Many like to walk the course to get a feel for the targets being presented. This adds up to an average of about three miles.

I realise that many of you will have buggies or golf carts but they bring their own impact to the equation. With the necessity to climb in and out of the cart some thirty-plus times, you may not walk as far, but the fatigue factor is still there.

Let's consider a worst-case scenario. You walk three miles over an average tournament time of four hours. The gun weighs eight pounds, add a bag containing a minimum of twenty pounds of shells, choke tubes, water, sun block, towel, gloves, glasses etc… So, let's say, thirty pounds carried, not in a well-designed and comfortable rucksack, but with one-third in a gun slip and two-thirds in a bag. Both have shoulder straps and the weight is badly distributed, unbalanced and inefficiently carried the three-plus miles. Then consider that all of this kit is put down and picked up thirty-two-plus times over the course of a four-hour event. Another big consideration is the standing-around time. Of the four hours, you will be standing and waiting your turn at the various stations most of the time. Ask anyone who stands all day on the job just how tiring it is.

In addition to all this activity, you will remove your gun from the rack or its slip and if you have a trial mount and swing before each shot, you will make over two hundred gun mounts and swings. With an eight pound gun that means lifting and swinging approximately 2,080 pounds or over one ton in weight!

If you take into account how far you travelled to the event, if you slept badly in a strange motel room, the event's duration, (maybe more than one day?) and the number of games you shot in the preliminary events, you can begin to see that Sporting Clays requires a high level of stamina and fitness. Ignore fitness and fatigue will set in and have a major impact on your performance.

The top competitors shoot every week, both in practice and competition. On their way to the top, they shoot many thousands of rounds per year. This, in its own way, is progressive resistance training. In effect, they shoot themselves into being fit. Many, however, still choose to supplement their shooting practice with an exercise regime to combat the fatigue inherent in major competition.

The average competitor cannot afford the time, targets, cartridges or competition fees to shoot themselves into fitness. But a simple exercise regime will definitely improve their scores. If put in place and stuck to, a fitness programme will reap dividends during next year's tournaments.

Fitness and Conditioning

Are the world's top guns supermen? No, but they *have* shot their way to the top. Consider how many thousands and thousands of times they have lifted and swung their guns in practice and competition. I know of top performers who in the early stages of their careers were shooting thirty thousand rounds a year in practice alone! By sheer frequency of practice, they gained the required stamina and fitness needed to win a major competition. If they had introduced a fitness regime into their training at the beginning of their shooting career, I personally believe they would have reached the top and won more majors shoots sooner.

Strength and conditioning play a vital role in the physical and mental aspects of any sport, and shooting is no exception. The fundamentals of correct stance, posture and gun mount that place the bones and muscles in their optimum position for ease of speed and movement (bio-mechanically efficient) are a must, but muscles must be developed for strength and endurance. By strengthening the major muscle groups involved in shooting, the competitor will not so easily concede targets to the effects of Creeping Fatigue Syndrome.

Physical training on its own cannot make you a better shot, but combined with the proper mechanics of shooting, it can have significant impact on your progress and improvement.

The Benefits of Being Fit to Hit

The Three Major Improvements:

1. Improves grip, hold and swing.
2. Improves endurance and fatigue resistance.
3. Improves relaxation and promotes a positive mental attitude.

These three improvements all increase your ability to hold and control a shotgun from the ready position through swing, mount and follow through. Your reaction times will become better coordinated and smoother. These benefits are especially important to the beginner, junior and female shooter.

The Eight Additional Benefits

1. Increased energy.
2. Better stress management.
3. Improved confidence in yourself and your abilities.
4. Suppression of doubts and anxiety control.
5. Increased ability to relax and control tenseness.
6. Better sleep patterns.
7. Better muscle condition and endurance.
8. Better weight control.

Having recognised the improvements and benefits derived from introducing exercise into our training regime, we need to consider what form this training should take.

There are as many methods of cardiovascular training as there are opinions on the best ways to shoot a springing teal. All work, though some work better than others. There is the traditional weight lifting or Marine Corps resistance training and, of course, there is swimming, cycling, aerobics and jogging. All work well and will improve your physical fitness and well-being, however, they do not specifically target the particular fitness requirements of shotgun shooting.

Targeted Training

The muscles used in mounting and swinging the gun, if performed correctly, are many. Starting with the feet, moving up through the legs to the hips, waist, torso, shoulders, and finishing with the arms, multiple muscle groups are used to get the gun comb to arrive at the correct position on the cheek, at the Zycomatic Process. The arms and hands play another vital role in the impact of recoil, absorbing much of this score-wrecking force.

The Shotgun Muscle Groups

We need to recognise the muscles that we use in shooting, to better understand their action and impact on more efficient shooting. Shotgunning utilises more of the body's muscles than the other aiming sports like rifle, pistol and archery. When shooting the FITASC and International disciplines where the gun-down position is mandatory, even more muscle action is required. Muscles that are properly exercised react to stimuli very quickly and powerfully.

The perfect shooting action begins with the feet which instigate initial rotation, continues up through the legs, hips and torso and culminates with the arms and shoulders delivering the gun to the cheek where the neck supports the head in the optimum position to allow hard focus on the target. Let us consider each of these muscles groups in their order of action.

1. **Gastronemious** Location: calves and lower legs. Function: walking and lifting of the heels. Begin the rotation of the body.
2. **Biceps Femoris** Location: the hamstrings, rear of thighs. Function: lifting of lower leg while walking. Continue the rotation of the body.
3. **Quadriceps** Location: front of thighs. Function: support the upper body, while walking. Provide the drive and push to continue rotation of the body in the direction of the target.
4. **Erectors** Location: lower back. Function: maintain the body in an upright position. Give the whole shooting action stability.
5. **Obliques** Location: sides of the waist. Function: rotate the body at the waist. Impacts our ability to shoot crossing targets and maintain balance throughout the shooting action.
6. **Abdominals** Location: abdomen. Function: maintain the correct posture to mount the gun and aid the obliques in rotation.
7. **Lattissimus Dorsi** Location: sides of upper back. Function: combined with the biceps, hold the gun into the body and bring the gun down from the shoulder position after firing.
8. **Trapezius** Location: between neck and shoulders. Function: shrug or lift the shoulders. Start the arms up and commence the gun mount.
9. **Deltoids** Location: side and front of the shoulders. Function: lift the arms, and maintain their position and that of the gun at the correct height – the major muscles in the gun mount and swing.
10. **Triceps** Location: rear of upper arm. Function: extend the arms, give the gun direction towards the target during the mount – major muscles in the gun mount and swing.
11. **Biceps** Location: front of upper arm. Function: working in opposition to the triceps, the biceps lift and hold the gun into the shoulder – major muscles in the gun mount and swing.
12. **Flexors and Extensors** Location: forearm, both under and over the lower arm. Function: work the hands, both gripping and extending. Grip gun and move it to the target, and absorb a good amount of recoil.
13. **Pectorals** Location: chest. Function: draw the arms together forming a proper frame for mounting the gun.
14. **Neck** Location: both front and rear of the neck. Function: to place the head in the correct position for the stock comb to be placed in the cheek at the Zycomatic process. Front muscles lean the head forward to the correct position while the back muscles stretch to help place and maintain this position. The head and neck should not move during the shooting action but should flow with the rest of the body's movements, ensuring that the eyes remain locked on the target. The neck muscles do not actually physically work, so they do not require resistance exercises, but stretching exercises are beneficial.

When making a shot, if proper form is shown, nearly all of the muscle groups play their role in maintaining both balance and smoothness. This is visually evident in the action of the top performers. Their proper form is present from the first target to the last of a competition. The Top guns are truly 'Fit To Hit'.

If you are still doubtful of the necessity to be fit to shoot well, then please consider this: Tom Migdalski in his book, *The Complete Book of Shotgunning Games*, writes 'If increased strength and reduced fatigue impact only five per cent of your shooting success, are you that good that you can afford to miss five targets out of every one hundred?' Migdalski has far greater in-depth knowledge on the subjects of nutrition, strength and conditioning for the shooting games than I ever will. I urge anyone who is prompted to begin an exercise programme to improve their shooting, to get a copy of his book and read it cover to cover.

With our busy life styles, attempting to spend several hours a week in the gym is impractical, if not

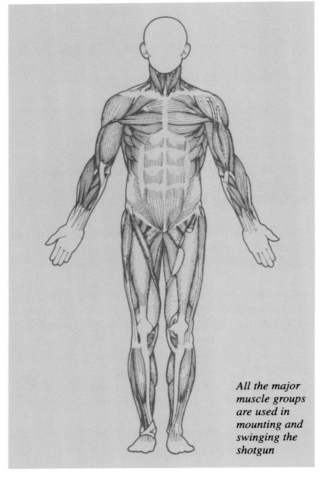

All the major muscle groups are used in mounting and swinging the shotgun

impossible, for most of us. What we need is a simple workout that increases our strength and endurance, without consuming an unmanageable amount of our time. The equipment should be compact, light and portable so that it may be included in your shooting kit when on the road. This rules out conventional resistance training tools such as free weights or machines.

In any muscle injury, low impact resistance training is a prerequisite to recuperation. A variety of equipment has been designed and used for this and has many advantages over more traditional methods. Many of these techniques have found their way into professional sports training, the balancing board and resistance ball being two of the better known.

One that lends itself perfectly to our requirements for shooting training is the rubber band resistance workout. A full kit is light and takes up little space on the road or at home. Because of their method of use, they allow us to use them to target specific muscle groups and work them in the action we use when shooting.

Using these rubber bands I have put together a simple, low impact resistance workout that takes only ten minutes and can be performed at home, in the office or on the road. If carried out three times per week, combined with a sensible diet and lifestyle, this workout will definitely add targets to your score, by making you 'Fit to Hit'.

Follow these simple rules to achieve maximum benefit from your workout:

1. Muscles need oxygen, so breathe normally.
2. For maximum strength and flexibility be sure to use the full range of motion for each exercise.
3. Be smooth; use a steady, slow motion when performing each exercise.
4. Emphasise this smooth, slow motion on the lowering part of each exercise. A controlled pace is most efficient.
5. Always maintain good posture while performing the exercises as shown in the pictures.
6. As with any exercise programme, consult your physician before beginning.

Start with one set of fifteen repetitions (Beginner).
Progress to two sets of twelve repetitions (Intermediate).
Progress to three sets of ten repetitions (Advanced).
Do not progress to the next set of exercises until you can comfortably carry out the full routine of your current level.

This is my recommended basic training programme. The exercises and programme can be customised to fit your personal fitness goals. It is essential that you rest between sets to get the full benefits from this work-out. Always space your workouts by one complete day, this will allow your muscle groups adequate time to rest and rebuild between workouts.

Rear Deltoid Pull
Grasp handles, hold in front of chest. Stretch hands out to sides, hold, and return to start then repeat.

Seated Rows
Sit on floor, extend legs, place one end of band around feet, grasp handles and extend arms over knees. Keep your back straight, pull handles to your chest, squeezing your shoulder blades. Return to start and repeat.

Seated Rows

Bicep Curl
Stand up, place one handle under your right foot, grip other in right hand, palm up, hand at thigh. Curl hand up to chest, squeeze and hold. Return to start and repeat. Switch hands after each set.

Tricep Kickback
In lunge position, grasp handles in each hand. Left fore-arm above knee and right hand at right hip, palm back. Extend right arm straight back and hold. Return to start and repeat. Switch hands and sides after each set.

Chest Press
Twist the band once, place around back and grasp handles, hands to side of chest, elbows at ninety degrees, extend arms forward then pull back to start, squeezing chest.

Bicep Curl

Rear Deltoid Pull

Chest Press

Squat Thrust

Stand in the middle of the training tube. With feet shoulder-width apart, bring handles up behind the arms and rest on shoulders. Maintaining a straight back and tight stomach, smoothly and slowly squat down until the thighs are parallel with the floor, making sure your knees do not extend over your toes. Return to start position and repeat.

Upright Rowing

Stand with the feet in the middle of the tube and hold handles in each hand. Start exercise with palms facing back towards your body. Pull upward with elbows out and handles up, close to your body, until the handles touch your chin and your elbows are level with your ears.

Specific Shooting-Specific Exercises

Opposing Hand Resistance

Helps in the absorption of recoil through the hands and arms, an essential requirement in control and gun mounting. Take the training band and twist it double. Take one handle in each hand and adopt your shooting stance and posture with your hands positioned as if holding the gun. Now pull your hands apart while making a smooth gun mounting action.

Opposing Hand Resistance

Rotation and Swing Resistance

Place your right foot in the loop and, taking the handle in your left hand, adopt your shooting stance, holding your hands in the gun mount position. Now, extend your left hand and make a practice mount, swinging to your left. Return to start position and repeat, swinging to your right. For the left-handed, please mirror the instructions.

Gun Mount Strength Resistance

Attach two training tubes to the foot loop, place right foot in the loop, then take both handles and adopt your shooting stance with your hands in the gun mount position. Now make your gun mount and swing, keeping both hands working in unison, swinging to your left and bringing the hands fully to the mounted position. Return to the start position and repeat to the right. For the left-handed, please mirror the instructions.

Rotation and Swing Resistance

Gun Mount Resistance

Be sure to perform all of these exercises slowly, smoothly and correctly. Pause at the peak of each movement and hold for a second before relaxing and repeating the exercise. This way you will achieve the maximum benefit from your Shooting Exercise Programme.

Chapter 17
Ladies

Being a female in a male-dominated sport can be intimidating. So it is refreshing that there has been a noticeable increase in the number of women taking up clay shooting. The introduction to this sport can be via encouragement from a parent, partner, or boyfriend, while others give shotgunning a try simply to join their partner at the gun club on weekends. What's important is that the first introduction to shooting is both enjoyable and educational.

What Sporting Clays offers the lady shooter, either recreationally or competitively, is the opportunity to have fun, even giving the men a run for their money on even terms. It is not a matter of who can lift the most weight, run faster or jump higher – but just hand and eye coordination skills as in catching a ball. Given the right start with the right equipment, some practical instruction, and the determination to practice, there is no reason why women cannot compete on equal terms with men.

It is often the introduction to this sport that proves most difficult for women. Far too many ladies are put off by an unsuccessful or even painful start. This can easily be avoided with an understanding of the extra – or rather different – challenges the majority of women face at the outset and how to overcome them.

More and more women are discovering the challenge of breaking clays

There are several areas that cause the initial introduction to shotgunning to be a make-or-break situation for women. Most boys, at some point, have had a toy gun. If from a shooting family, this would have been replaced, with age and responsibility, by an air gun and eventually, a small-gauge shotgun. This experience with guns gives men an advantage when they begin clay shooting because they are already familiar with the weight, handling and shooting of a shotgun.

Only a small percentage of women have had these opportunities, and most come to the sport in their late teens or older and have a natural apprehension of shotguns. Even if it is used recreationally in the same manner as a tennis racquet or golf club, it is still a lethal weapon. This unfamiliarity with guns is the first hurdle to jump, but approached correctly, the foundations can be laid for a smooth introduction and steady progression in the sport.

Clay target shooting is one of the warmest and friendliest of sports. Can you imagine walking into a golf club and announcing that you were a beginner and would like to play? You would not find many scratch players rushing to help. Not so at the clay club! You could be maimed in the stampede to help, particularly if you are a female. A lady may want to begin as a spectator, observing a competition. This would help in understanding the sport and its challenges as well as provide an opportunity to ask questions. With some experience as an observer, it is easier to see how instruction is designed to provide the tools to break clays.

Women and Eye Dominance

Women are multi-taskers, usually able to carry out several activities at one time. Nature pre-programmed them this way to be able to cope with nursing and raising children and still maintaining the 'flight or fight' survival awareness.

In the brain the *corpus callosum* is a network of nerves that transmits messages between the right and left halves of the brain. It is better integrated in women than in men, enabling women to use both sides of the brain at one time. However, this ability has a downside: almost ninety per cent of women are either cross-dominant or have central vision. Eye dominance must be checked and if

There is a higher incidence of cross-dominance in women than in men

opposite the shoulder shot off, the options are to change shoulders or obscure the dominant eye.

The most simple and effective cure for cross-dominance is the application of a small piece of opaque tape cut in a triangular shape and placed on the lens of the shooting glasses over the dominant eye. So when the head is on the stock, ready to take the shot, the tape is directly in front of the centre of the pupil. The advantage is that until the shot is ready to be taken, the brain is receiving binocular signals and can better identify the target in space and distance.

Under supervision, with a known-to-be-unloaded shotgun, the lady shooter will learn its parts, their function, and how to open and close the gun. Next, she should move on to loading the shotgun using snap caps (dummy cartridges), then firing it, and unloading it. It is at this time that safety and the Rules of clay shooting are learned, along with the basic skills needed to shoot a simple target. This information will build confidence, familiarisation, and knowledge, helping to overcome the natural apprehension felt when first learning to shoot.

Gun Fit

Overall, gunstocks are built to fit men. Alteration is required to make them comfortable for most ladies to shoot. Stock fit for ladies is not simply a matter of a shorter stock as there are obvious differences in body shape between the sexes. Ladies have a different skeletal shape to men, lighter and more petite; everything is scaled down, including bone length and diameter and muscle mass. This means ladies move differently – compare the actions of a man and a woman throwing a ball.

These differences impact on a woman's choice of gun, its fit and the gun mounting action. High cheekbones and a long neck, requires a gun to have a high comb to achieve proper alignment of the eye and rib without having to drop or roll the head. With many women, a Monte Carlo stock works well.

Small hands mean that the thick grips and forward trigger placements of some modern competition guns are not suitable for ladies. A slimmer, semi-pistol grip is needed to give proper comfort and control, with a trigger that is adjustable forward or backward.

The shape and soft tissue of a woman's chest requires careful adjustment to the pitch (angle of the rear portion of the butt that contacts the shoulder) on the stock. Too much pitch and all of the recoil forces are concentrated through the toe (bottom of the butt) of the gun. Not only is this painful and bruising, but can result in twisting or canting the gun or, worse, placing the butt of the stock out onto the bicep. This fitting problem can be further compounded by the adjuster or buckle on the bra strap. This clip is often exactly where the toe of the gun rests, adding to the discomfort and bruising.

A minimum of six to eight degrees of pitch is recommended, along with a sports bra with no strap adjustments and a KICK-EEZ recoil pad to further displace recoil. While it is not possible to lay down any hard and fast rules, years of gun fitting have given me these yardstick dimensions for the average lady shooter:

Length of Pull: 12¾ inches to 14½ inches with negative pitch of six to eight degrees
Drop: at precisely where the face contacts the top of the comb – 1⅜ inches, give or take ⅛ inch
Cast – ⅛ inch at the heel, ⅜ inch at the toe.

Gun Weight

'It's so heavy!' is one of the most common comments I hear when ladies take part in a first lesson. Yes, the sporting shotgun is heavy, designed to be carried a little and shot a lot. The average of 7½ to 8 lb, combined with what really is an unusual position to both hold and support weight – at arm's length – leads ladies to shoot off the back foot. Because of the weight of the gun, women and other shooters of small stature tend to lean backwards, pushing their hips forward, using their upper body to counter the gun's weight.

The length of the gun really impacts on its perceived weight. If the butt stop is too long, the gun is farther from the axis of the body, increasing this subconscious need to push the hips forward and transfer more weight to the back foot to counter-balance the weight of the gun.

Proper posture is required to absorb recoil, create better access to the cheekbone and create a good pocket for the gun in the shoulder. This calls for a slight inclination or angling of the body towards the target. Simply shifting the hips backward achieves this proper posture. Exercises may be required, aimed specifically at the shooting action. These will increase strength and teach the lady shooter to mount the gun firmly and consistently into the same proper place in her cheek and shoulder (see Chapter 16).

Gun Selection

A lot can be achieved with proper gun selection. A twenty gauge semi-automatic shotgun, particularly with an alloy action, is a great choice for a lady, offering reduced weight and recoil.

If strength will allow, a light twelve gauge with a suitably light cartridge would really be my recommendation. The margin for error is so much more with a twelve gauge than a twenty gauge and success is so important for the beginner.

The Beretta AL391 youth model

Cartridge

Recoil is controlled by the combination of the gun's weight and cartridge velocity. Use the heaviest gun that can be comfortably controlled with the softest-shooting cartridge.

Recoil Reaction

Recoil anxiety is always an element of that first experience or lesson. The *anticipation* of recoil can cause as many flinches and trigger freezes as the *actual* recoil.

The control of recoil is achieved by a suitable gun that is properly fitted, lighter cartridge selection, good ear protection, correct posture, good positioning of the hands for control and grip, and a solid gun mount.

Clothing and Accessories

Most shooting vests are designed to fit the male form, with ladies' models simply coming in smaller sizes and brighter colours. This makes no allowance for the fit required for women to be comfortable and to perform at their best. The typical cut of a vest: big in the shoulders, adequate across the chest, then falling straight to the hips, does not accommodate the shape of the female form.

This poor fit at the waist and torso means that surplus cloth is gathered under the armpits when a lady attempts to mount the gun, making it snag or hang up. This male orientation in design is apparent in guns, earmuffs, earplugs and shooting glasses too. However, there are now several companies that offer shooting clothing especially for women. They have recognised the different needs of the lady shooter. In a pinch, if you are good with a needle and thread, you can restyle an off-the-rack vest to fit better by removing the surplus material. Even a safety pin can work wonders.

Today's lady shooter has a wide choice of equipment

A simple pair of earplugs that fit can be difficult to find, earmuffs, gloves and shooting glasses equally so. Do not compromise on quality, but be sure to find those accessories that do fit. By trial and error, you can find the shooting equipment that offers the best fit and the most comfort.

Lead

I cannot recall where I read it or who wrote it, but I remember this remark caused quite a debate among instructors. The statement was: 'women see target lead at the barrel, whereas men see it at the target'. There is no doubt that, regardless of gender, we each have our own individual perceptions of lead or forward allowance, and learning what it is for us is an essential ingredient of successful shooting. I cannot say that women see lead in a different way than men, but I have found that they need a little more help in understanding what they *are* seeing.

Trying to describe what you see to another person, particularly one just beginning to shoot, is tough. With ladies, I have found a simple method that appears to work and is easily understood.

I start out working with a simple incoming target, like a low-house station two on a Skeet field. Now, I know the picture that breaks this target. I have the lady shoot the target and, regardless of the miss or hit, ask her what she saw. I do this while showing a to-scale target at the end of the muzzle. I then ask her to adjust the picture to match the one she saw. One or two shots in this way, and I know how she sees lead. Be it in inches or feet, this becomes her own individual unit of lead.

I then ask if there is something in her everyday life that is comparable in length to what she perceived. This can be anything from a car to a half or full loaf of bread. From then on, simply helping the shooter to learn her individual picturing is easy. I just ask her to increase or decrease the forward allowance by her own perception of lead, such as 'give it two full loaves on the next shot', or 'reduce it to one on the next shot'.

Gun Mount for Ladies

Finally, I offer two tips for the lady shotgunner looking for extra targets. Get a five-pound dumbbell and, holding it in your left hand (if you are a right-shoulder shooter), extend your arm to the natural shooting position and begin tracing lines and shapes until the muscles begin to complain.

Repeat this exercise as often as you can. Keep one dumbbell in the office and another at home and whenever you have five minutes on the phone or are watching television, exercise. This will increase the strength in the leading hand, ensure a better gun mount, give you more control of the gun and develop the ability to establish the all-important eye-target relationship.

The second tip is, if shooting gun down, hold the gunstock in the ready position an inch or two off or away from your body. This way you will avoid hitting your chest and your mount will be unimpeded and much smoother.

A Final Word for Ladies

The requirements that let a lady compete on an even playing field with the men are a structured introduction, learning and understanding the fundamentals, the correct gun properly fitted, a soft-shooting cartridge, then exercising and shooting to learn a smooth and controlled move to the target.

Chapter 18
Young Guns

E very parent or grandparent knows the pleasure of sharing a hobby with their children or grandchildren. Spending time together, passing on experiences, is a gift that will last both adult and child a lifetime.

The enthusiastic clay shooter is no different and is usually quick to encourage his children to join him in his favourite sport...and this is where it can all go wrong. Today with the multitude of recreational activities that children can participate in, from the Internet and video games to conventional sports, the child can be an unwilling participant. Sometimes they only participate to make or keep their parents happy.

To begin to teach a child to shoot, first be sure that your child really wants to learn to shoot. Please do not confuse this with

The big shot is a little shot who kept shooting

simply letting them 'have a go' at it, which is an entirely different scenario. However, much of this advice is still applicable. Here I am addressing the introduction to the sport for a young gun who may intend to shoot competitively.

Safety Comes First!
Teach them the safety rules and show them competent and correct gun handling. Never, ever leave them alone, even for a minute, while at the shooting grounds. There are dangerous out-of-bound areas and potentially dangerous mechanical equipment is everywhere. Keep them with you at all times!

Equipment
Just like the lady shooters, young shots will have to experiment to find equipment that fits and works for them. Ear and eye protection is mandatory but much can be done to alter adult clothing to fit and function better for a young shooter.

What Is the Best Age to Start?
This should be more accurately stated what is the best size to start shooting? Children need encouragement and progress – this comes from success. If they do not have sufficient strength to control and swing a gun consistently, they will not achieve this success. They will quickly become frustrated and disillusioned with the sport, usually going back to something at which they are already successful.

Regardless of what age the child is, they should be a minimum of one hundred pounds to be able to properly control and swing a gun. I have had eight-year-olds who could do so and twelve-year-olds who could not. There are no hard and fast rules on age but there are definite criteria as to size and strength.

There is nothing worse than seeing a young person leaning back, trembling with effort, trying to support a too-heavy gun, attempting to shoot an unsuitable target. It is unfair and unkind to subject them to this. It is far better to allow them to accompany you as you shoot, learning safety, proper gun handling as well as the etiquette of the gun club and the rules of competition. Then, as they build their strength and practise correct gun handling, they can move on to learning the correct method of the mount and swing. Their progress, when they are strong enough to manoeuvre the gun, will be swift and enjoyable and they will be better shots, all for a little patience on the part of the enthusiastic parent.

Which Is the Best Gun for the Beginner?

There is very little difference in the weight of guns and gauges of the .410, twenty-eight and twenty gauges, but there is a great difference in the pattern they throw. The twenty bore in this case is the best, offering the optimum weight-of-gun-to-pattern ratio. On the other hand, if the child is strong enough and can competently control and swing a twelve gauge, then let them do so as soon as possible. As progress is made, you will see that only one gauge is used in major competition and that is for good reason; the twelve gauge is king in range and pattern.

Recoil is one of the biggest challenges that faces the young gun and recoil is controlled, not by shooting a small gauge, but by the cartridge selection, the type of gun and its fit.

The semi-automatic Berretta Urika 91 Youth Model in twenty bore, fitted with a KICK EEZ rubber recoil pad is the gun of choice. Combine this with a light load of 24 grams (7/8 of an ounce) and, if possible, no more than 1,050 feet per second. This gives the beginner a gun with maximum recoil control and minimum weight, as well as a reduced grip and fore-end, which is excellent for small hands.

The Beretta AL391 Youth Model

What About Gun Fit?

With regard to gun fit, there are no set parameters and all I can offer is general advice. Children grow at an alarming rate and their gun fit dimensions will be constantly changing. So at the start, the gun should be shortened to the correct length and the wood that is removed should be kept and cut into half-inch slices. This way, as the child grows and extra length is required, the slices can be replaced, one at a time, exactly matching the size and grain of the stock. The height and cast alterations are easily achieved and altered to match changing dimensions by using Beretta's easily-adjusted shim system.

What is the Best Way to Practise?

Practise the fundamentals, emphasising footwork, stance, good posture and head position. Practise the gun mount and move to the target. Use a drawing board to explain the basics of hitting a moving target and, when understood, begin with easy targets.

Low house one is an excellent place to start and, if you can wind the spring off and raise the elevation of the target, so much the better. Create visual prompts to emphasise the Visual Hold, the Gun Hold, and Break Points. This can be done with stacks of fifteen to twenty clays at these positions.

Concentrate on good form – better to have three successful good shots than a box full of mediocre hits and misses. You are putting in place the building blocks of good technique. You do not need to shoot a great deal to do so. Little and often is the secret with young guns.

Keep it fun – do not overload them with technicalities. They do not need to know about chokes and cartridges or other trivia, but they do need success. Keep lessons short and be ever watchful for fatigue, usually demonstrated by sloppy gun handling as muscles tire.

Be sure to finish every session on success. I will often set several rabbit targets on edge at different ranges and start the beginner out with these stationary targets. If fatigue starts to set in, I will often finish a session with a wager…five straight at these targets for a soda or snack. This ensures that every session concludes with broken targets and a boost of confidence.

Better, better, best – never let it rest

Chapter 19
Instruction

T here is no such person as The Natural. I will allow that there are a few participants in any walk of life who can learn a motor skill quicker than the average person. But there is still a ceiling to their progress – they just reach it quicker. The learning curve of any activity is never a straight line; it consists of peaks and troughs and very often long plateaus of little progress.

A book like this is never purchased by the Top Shots…they consider that they know everything there is to know on the subject. This is a book for the Beginner through C, B and A Class shooters – those looking for insight and ideas on how to improve and move up in class. Well, the AA and Master Class competitors were not born with their skills and knowledge, they acquired them over time and so can you.

There is not one top competitor in any discipline who has not sought advice or taken instruction. To achieve the high standards they display has taken years of dedicated practice and a great deal of hard work. I would compare it to the martial arts; they have successfully progressed through the belts to black. However, just like the martial artist, no matter how good you are there is always room for improvement. I can assure you the top shots are always looking for an insight or tip that can sharpen their skills and break bad habits.

Group lessons with a qualified coach are a good way to learn the fundamentals

Getting Started

If it is your intention to become the best you can be at breaking clays, you need to follow their example and recognise that the quickest way to make progress is to take instruction and practise the lessons learned.

There are two distinct introductions to clay shooting: the first is usually through friends or family who already shoot or by exposure from a 'have a go' day or corporate event. At first your only concern is to break a target, just one will do! Then as you choose a discipline, if you can break half the targets you shoot at, you are happy. But as skills increase, you start to make better scores. And when you come close to a straight or winning a class or event, the game has changed. Shooting goes from being a recreational sport where the scores where immaterial, to a competitive sport where good scores are imperative!

If only you could find that consistency on High house two at Skeet, the hard right-hander on Station five at Trap or beat the Battue in Sporting Clays! This is often the motivation for considering instruction or getting that placebo for all misses…a gunfit.

The problem is you now have established muscle memory. There is no such thing as bad muscle memory, but there is incorrect muscle memory. Often when you first take instruction, the coach is faced with a dilemma:

you do not have the sound fundamentals in place for him to be able to teach you the correct technique and method to shoot your bogie target. So, he can either teach you a trick to do so – Quick Fix or Short-Term Coaching – or he can take you back to basics and help you to understand the fundamentals – Long Term Coaching.

Short-Term Coaching or Long-Term Coaching
The Short-Term Coach

Take a short-term coaching example: suppose you want some instruction on a long crossing target – they always give you trouble, they soften your scores in competition and have become the target you dread. The coach asks you to shoot a couple and instantly tells you, 'You're behind that'. Before that sentence is finished, he says 'Double your lead!' And if that is not successful, 'Treble it!'

This theme is continued until he 'dials' you in and you break the target. For the next hour you visit several stations presenting similar targets and the coach works his 'magic' for you every time. You leave, delighted with your progress, and looking forward with anticipation to the next competition.

The big day arrives; you are shooting well with renewed confidence. You get to the long crossing presentation... you enter the stand and begin to miss! The target is *still* a mystery! You recall the coach's advice and double the lead, treble it and still you cannot connect. You blank the stand and as you leave the stand, you see a friend watching and ask 'Where was I on those?' His reply...'You missed them a mile in front!' How could that happen? You had an excellent lesson only last week where you were crushing them!

What happened was, you received Quick Fix or Short-Term Coaching. When the coach stands behind you he sees where you are missing, but he does not look for the reason why. He puts you right by talking you into putting the gun in the right place, in effect, shooting the target for you. You may be pulling the trigger but he is the one calling the shot. Yes, it can be a very successful lesson, but when you are on your own without the coach there to correct your mistakes, you are back where you started!

The Long-Term Coach

A long-term coach will explain the importance of learning sound fundamentals and how to practise the moves until correct muscle memory is established. This ensures that your shooting skills will not break down under the pressure of competition. Lack of the key fundamental skills is usually the cause of missing.

The long-term coach, in contrast, will look for the cause of the miss, running through a check list of possible faults, starting from your feet up. When he has analysed the problem (or problems) he will explain them to you. It could be fundamentals, technique, method or set up. He will then explain the solutions, working with you to correct your problems to the point that you can shoot those 'problem shots' on your own. This may take one or several coaching sessions, but once these changes are grooved, they are permanent.

Always try to find a long-term coach who 'Looks for the fault, analyses the cause and offers the correction'. Find the right coach and he can improve your performance quickly, find the wrong one and he can set you back just as fast.

Fundamentals First

The most important lessons are the first. If possible, try to begin your shooting career with a series of lessons from a long-term coach. You will learn the fundamentals of foot work, stance, posture and head position, gun mount, technique and methods, proper set up and address to the target, together with advice on equipment and gun fit.

This good beginning will instil the correct muscle memory and pay great dividends over the years. Future lessons can be targeted at specific problems in your chosen discipline. The top shots got where they are through instruction and practice...follow their lead and you can succeed as well.

How Do You Find a Good Instructor?

To find a good instructor, look in magazines and on the Internet, read articles, ask fellow shooters for recommendations and ask the winners who coached them. When you have made a couple of choices, ask the pertinent questions:

1. How long are the lessons? (One hour, two hours, half-day, full day?)
2. What is the cost of shooting instruction?
3. What is included? (Ammunition, cartridges, targets, gun club fees?)
4. Do the lessons include the use of a gun, as well as eye and hearing protection?

There are one and two day schools you can attend as well. When considering these, be sure to ask about accommodation and meals, the size of the class and the ability level of the students. Does the school include gun fitting?

There is not a top competitor who has not sought advice or taken instruction

The Right Coach at the Right Time

We are all different and receive and react to instruction in different ways, so finding the right instructor is very important. You should consider that one's personal interpretation of these instructions may not be in line with how they where meant to be acted upon. The experienced coach recognises this and if one instruction is not working, will try another.

Sometimes the coach may need to step back and consider if his instructions are being understood. Can he explain them in another way to help the pupil make the breakthrough they are looking for? If he is unable to, either through lack of experience or just not being able to communicate well with a particular student, he should recognise this and recommend the pupil to a colleague or peer.

This ability to recognise that we do not have all the answers is one of the gifts that the Master Coaches have. They recognise that another coach may be better able to communicate with or have the greater experience needed to bring out the best in a particular student. Students who seek instruction from a variety of coaches, in effect, ensure that they will find the coach that they can 'gel' with. If they can understand the coach's instructions and communicate with him, they can put those instructions in place.

The individual who does not find this personal relationship, however, can still derive great benefit from a variety of coaches' instruction. The student may have been told a thousand times not to do something by one coach and another coach may deliver the same message, using different words, and a mental light bulb turns on for the student.

Was the second coach a better instructor? Not necessarily, but he benefited from all of his predecessors' hard work. He simply found the words that got the message through to that pupil.

Instruction can be expensive. If the cost is temporarily out of your range, all is not lost! At your club look for the competitors who consistently shoot high scores, demonstrate good form and make their shooting look smooth and easy. When one of these good shooters has finished for the day, approach him and ask if he would have the time to work with you occasionally to help you get a grip on the basics. I am sure you will find one who would be delighted to do so. Be aware, however, that being a good shot does not guarantee being a good teacher. So keep the fundamentals in mind at all times.

Coaching Qualifications

In the UK the CPSA and in the USA the NSCA have Coaching Certification Programmes offering three levels of instructor qualifications:

Level 1: Qualified to provide instruction to the beginner or novice shooter.
Level 2: Qualified to provide instruction to intermediate shooters.
Level 3: Qualified to provide instruction to shooters of all levels.

I would urge everyone who thinks about getting some instruction to do so, one lesson can save years of frustration. Try to find a coach with whom you feel comfortable and can readily communicate. As your skill increases, plan to spend time with several coaches, listening to their ideas. If you learn to take one extra target it will be money well spent.

*Look for instructors with
qualifications from the
governing body*

Find a coach to match your abilities

Governing Bodies

United Kingdom:

Clay Pigeon Shooting Association (CPSA)
Edmonton House
Bisley Camp
Brookwood
Woking Surrey
GU2 ONP – UK
Phone: +44-(0)1483-485400
Fax: +44-(0)1483-485410
info@cpsa.co.uk

The British International Clay Target Shooting Federation (BICTSF)
11, Beech Crescent
Darrington
Pontefract
West Yorkshire WF8 3 AD – UK
Phone: +44-(0)1977-791242
Email: bictsf@globalnet.co.uk

The Welsh CTSA
45, Picton Road
Hakin
Milford Haven
Dyfed SA73 3DY – UK
Phone: +44- (0)1646-693076

The Scottish Clay Target Association
Box 400
24, Station Square
Inverness IV1 1LD

The Irish Clay Pigeon Shooting Association
Kilsallagh
65, Glendoher Drive
Rathfarnham
Dublin 16 Eire
003531-4931484

The Institute of Clay Shooting Instructors (ICSI)
Fairview
Church End
Main Road
Parson Drove
Cambridge
PE13 4LF

France:

Federation Internationale de Tir aux Armes Sportive de Chasse (FITASC)
10, rue de Lisbonne
Paris 75008
France
Phone: 00421-934053
Fax: 00421-935822

Federation Francaise de Balle Trap (FFBT)
20, Rue Thiers
92100 Boulonge Billancourt
France
Phone: 0033-141410505
www.ffbt.assoc.fr

Germany:

ISSF
Bavariering 21
D-80336 Munich 1
Germany
Phone: 004989-5443550
Fax: 004989-5435544

USA:

National Sporting Clays Association (NSCA)
& National Skeet Association (NSSA)
5931 Roft Road
San Antonio
Texas 78253
USA
Phone: 210-688-3371
Fax: 210-688-3014

Amateur Trapshooting Association (ATA)
601 W. National Road
Vandalia
Ohio 45377
USA
Phone: 937-898-4638
Fax: 937-898-5472

Sporting Clays of America (SCA)
9257 Buckeye Road
Sugar Grove
Ohio 43155-9632
Phone: 740-746-8334
Fax: 740-746-8605

U.S.A. Shooting
Olympic Training Center
One Olympic Plaza
Colorado Springs
Colorado 80909-5762
USA
Phone: 719-578-4883

Bibliography

Adams, Cyril S., Adams and Braden, Robert S. *Lock Stock and Barrel*. Long Beach: Safari Press,1996.
— *Clay Pigeon Shooting*, Kaye & Ward Ltd, London 1973.
Atwill, Lionel, *Sporting Clays*, An Orvis Guide, The Atlantic Monthly Press, NY, 1990.

Barnes, Mike, compiler, *The Complete Clayshot*, David & Charles, Newton Abbot, Devon, 1993.
Bassam, Lanny, *With Winning In Mind*, Xpress Publications, San Antonio, TX, 1988.
Bentley, Paul, *Clay Target Shooting*, A. & C. Black Ltd, London, 1987.
— *Competitive Clay Target Shooting*, A. & C. Black Ltd London 1991.
— *Clay Shooting with the Experts*, B.T. Batsford Ltd, London 1994.
Bidwell, John, and Robin Scott, *Move: Mount: Shoot*, The Crowood Press, Marlborough, Wiltshire, 1990.
— *Black's Wing and Clay*, Ehlert Publishing Group Inc, Maple Grove, MN, 2004.
Bowlen, Bruce, *The Orvis Wing Shooting Handbook*, Lyons & Burford, NY 1984.
Brindle, J., *Shotguns and Shooting*, Nimrod Book Services, 1984.
Brister, Bob, *Shotgunning: The Art and Science*, Winchester Press, Tulsa OK, 1976.
British Proof Authorities. *Notes on the Proof of Shotguns and Other Small Arms*, The Worshipful Company of Gunmakers, of the City of London and the Guardians of the Birmingham Proof House, The Proof House, Commercial Rd, London, The Gun Barrel Proof House, Banbury Street, Birmingham.
Buckingham, Nash, *Mr Buck: The Autobiography of Nash Buckingham*, Dyrk Halstead and Steve Smith, Countrysport Press, Traverse City MI, 1990.
Burrard, Maj. Sir Gerald, Bt, *In the Gunroom*, Herbert Jenkins, London 1930.

Carlisle, Dan, and Dolph Adams, *Taking More Birds: A Practical Guide to Greater Success at Sporting Clays and Wing Shooting*, Lyons & Burford, NY 1993.
Churchill, Robert, *Churchill's Shotgun Book*, Alfred A. Knopf, NY, 1955.
— *Game Shooting*, Michael Joseph Ltd, London, 1955.
Clay Pigeon Shooting Association, *Safety Officers Manual*, CPSA, Corby, Northamptonshire, c1998
— *Senior Coaches Handbook*, CPSA Buckhurst Hill Essex, 1990.
Cradock, Chris, *Cradock on Shotguns*, B.T. Batsford Ltd London 1989.
— *A Manual of Clayshooting*, revised edn, B.T. Batsford, London 1988.
Crews, Dr Debbie, *Balanced Brain*, Research Paper, Arizona State University, 1997.

Davies, Ken, *The Better Shot*, Quiller Press, London 1992.
Deacot, Robert, *'Bud', Writings*, Decot-Hywyd, Phoenix, Arizona, 1996.

Evans, George, *The Best of Nash Buckingham*, Winchester Press, NY, 1973.

Greevy, Les, *The Mental Game of Clay Target Shooting*, Self Published, Williamsport, PA. 2001.
— *Shooting in the Zone*, Self Published, Williamsport, PA, 2002.

Hartman, B. C., *Hartman on Skeet*, McCelland and Stewart, Toronto, 1967.
Hastings, MacDonald, *How to Shoot Straight*, A., Barnes and Company, NJ, 1970.
Hawley, John and Louise Burke, *Peak Performance*, Allen and Unwin, St Leonards, NSW, 1998.
Hearn, Arthur, *Shooting and Gunfitting*, Herbert Jenkins, London, 1930.
Hoare, Tony, *Successful Clay Pigeon Shooting*, The Crowood Press, Marlborough Wiltshire, 1991.

Jackson, Susan and Milhaly Csikszentmihalyi, *Flow in Sports*, Human Kinetics, Champaign, Illinois, 1999.
Janelle, Christopher and Charles Hillman, *Quiet Eye Phenomenon*, University of Florida and University of Illinois, Research Paper. 1996.
Jarett, Alan, *Shooting at Clays*, Stanley Paul, London, 1991.

Kayes, Michael, *Mental Training for the Shotgun Sports*, Shotgun Sports, Auburn, CA, 1995.
King, John, *Clay Pigeon Shooting*, The Sportsman's Press London 1991.
Knight, Richard Alden, *Mastering the Shotgun*, E.P. Dutton Co, NY, 1975.

Lancaster, Charles, *The Art of Shooting*, McCorquodale & Co, London, 1954.
Lind, Ernie, *The Complete Book of Trick and Fancy Shooting*, Citadel Press, Secaucus, 1972.
Linn, John R. And Stephen A. Blumenthal, *Finding the Extra Target*, Shotgun Sports Magazine Book, Shotgun Sports Inc, Auburn CA, 1989.
Little, Frank, *The Little Trapshooting Book*, Shooting Sports Magazine Book, Futher Adventures Inc., Auburn, CA, 1994.

Marshall-Ball, Robin, *The Sporting Shotgun: A User's Handbook*, Saiga Publishing Co, Surrey, England, 1982.
Martin, Dr Wayne F., *An Insight to Sports: Featuring Trap Shooting and Golf*, Sports Vision Inc., Seattle, WA, 1987.
McCawley, E.S., Jr. *Shotguns & Shooting*, Van Nostrand Reinhold Company, NY, 1965.
Meyer, Jerry, *The Sporting Clays Handbook*, Lyons & Burford, NY, 1990.
— *The Clay Target Handbook*, Lyons Press, NY, 1992.
Migdalski, E, *Clay Target Games*, 1978,
Migdalski, Tom, *The Complete Book of Shotgunning Games*, Masters Press, Indianapolis, IN, 1997.
Miller, Brian, *Gold Minds*, Crowood Press, London, 1992.
Missildine, Fred, with Nick Karas, *Score Better at Trap*, Winchester Press, NY, 1972.
— *Score Better at Skeet*, Winchester Press, NY, 1972.
— *Score Better at Trap and Skeet*, Winchester Press, NY 1971.
Montague, A. Andrew, *Successful Shotgun Shooting*, Winchester Press, NY, 1971.
    The Derrydale Press, Lanham, Maryland, 2000.

Nichols, Bob, *Skeet: And How to Shoot It*, G. P. Putnam's Sons, NY, 1947.

Orberfell, George G. and Charles E. Thompson, *The Mysteries of Shotgun Patterns*, Oklahoma State University Press, Stillwater OK, 1957.
O'Connor, Jack, *Complete Book of Shooting*, Outdoor Life, NY, 1965.

Pearce, Michael, *Sporting Clays*, Stackpole Books, Harrisburg, PA, 1991.

Reynolds, Mike, with Mike Barnes, *Shooting Made Easy*, The Crowood Press, Marlborough, Wiltshire, 1989.
Rose, Michael, *Guncraft: Clay and Game Shooting*, Chancerel Publishers Ltd, London, 1978.
— *The Eley Book of Shooting Technique*, Chancererel Publishers Ltd, London, 1978.
Rottella, Bob, *Golf is not a Game of Perfect*, Simon & Schuster Inc, NY.
Ruffer, Maj. J. E. M., *The Art of Good Shooting*, David & Charles Publishers Ltd, Newton Abbot, Devon, 1972.

Scherer, Ed, *Scherer on Skeet*, Ed Scherer, Waukesha, WIS, 1991.
Smith, A. J., *Sporting Clays*, Argus Books, Hemel Hempstead, 1989.
Smith, A. J. and Tony Hoare, *A. J. Smiths Sporting Masterclass*, Argus Books, Hemel Hempstead, 1991.
Stadt, Ronald W., *Winchester Shotguns and Shotshells*, Armory Publications, Tacoma, 1984.
Stanbury, Percy and G.L. Carlisle, *Shotgun Marksmanship*, Stanley Paul & Co. Ltd, London, 1986.
— *Clay Pigeon Marksmanship*, Herbert Jenkins Ltd, London 1982.
— *Shotgun and Shooter*, Barrie and Jenkins Ltd, London 1970
— *Clay Pigeon Marksmanship*, Barrie and Jenkins Ltd, London 1982.
Stewart, Jackie with Mike Barnes, *The Jackie Stewart Book of Shooting*, HarperCollins Publishers, London 1991.

Taylor, John, *The Shotgun Encyclopedia*, Safari Press Inc, Long Beach, CA, 2001.
— *Shotshells & Ballistics*, Safari Press Inc, Long Beach, CA, 2003.
Taylor, Mark H., *Clay Target Shooting: The mental game*, STP Books, Tucson Arizona, 1997.

Yardley, Michael, *Gunfitting: The Quest for Perfection*, The Sportsman's Press, London 1993.
— *Positive Shooting*, The Crowood Press, Marlborough Wiltshire, 1994.
— *The Shotgun: A Shooting Instructors Handbook*, The Sportsman's Press, 2001.

Zutz, Don, *Modern Waterfowling, Guns and Gunning*, Stoeger, Publishing Co, South Hackensack, NJ,1985.
— *The Double Shotgun*, Winchester Press, NY, 1985.
— *Shotgunning: Trend in Transition*, Wolfe Publishing Co. Inc., Prescott, AR, 1989.
— *Shotgun Stuff*, Shotgun Sports Inc, Auburn, CA, 1991.

Periodicals

Clay Shooting Magazine (UK)
UK: Brunton Business Publications Ltd
Thruxton Down House
Thruxton Down, Andover
Hampshire, SP11 8PR
Email: info@clay-shooting.com

Clay Shooting (USA) – Incorporating the Clay Pigeon
USA: Clay Shooting USA
8535, Wurzbach, Suite, 203
San Antonio, Texas78240
Email: info@clay-shootingusa.com

Pull (UK)
Official Magazine of the Clay Pigeon Shooting Association
Bourne Publishing Group
Roebuck House
33 Broad Street
Stamford
Lincolnshire

Sporting Clays (USA)
5211, South Washington Avenue
Titusville
Florida 32780
USA
www.sportingclays.net

Shotgun Sports (USA)
PO Box 6810
Auburn
California 95604
USA
www.shotgunsports.com

Sporting Gun
IPC Magazines Ltd
Kings Reach Tower
Stamford Street
London SE1 9LS

Index